ALL THINGS NEW

Robert S. Fogarty

ALL THINGS NEW

American Communes
and Utopian Movements
1860–1914

The University of Chicago Press
Chicago and London

ROBERT S. FOGARTY is professor of history at Antioch College and editor of *The Antioch Review*. He is the author of the *Dictionary of American Communal and Utopian History* and *The Righteous Remnant: The House of David* and the editor of the series American Utopian Adventure.

THE UNIVERSITY OF CHICAGO PRESS, CHICAGO 60637
THE UNIVERSITY OF CHICAGO PRESS, LTD., LONDON
© 1990 by The University of Chicago
All rights reserved. Published 1990
Printed in the United States of America
99 98 97 96 95 94 93 92 91 90   5 4 3 2 1

Library of Congress Cataloging-in-Publication Data
Fogarty, Robert S.
    All things new : American communes and utopian movements,
1860–1914 / Robert S. Fogarty.
        p.   cm.
Includes bibliographical references.
ISBN 0-226-25654-5 (cloth)
    1. Collective settlements—United States—History.   2. United
States—Social conditions—1865–1918.   I. Title.
HX653.F63   1990   89-48996
335'.973—dc20   CIP

This book is printed on acid-free paper.

Contents

Acknowledgments

For a book that has been long in the making, there are many debts, both personal and professional, that need to be acknowledged. First and foremost, I want to thank the numerous librarians who answered my queries, sought out obscure ephemera files, and helped me track down little-known or -recognized groups. Over the years, the librarians at the Olive Kettering Library have helped with problems and interlibrary loan requests, and I am indebted to Joe Cali, Bruce Thomas, Kim Iconis, Ruth Bent, Jadine Surette, Nina Myatt, and Mary Kidd. Student assistants helped along the way, most notably, Kim McQuaid. My colleagues in the History Department at Antioch were always supportive and encouraged me at difficult junctures. Fred Hoxie, Frank Wong, Hannah Goldberg, Michael Kraus, and Louis Filler all contributed to the making of this volume. Editorial assistance from Gerda Oldham, Sharon Hollister, and Sandy Long at various junctures improved the look and style of the manuscript. A host of utopian scholars supplied me a steady stream of notes, with their own work in progress, and with fresh insights. Such scholars as Alexandra Aldridge, Carl Guarneri, Mario DePillis, Michael Barkun, Joseph Blasi, Yaacov Oved, Robert Hine, H. Roger Grant, Laurence Veysey, Lyman Tower Sargent, Howard Segal, Ray Reynolds, W. H. G. Armytage, John F. C. Harrison, Bryan Wilson, John Ott, Oto Okugawa, Jack Salzman, Dolores Hayden, and Taylor Stoehr all shared their work. Support for this research has been provided by the Faculty Fund, Antioch College; the American Council of Learned Societies; the American Philosophical Society; and the National Endowment for the Humanities, whose fellowship support provided a year's leave at a crucial point. As a visiting fellow at All Souls College, Oxford, I was able to put the final touches on this work. I am grateful to the warden and the fellows for their hospitality. Finally, I want to give a special place to Katherine Kadish, who continuously encouraged and cheered on this work.

1 "Enclaves of Difference": The Communal Pattern

I will not prejudge them successful. They look well in July. We shall see them in September. I know they are better for themselves than as partners. Their saying that things are clear, and that they are sane, does not make them so. If they will serve the town of Harvard, and make their neighbors feel them as benefactors wherever they touch them, they are as safe as the sun.

R. W. Emerson, "On Brook Farm," 1843

We have been talking and writing a long time now about the social equality of women and freedom and justice, and considering what we must do to bring about those much desired objects. And many of us, are waiting for the time to come when we can do something; we are waiting for Association, for community, for social reorganization of some sort. . . . Are we not beginning to see that, instead of this waiting we must go to work right HERE and NOW.

James Towner, *Social Revolutionist*, 1857

And yet my own conviction is strong that Co-operation is the true goal of our industrial program, the application of Republican principles to labor, and the appointed means of reducing the laboring classes from dependency, prodigality and need and establishing it on the basis of forecast, calculation, sobriety and thrift, conducive at once to its material culture and moral education.

Horace Greeley, "Moral Aspects of Cooperation," 1867

Arthur Bestor's assumption that, "for most reformers in an industrial age, communitarianism was a tool that had lost its edge, probably forever," has become an unchallenged historical truism. His contention that communal projects in the post–Civil War decades were irrelevant to the needs of the time and that there were no enduring societies along the lines of the Shakers, Oneida, or Harmony is based on his assumption that "social patterns became so well defined over the whole area of the United States that the possibility no longer existed of af-

1

fecting the social order by merely planting the seeds of new institutions in the wilderness."[1]

John L. Thomas has written about the "collapse" of communitarianism in the 1850s, and suggests that the perfectionist impulse to create "anti-institutional institutions" failed to sustain itself after the Civil War. Mark Holloway asserts that communes established after 1865 were essentially ephemeral and that the Topolobampo colony was the only attempt on a grand scale—in short, that the July of communal activity had been in the 1840s and that, when one looks at the September of that century, one finds weakness or, at best, romantic rhetoric.[2] My research into archives, newspapers, and monographs (many published since 1970) presents another picture. A convincing argument can be made that such broad generalizations about the communal tradition after the Civil War are unfounded and that instead of discontinuity there was continuous colony organization, that instead of a few there were numerous collective settlements, and that instead of weakness and irrelevance there was strong social purpose and a serious intent to respond directly to emerging social conditions by both spiritual and secular leaders.

For some reformers, like Henry Demarest Lloyd, they were a significant element in the reform equation: "Only within these communities has there been seen, in the wide borders of the United States, a social life where hunger and cold, prostitution, intemperance, poverty, slavery, crime, premature old age, and unnecessary mortality, panic and industrial terror, have been abolished. If they had done this for a year, they would have deserved to be called the only successful 'society' on this continent and some of then are generations old. All this has not been done by saints in heaven, but on earth by average men and women." Later historians, like Bernard and Lillian Johnpoll, have argued that the political utopians like Lloyd were woefully inadequate to the task of understanding the dynamic transformation of industrial America, but try they did.[3] Lloyd and Bellamy tried, as John Thomas has suggested, to sustain an arcadian style of village life that was then in decline. There were virtues in such settlements, and, however mistaken in their political prognosis, reformers found those small-town virtues compelling and worth both cultivating and sustaining.

It is within this context that I examine the social sources and history of communal groups from 1860 to 1914. Some groups left voluminous records and have been the subject of substantial histories. Others have had brief notice except in the radical press of the day and in folklore, and precious little has come down to us in the way of biography and autobiography. The historical record for groups founded in this period is uneven, and one of the major purposes of this book is to set it straight, to rescue some of the lesser-known groups from obscurity and try to place them and their fellow travelers within a larger framework.

I hope that this study can throw some light on the nature of charismatic authority, on the relationship between leaders and followers, and on the tensions between ideology and utopia. All historical periods are periods of change, but the last half of the nineteenth century saw changes that simultaneously threw American culture back on its heels and set it in motion. The 140 communal groups founded during this period were both rocked by the events of those decades and poised to advance to meet them. A few planted roots deep enough to sustain a collective life for a generation, while others struggled just beyond infancy, failing to reach their adolescence and maturity. All were inspired by the exhortation found in *Revelation* that the time had come to make "all things new."

Alan Trachtenberg has written that the meaning of utopia lay at the base of political and social controversies throughout the nineteenth century: "Was the true America best represented by its most successful citizens, those for whom laws protected the private means of employment—private property and contrast—and permitted accumulation of private wealth? Or did utopian 'America' demand for its realization a new social order, the abolition of private property, the emergence of the nation as a collective body of shared wealth as well as culture."[4] For the charismatic perfectionists, the cooperative colonizers, and the political pragmatists (all different stripes of utopians), the logic of history was both clear and on their side—community was on the rise during the period and would rescue America from itself.

In a series of provocative studies, Robert Wiebe has argued that American society in the late nineteenth century, through segmented (to use his own word), operated under a set of common assumptions and general principles that fostered both change and continuity. What he has called the "units of life" did in fact undergo change over time. In the eighteenth century, the family living in a small community was the norm, whereas, by the nineteenth century, not only had the pace of life quickened, but there were other units of life that had their origins in the growth of towns and cities, in the immigrant diaspora that made America more diverse, and in new commercial arrangements that forced different patterns of entrepreneurship.

All these forces created a society that seemed to reshape itself in continuous fashion and appeared, at times, at war with itself. It was a society that encouraged diversity, and diversity was its guiding principle: "A properly ordered society, therefore, would comprise countless isolated lanes where Americans either singly or in groups, dashed like rows of racers towards their goals. What happened along other tracks might be a matter of intense interest for competitors, for they were all sprinting there, but it was seldom a matter of emulation. Each lane, testing a unique virtue, would trace a unique experience."[5]

According to Wiebe, five fundamental conditions in American life provided the basis for the race and the different units of life: an expanse of land, cultural diversity, military security, the absence of feudal traditions, and economic abundance. Communal and cooperative societies formed during this period faced in both directions, however, as they both participated in the segmented society and resisted it. On the one hand, they represented an alternative path, a distinct set of values that allowed their members to distinguish themselves from the others in the race, yet, on the other, they hoped that others would emulate them. As a rule, they resisted the tendency toward competitive individualism so much in evidence around them. Many who organized and many who joined such groups were rejecting the national model, one based on elite leadership, on professional competence, and on national values. There were elements of decentralism, of a resistance to dominant trends, and of a search for spiritual values in community. These groups chose to be marginal and organized themselves into collective settlements that promised them a new life, but in doing so they also further emphasized their marginality.

American pluralism, a tradition of political liberty, and the continuing abundance of land allowed some groups, according to Wiebe, to define themselves by "networks of family and friends or ethnic affiliation rather than by categories of skill, by a single core of character rather than a multiplicity of roles, by the creeds of religious or mystical truth rather than the codes of an occupation." By joining a utopian community individuals defined themselves, by moving West or South the group forged a new identity en route, and by adopting a new identity group members rejected the emerging corporate one. Wiebe's assertion that "what they sought in each instance was an enclave of difference, a small preserve in the larger system where their special values would have sovereignty," could be applied equally to the small town and to the communal society in late nineteenth-century America.[6] Both were part of the main, yet both tried to maintain their island values.

Even though such utopian communities were often ideologically and socially in opposition to American society, they were, by and large, left alone to carry out their own destinies and to run their course with a minimum of interference. There were times, of course, when they came into conflict with local attitudes or with deep-seated social patterns. Most established themselves on the physical margins of the American landscape, and it was not until 1900 that the first urban communal societies made their appearance. Certain communities—those that I have called the cooperative colonizers and the political pragmatists—acted as a conservative force to blunt the calls for class action that were heard increasingly in the 1890s. By opposing such calls and upholding the ideal of the common good, they signaled their allegiance to an older and more egalitarian society that had within it elements of John Eliot's praying villages.

Within these communities, there were various leadership patterns and an equal number of strategies advocated for achieving a perfected society. There was no one community paradigm, and several coexisted during the same period. The impulse to create new communities remained a strong one, and Wiebe has noted this continuing tradition: "The communitarian impulse of the nineteenth and its modifications in the twentieth century simply extended this normal American pattern. From New Harmony to Pullman, from exurbia to the student communes the appropriate means of following a different persuasion were secession and isolation."[7]

While secession was an essential part of both the utopian and the colony-building process, complete isolation was always impossible, and beyond that there were groups that resisted such withdrawal and sought to become centers of influence and culture. Some communal and cooperative groups sought to escape the pressures and developing patterns of late nineteenth-century society and to protest against the forces of consolidation represented by the trusts by organizing themselves into "good trusts." If they could not control the forces at work in the economic sphere, they could constitute themselves into a new moral order in which work, family life, and social aspirations could be merged.

Yet it must be emphasized again that they did not emanate from a single source or speak a single language. William Demarest Lloyd's description of his own philosophy, for example, might be used to describe the political sources of the various groups that had a political agenda; he was a "socialist-anarchist-individual-collectivist-individualist-communist-cooperative-aristocratic-democrat."[8] One might say that Lloyd was confused; however, his confusion represents the varieties of community experience that flourished.

As much as the Lloyds of the period tried to distinguish themselves and chart a different course, they were also wedded to contemporary assumptions about how the good life might be achieved. One finds, for example, that the socialists embraced the economics of abundance, believing that the production of consumer goods and the utilization of new technology would lead to the expansion of the market place—their marketplace. They realized that they had to enter the world in order to protect their place in it, but they hoped that they could infuse it with their values (in a sense spiritualize the capitalist economy). Despite the rhetoric of social revolution, many cooperators hoped to become competitive, to buttress traditional individualist values in the name of American liberty.

Not all who joined sought to change the material world; theirs was the politics of adjustment, accommodation, or retreat. These individuals sought salvation in community and solace in an intense religious life. R. Laurence Moore has argued that the distinction between mainline and sect congregations fails to come to grips with the essentially pluralistic and shifting character of American religious life and spiritual development. It was a much more complex phenomenon than the categories suggest. Religious and social identification with a fringe group often took place within the context of a social environment in which the boundaries of faith and commitment were both fixed and open ended: "What the proliferation [of religious groups] did was provided ways for many people to invest their lives with a significance that eased their sense of frustration. For many, no doubt, that meant coming to terms with and accepting social and political powerlessness. For others, it led directly to gaining conventional forms of power in a world that was no longer primarily religious."[9] This is not the same as identifying sects as "religions of the oppressed" or saying that cult activity arises simply out of social stress; rather, identification with either cult or church was an expression of religious values in a world where religion had lost its moral potency. Clearly, spiritualism and the belief in spirit phenomenon emerged as a major religious force in this period, and other spiritual forces—some domestic, others foreign—appeared.

On another note, Page Smith has pointed out in his study of town development that those that grew in cumulative fashion showed less variation than the colonized towns (some of which will be discussed).[10] During the 1860s, the Kansas Territory was opened by both cumulative and colonized towns, and there were few restrictions placed on either pattern. The belief in community, in the possibility of establishing a sanctified band, remained potent in this period despite the existence of larger and more powerful movements. These groups did not run in the fast lane, and they had few winners; they did set, at times, a fast pace, were out in front for a while, and, by their sometimes erratic behavior, made the whole race certainly livelier and more interesting. Like their predecessors in the 1840s and 1850s, they did not affect the final outcome of the national race. It must be said that they mirrored both dissatisfactions and new possibilities, that they contained elements from the mainstream and the margins, that they were a compound of radical and conservative notions, and that they were more heterodox than orthodox.

One of the most powerful images that one finds in late nineteenth-century literature is the one used by Edward Bellamy in his 1888 classic, *Looking Backward*. He describes a "prodigious coach" to which were harnessed the mass of humanity. It was driven up a hilly and sandy road by hunger, who "permitted no lagging though the pace was necessarily slow." The top of the coach he describes as being covered with passengers who never got down, "even at the steepest ascents." The greatest misfortune for the coach riders was to "lose one's seat and the apprehension that this might happen to them or their friends was a constant cloud upon the happiness of those who rode."[11] There were, of course, others on that road, some who had leaped willingly from the coach to walk on foot, others who thought the coach too commercial and sought a more spiritual vehicle. Still others, like the members of these communal societies, had elected to move about in caravans, to travel together, to choose their own driver, and—if they wanted to—to take another road.

The township ideal was still a powerful one during this period, and so was the ideal of the covenanted community of saints. Establishing a city on a hill still seemed possible, and many tried to do so—some because they had fallen off the coach, others (like the Hutterites) because they had visions that took them down other roads. There was no uniform vision, no uniform way. In his second of ten Gifford Lectures on natural religion at the University of Edinburgh in 1901–2, William James defined his subject (later published as *The Varieties of Religious Experience*) in a talk titled "Circumspection of the Topic." James said that the term *religious experience* encompassed phenomena "so many and so different from one another; it did not stand for any single principle or essence, but was rather a collective name."[12] The same can be said for the varieties of community experience during the period 1860–1914. Keith Thomas has noted that "we are still, I think, very much in the dark, historians and anthropologists alike, as to the precise mechanisms by which collective beliefs change over long periods of time."[13] One of the major purposes of this book will be to examine collective settlements as one example of collective belief and to describe—in narrative fashion—how such groups came into existence, how they attracted their members, and what, finally, became of them. They did not arise from the air, though many had an airy quality about them. They grew organically from a utopian tradition that was deeply rooted in American history.

That tradition was reflected most obviously in John Winthrop's speech aboard the *Arbella* in 1630, when he spoke about the meaning implicit in the colonization of North America: "We must consider that we shall be a City Upon a Hill, the eyes of all people are upon us." The early settlers at the Massachusetts Bay Colony were, in the words of Kenneth Lockridge, "conservative, Christian and Utopian."[14] The millennialist assumptions of eighteenth-century settlers and leaders have been outlined again and again by commentators on American life.

One central tension in American life has been between the forces of individualism and the demands of community. Tocqueville, for example, noted the importance of townships—"a middle ground between the commune and the canton of France"—in mediating these opposing forces; they were "not so large, on the one hand, that the inhabitants would be likely to conflict and not so small, on the other that men capable of conducting their affairs may always be found among its citizens." In France, such townships were model political and social environments because they elicited both support and participation from citizens. In America, they could, Tocqueville stressed, provide the social glue so essential for a society that had within itself the seeds of social chaos: "Because beyond the people nothing is to be perceived but a mass of equal individuals."[15] Such equality had produced enormous liberty, but there was little that held it together. Within a small settlement, however, it was possible to counteract that tendency because both collective and individual responsibility were assumed as vital elements in social life. In one sense, many of these new settlements in the post–Civil War period were efforts to create new townships and return to a tradition that emphasized participation, shared symbols, common rituals, and common goals; the ideal of the township was the ideal of the perfected community. Those that were successful had all the characteristics that Rosabeth Kanter notes in such utopian communities: sacrifice, investment, reunification, mortification, and transcendence.[16]

John L. Thomas has argued that the utopian tradition in late nineteenth-century America as exemplified by Edward Bellamy, Henry Demarest Lloyd, and Henry George attempted to present a vision of a new America based on a redefined social and political economy. This new model commonwealth drew its inspiration from three separate traditions: the Jeffersonian, the Protestant evangelical, and the artisanal. Jefferson's decentralized society was based on a political model rooted in the township with its freely elected representatives. The evangelical vision took the form of a perfected religious body made up of visible saints aligned against a corrupt civil order. The third ideology—the artisanal—was grounded in a "philosophy of true producers who formed a naturally cooperative community based on shop floor solidarity."[17]

Bellamy, George, and Lloyd were all political economists and publicists who hoped to create an adversary culture (to use Thomas's phrase) able to combat the growing power of the trusts. In a letter to the Populist-feminist Annie Diggs, Lloyd wrote that "cooperatives, trade unions, farmer, Granges and the churches must supply us with the material for the new social union to which we are moving."[18] Bellamy's defense of small-town virtue and his appeal to form an industrial army steered a middle course that preserved local values and promoted martial efficiency. George's single tax plan offered the way out to agricultural and urban producers alike. For George, the proper distribution of wealth would enable men to maintain their independence and integrity while also allowing village life to flourish for a middling class that was then torn between two forces, the rising metropolis and the bonanza farm. According to Thomas, George believed that the essence of American liberties remained linked with small towns and local government. Town and country might be joined to create an industrial village where a true community of interests reigned rather than the contemporary and growing community of calculation, commodities, and land speculation. Although both George and Lloyd distrusted state socialism, they shared millennialist assumptions about the possibility of a perfected society based on Christian ethics and salvationist prophecy.

Though it is often asserted that utopian writers and colony builders operated in different worlds, there is considerable evidence that during the period 1860–1914 they shared a set of common concerns. There was, in fact, a common faith, a common sensibility, and a series of common characteristics shared by the literary utopians and the practical communists. One was their belief in the inevitable historical development of society toward a cooperative state. That development was based on man's progressive nature, on his ability to overcome social obstacles, and on his desire for a higher and more spiritual life. Community was discussed in both *Looking Backward* and in the pages of Albert Kimsey Owen's journals as the place where superior values would be put into practice. True community could emerge if mankind conquered its lower instincts, its propensity toward acquisitiveness, and its desire to dominate others.

A second shared belief was that the frontier still offered both land and social space for launching new ventures. From 1867 to 1914, communal settlers turned their faces toward the West and the South. The settling of Kansas and Colorado in the 1860s and 1870s involved both individual and collective patterns, and, beginning in the 1880s, California exerted a strong pull on the imagination of these paradise planters. Clearly, the continuing availability of cheap land played a major part in the colony plans, but one also sees that some communities advertised the attractions of the climate, of the fruitfulness of the land, and of the garden that the cooperators would settle and help bring to blossom.

Another significant element was the "patent-office model" approach that Arthur Bestor noted was the major characteristic of the earlier Owenite and Fourierist movements. It centered on the belief that communal and cooperative settlements could serve as social laboratories and that by experimenting on a small scale the reformers might teach the larger world some lessons. Just as the utopian novels of the period were shot through with moral didacticism, the social experiments, for example, de Boissiere's Silkville, presumed that others would follow their lead.

Fresh opportunity, fresh land, and fresh ideas fueled the spirit of community development during this period. George feared the disappearance of free land and what it meant for the American psyche: "The Single Tax and millennium it pictured," writes Thomas, "offered an escape fom the confinements of time and indeterminacy in a simple device for restoring strength and purpose by returning Americans to the soil."[19] Land—cheap land—was still available despite what George and later Turner argued, and it was taken up by communal settlers, particularly during "hard times." It was not until 1900 and the emergence of the Straight Edge Society that one sees the city embraced as a locus of cooperative activity— village life was the dominant utopian mode.

There was a curious mixture of idealism and opportunism evident in some schemes, particularly in the 1890s, when land development plans and socialist hopes came together. As Roger Grant has noted, the rise of insurance schemes was clearly related to the uncertainties of the age. Security played a large part in the appeal that certain groups had, particularly to workingmen and their families. Many families sought a caring community in a world where economic chaos ruled. "A secure future in a new land" was a theme used not only by the cooperative colonizers and the political pragmatists but also by the charismatic perfectionists who offered a secure grounding with a holy person and a body of religious believers. Jewish communards came to the American West because it offered them what Czarist Russia could not—bread and land. Beyond that, the Am Olam movement was motivated by a millennialist vision rooted in socialism and the creation of a special place for Jews. Its idealistic and practical elements were complementary.

The romance of socialism also included a variety of plans to lighten the burden of industrial labor. One of those schemes was the cooperative plan outlined by Walter Thomas Mills in *Product Sharing Village*.[20] Variations on that theme were in evidence in the 1870s and 1880s and became full blown between 1887 and 1896. Tied closely to the industrial problem was the urban problem. It was, however, more clearly stated as a problem in ethics and morality than as a problem in economics. Elizabeth Rowell Thompson's concern about the fate of urban children, which led to the creation of the mystical community of Shalam in New Mexico, was one that agitated spiritualists and socialists alike. But it was the spiritual dimension of the problem that concerned her. Cities were places of corruption, and that view did not arise simply out of the industrial crises of late nineteenth-century America; it was derived from a Jeffersonian worldview.

Mystical dreamers, inspired prophets, and radical visionaries have always played a large part in the utopian tradition. Looking backward over this period, it is obvious that God, or the Oversoul, continued to speak to would-be communal leaders as frequently as before. Thomas Lake Harris's inspiration was found in the Swedenborgian dream mansion and continued to sustain his settlement into the 1890s. Cyrus Teed, Charles Sandford, and Benjamin Purnell were all different personalities and clearly appealed to different religious constituencies, but appeal they did. One does see the spiritualist and Eastern-oriented belief systems take on a more prominent role at the century's end with such romantic figures as Katherine

Tingley, Jacob Beilhart, and George Littlefield, all influenced by books and ideas from mystical realms. Laurence Veysey has documented this mystical shift by looking at the Vedanta movement and its appeal to upper-class women.[21] Zen Buddhism was an arcane and exotic belief system in the year 1900; today it is a growing part of the American alternative religious scene. It is not mainstream (to use the conventional language of religious affiliation); however, it has an appeal for the therapeutically inclined new professional class—the new mainstream.

There were quirky visions that were a compound of private vision and biblical inspiration and had a symmetry that reminds one of the sculptural vision of the black primitive artist James Hampton whose construction, "The Throne of the Third Heaven of the Nations' Millennium General Assembly," has grandeur and dignity. Some were jerry-built affairs, while others, such as William Frey's Positivism, were rational and formal. John Thomas describes all these visions as being part of an oppositional culture that in its most rational form was led by Lloyd, Bellamy, and George: "Here was the oppositional culture that the utopians codified for an entire late nineteenth century community comprised of displaced artisans and mechanics; small tradesmen and local entrepreneurs; yeoman families particularly in the South; and increasing numbers of European immigrants at one or two removes from the soil and bringing with them memories of a communal life and its traditions."[22]

Those who joined the colony at Burley in Washington State we know had all read Bellamy, George, and Gronlund, and the pages of every socialist journal were full of illusions to their work. Although no single text other than *Revelation* appeared to have inspired the charismatic perfectionists, it is possible to see this oppositional culture from a historical perspective that suggests that they were part of a covenanted theory that stretched back to 1630, of a thirst for community that was in evidence in the 1820s. Thomas Lake Harris and his disciples had moved to Santa Rosa and George Littlefield from the labor battles of Haverhill, Massachusetts, to Santa Barbara. Clearly, California offered a whole new venue for utopians, and Florida seemed to attract the socialists. As Kevin Starr (and Carey McWilliams before him) has noted, southern California was "Lotus Land" at the turn of the century.[23] It offered land, luxurious scenes, and the promise of new things. It was the land that Columbus had set sail for in his imagination, a land that promised to release men and women from the shackles of labor, from oppressive government, from hunger and exploitation. It is not surprising that, when the

Oneida Community became unglued in the 1880s, a contingent of these latter-day utopians left New York and headed for Anaheim. Those communards—like many other Americans of their day—found California irresistible. Eventually, many of the Oneida settlers were drawn back to their Puritan roots and laid to rest in the community cemetery. What had begun as both a reaction to Puritanism and a reflection of it ended the same way. Utopianism and one practical expression of it, communal settlements, represented a continuous phenomenon, one not to be denied. During the post–Civil War period, it flourished in unlikely corners of America, drawing its inspiration from both classic dreams and contemporary realities. Such communities allowed Americans to experiment in ways both practical and expressive of the process of making the world new again—*novus ordo seclorum*.

Such communities were, like the country, in transition. Their residents were in transition to a better world and hoped to construct better communities than the ones that they had lived in. They were not purely reactive, nor were they simply escapists. There were those who had visions and convinced others to embark on a journey; there were those who saw landed settlements as a solution to the vexing "labor" question; there were those who, particularly at the turn of the century, took their mission to the city and the world; and there were those who, as Bryan Wilson has noted, retreated to cultivate their own holiness.[24] Some, like the members of Brook Farm, started out with one strong set of beliefs and then had to modify them in the face of practical necessities. Of course, there was always the pressing issue of survival, an issue that communal settlers from every generation had to confront.

One of the earliest descriptions surrounding the founding of Brook Farm is recorded in an October 1840 letter from Henry Wadsworth Longfellow to his father. Young Longfellow wrote about the "sundry novelties" that were appearing in "his quarter of the world," chief among them the activities of some "Practical Christians" who were planning a utopian community. Though somewhat skeptical about their ability to manage such a venture, Longfellow was sympathetic to their efforts. Yet where it would all lead and what impact it would have were still open questions in his mind: "What will be the final outcome of all these movements it is impossible to foresee; some good end, I trust, for they are sincere men, and have good intent."[25]

Likewise, Ralph Waldo Emerson's notation in his 1843 journal questioned neither the sincerity nor the intent of such efforts but, more important, the eventual impact and outcome of utopian and collective schemes: "They look well in July. We shall see them in September." He was writing about Bronson Alcott's Fruitlands community, and he reflected a commonplace caution about communal ventures and their ability to survive the ravages of time and internal strife—namely, that the heat of cooperative passion was often insufficient to sustain a community through later problems of changing perspectives, weak natures, and difficult economic circumstances.[26]

A different view was put forward by Emerson's contemporary Frederick Douglass toward the end of his distinguished reform career when he was asked to speak about the Northampton Association. It had been organized in 1835 as a commercial silk venture and later metamorphosed into a communal society. Among its members were David Ruggles, the black reformer who had befriended Douglass after his escape from slavery. Douglass's journey toward freedom had given him a keen awareness of environments that nourished equality, and he remembered with fondness his visit to the Northampton Association a half century earlier: "I found too that men and women who were interested in the emancipation of civilization were also deeply interested in the emancipation of slaves; and that this was enough to insure my sympathy for these universal reformers. . . . The people and the place struck me as the most democratic I had ever met. It was a place to extinguish all aristocratic pretensions. There was no high, no low, no masters, no servants, no white, no black. . . . The cordial reception I met with at Florence was therefore much enhanced by its contact with other places in that commonwealth. Here, at least, my color nor my condition counted against me."[27]

Northampton had a short history (1842–46) as a communal society, yet it made a profound impression on Douglass, who was sensitive to the nuances of democracy as they related to equality of condition. Not only Ruggles but Sojourner Truth ("God's Faithful Pilgrim") had found a home at Northampton. Before that, Truth had been a member of the infamous Matthias sect and a principal witness in the murder trial of Robert Matthews (Matthias), who was accused of killing sect member Elijah Pierson. Truth (known then as Isabella von Wagener) had defended Matthews against his accusers.[28]

When asked to speak about Northampton, Douglass was remembering a time when the forces of Fourierism, Swedenborgianism, Grahamism, Transcendentalism, and, in the case of the Northampton community, Unitarianism had made individuals reconsider

14

their moral and social convictions. Writing in 1889, Douglass must have been keenly aware of the transformations in the social and industrial life of Massachusetts and the excitement surrounding the publication of a novel by another Massachusetts son, Edward Bellamy. *Looking Backward* was then serving as a catalyst for social reform and the development of utopian colonies even though Bellamy disapproved of such ventures. In his remarks, Douglass failed to mention any communal or cooperative schemes that were carrying on in the Northampton tradition. His failure to note them highlights the view that communal societies did not survive the Civil War and the changing social climate brought on by industrialization. Had the tradition died? No. What Douglass had failed to do was look beyond New England, for, if he had, he would have seen a varied and vital communal world to the West and South.

The continuity of the tradition may be emphasized by looking at the activities of three communists and publicists during the summer of 1868. Men like John H. Noyes and Horace Greeley and women like Marie Howland bridged the gap between the two periods, representing effective voices in support of the proposition that communal settlements were a viable alternative for individuals seeking collective solutions to collective problems. Both Noyes and Greeley had been propelled into community organizing by experiences in New York City in the 1830s. Noyes had "talked familiarly" with "abandoned men and women" in the Five Points District while engaged in a spiritual battle with the forces of evil.[29] He emerged from the experience purified enough to start a religious paper, *The Perfectionist,* and develop a theology that led to the formation of communes first at Putney, then at Oneida. Greeley had witnessed the chilling effects of the Panic of 1837 on poor New Yorkers, and the experience had opened him up to Albert Brisbane's plan for social renewal based on Fourier.[30] Marie Howland's career is considerably less well known than the others. She lived at Stephen Pearl Andrews Unity House in New York, married the radical lawyer Lyman Case in the 1850s, and traveled in artistic circles.[31]

By 1868, all three had witnessed the successes and failures of communes, yet they continued to work for projects that would enlarge the cooperative spirit. For Noyes, it was continuous encouragement to new religious groups, his press, his eugenics plan—all directed toward producing a new race of communists capable of carrying on "Bible Communism."[32] For Greeley, it was increased agitation in favor of cooperation in the pages of the *New York Weekly Tribune* and his outspoken support for agricultural colonies. Howland, who had lived at Pierre Godin's experiment in worker's cooperatives at Guise, France, during the Civil War, was working on her novel *The Familisterie*, published in 1873, which was an ode to liberated women and the communal life.[33] During the 1880s, she became acquainted with Albert Kimsey Owen and then became the chief publicist for Topolobampo. She joined that colony in 1889 and after its disintegration spent her last years in the single-tax colony of Fairhope, Alabama. All three (Greeley died in 1872, Noyes survived beyond the end of Oneida as a communistic society in 1879, and Howland lived until the 1920s) believed that cooperation, tempered by a scientific and progressive spirit, could usher in utopia. In 1868, Noyes was on the verge of revitalizing (or destroying) Oneida with his stirpiculture plan, Howland was promoting Godin's plan and neo-Fourierist ideas, and Greeley was encouraging settlers to move westward into Colorado (or at least as far west as the Hackensack Meadows) using cooperation as the vehicle for that move.[34]

They were not the only ones directing efforts toward cooperative projects. Thomas Lake Harris founded his long-lived Brocton (later renamed the Brotherhood of the New Life) community in 1867 after having led a spiritualist community in Virginia in the 1850s.[35] In that same year, William Davies declared his son James the reincarnation of Jesus Christ, and the Kingdom of Heaven colony under the divine inspiration of the "Walla Walla Jesus" began its thirteen-year history.[36]

Communal societies founded in the post–Civil War period can be grouped under three general categories that reflect leadership style and membership interest.[37] There were cooperative colonizers, charismatic perfectionists, and political pragmatists. The first group—the cooperative colonizers—were individuals who, in the tradition of Robert Owen, believed that secular salvation could be attained by establishing groups in new settlements and that, by collectively assuming responsibility for the financial future of their communities, the colonists would improve both their moral and their economic conditions. The leaders and sponsors of such societies saw them as ordered environments in which predator habits developed in cities would be eliminated, in which the bonds of family and marriage would be strengthened, and in which the conditions for moral growth would exist. Such settlements usually emphasized economic cooperation and addressed themselves to immediate social and ethical problems. Such colonies were often promoted as an antidote to radicalism and social disorder, but more often as a means by which permanent economic security could be guaranteed to families caught in a web of economic depression and urban decay. In some cases, they were promised a form of secular salvation through cooperation.[38]

Until his death in 1872, Horace Greeley championed this approach, and, during the 1870s and 1880s, Robert Collyer, R. Heber Newton, Elizabeth Rowell Thompson, George Jacob Holyoake, and Thomas Hughes urged its adoption. In the 1867 essay "Moral Aspects of Cooperation," Greeley directed the cooperative message to the journeyman of New York, whose life was being dissipated on "ball games, saloons, grog shops, gaming houses and even more shameful haunts." The answer to this moral and social disorder lay in cooperation: "Now, I would urge good men everywhere to promote, encourage and give their names and efforts to help, direct and sustain cooperative movements, primarily because of their moral influence." In 1869, he reiterated the message: "And yet my own conviction is strong that Co-operation is the true goal of our industrial program, the application of Republican principles to labor, and the appointed means of reducing the laboring classes from dependence, prodigality and need and establishing it on the basis of forecast, calculation, sobriety and thrift, conducive at once to its material culture and moral education."[39] Sentiments similar to these would be echoed by reformers and community experiment advocates over the next forty years, particularly during the upsurge of the Social Gospel in the 1890s.

The second category—the charismatic perfectionists—represents the largest number of groups and those that survived for the longest time. Such colonies were charismatic in one of two ways: they were based either on the personal sanctity of the membership as a whole or on the personal sanctity, special gifts, or powers of a forceful leader. They were perfectionist in their promise that the perfected life could be attained within the confines of a community. Such communities quite often served immediate religious needs and operated within a spiritualist or millennialist tradition.[40]

Their concern for social questions was always secondary to an emphasis on the personal and religious development of the membership as outlined by an inspired leader. Their appeal was wide, however, and cut across class lines. For example, Jacob Beilhart's justification for the Spirit Fruit Society (1900) was essentially a statement about personal holiness and the possibilities of attaining it within a community: "I have studied various religious cults and -isms, and came to the conclusion that all professions are vain unless we teach that man must obey the law of his own being and grad-

17

ually move away from the lower nature into the unselfish spirit and subdue all passions which rule our natural man."[41] Beilhart's message attracted a millionaire and a labor leader.

Commenting on the special role that his mother played in the spiritual life of the Women's Commonwealth that she founded in 1876, Robert McWhirter said, "The religion teaches that the Almighty appears in dreams and these dreams are interpreted by any member of the band. . . . While Mrs. McWhirter's opinions have more weight, yet other members may interpret the dreams and on their own opinions."[42] Martha McWhirter was clearly the leader and dominating figure in this feminist collective, but it was her spiritual insights that brought her followers and coworkers. Regrettably, such charismatic and perfectionist groups have been overlooked in cultural and social studies of the period.

The political pragmatists consisted of political and social radicals who were seeking an arena within which to test their principles and publicize their ideals. They were most numerous during the 1880s and 1890s, when American labor leaders and socialists sought an outlet for political and social energy that was impatient with (and discouraged by) the pace of American democracy. They wanted to show the world and their fellow radicals that cooperation could work and that there was a way to implement socialism in hard times, particularly when the ballot box failed to gain desired results. They emphasized cooperation in the face of a growing Marxist emphasis on the inevitability of class warfare and social strife. The cooperative commonwealth became an alternative to ballot-box democracy and ineffective unionism. However, they were not just parlor socialists but often workingmen weary of the struggle against capitalism and desperate to find a way out of the competitive trap for them and their families. Many were idealists eager to test their faith.[43]

Albert Kimsey Owen, the founder of the commercially inspired Topolobampo colony on the west coast of Mexico, stressed the moral and practical qualities of colonization for his members: "The mission of the Socialists is to force upon the consideration of our people of every class the vital issues underlying the second great problem of civilization (wages, transportation) and to urge by organizing cooperative industries and exchanges the application of equity in the affairs of mankind, at the same time that our home industries are protected."[44] For Owen, the first great problem was to provide a secure home for every individual.

These political pragmatists ranged from Christian socialists to anarchists, and they often saw their efforts resulting in model communities (the kind that Arthur Bestor believed had gone out of favor) that others would copy. Marked often by internal disputes and slipshod admissions policies, such colonies were often shortlived and volatile. Most were conservative on the marriage question and conventionally moral and were allied with the cooperative colonizers in their belief in the moral utility of such colonies. Throughout the period there were, of course, communities founded that failed to fit any convenient category, and they stand as monuments to eccentricity, to a singular vision, and to idiosyncratic communal behavior and inspiration.

If there is a single idea that holds these disparate utopians together, it is the notion of journeying. When we consider the diverse motivations, memberships, and settlement patterns, one impulse does seem to emerge. It is the impulse that moves the pilgrim, the impulse that suggests that a group might explore new territory together. They believed that it was possible to redeem oneself by undertaking a journey, that migration in both a physical and a psychological sense could create community. Just as Sojourner Truth and Frederick Douglass claimed new identities in order to further their cause, these utopians all struggled to redefine themselves, to make "all things new" in the words of *Revelation*, to secure a collective foothold in the world, and then to announce that they had the truth and that they were rooted in Zion.

There were a few communities—and here I use the word *communities* advisedly—made up of individuals who printed pamphlets announcing the birth of their colony and detailing the principles of organization but who failed to generate a body of believers. In addition, there were individuals who hatched colony schemes throughout their careers and who hatched projects wherever they landed. Alcander Longley, of St. Louis, was associated with at least seven colonies in his long life, and his last effort in the 1890s (the first had been in the 1850s) consisted of "himself and an elderly woman stricken with paralysis and rheumatism, bedridden, but enthusiastic."[45]

Some communities owned extensive property, and a few were clearly entrepreneurial in character. The Amana colonies covered twenty-four thousand acres of productive farmland, while Bishop Hill occupied one of the tallest buildings outside Chicago in the 1860s. The "Pacific City" scheme at Topolobampo was part of a vast land and railroad project, and much of its appeal was to Socialists who caught the speculative fever and who wanted to own their homes. John Humphrey Noyes, founder of Oneida and author of the

History of American Socialisms, wrote that the principal cause for the failure of utopian communities could be attributed to "land mania." Too many communities were carried away with their material vision of utopia and allowed their domain to extend as far as the speculative land market would allow. Returning to the land was, in fact, a major thrust of colonies that promised to protect workingmen against the shifting currents of a capitalist economy. Self-sufficiency was often touted as a bulwark against the economic panics that characterized the period.

Groups defined themselves by moving and in that process created a bond and an experience that solidified colony life. By the simple act of journeying, they gave their enterprise a new significance. They embarked on a hegira, usually to what became a holy place, one that they could invest with new meaning. They did not have to call it Zion, or New Jerusalem, or New Odessa, although some did; such a move signified new beginnings, new hope, and a rejection of the past. Even the secular utopians engaged in this process and saw in their march to the new commonwealth a religious affirmation of their pledge to socialism. These journeys, whether religious or secular, were shaped by the expectations that the communists brought to the communities, and they in turn reshaped those collective entities to serve their messianic dream.

One of the tasks of this book is to see where individual aspirations and collective goals met and where, in this age of intense urbanization, industrialization, and industrial warfare, they diverged. It was an era of options and an era of limits—cooperative communities seemed to offer both.

The direct effect that these groups had on national affairs, on public policy, and on major structural change was slight. Yet their raison d'être can tell us something about trends and tendencies that forced workingmen and -women to embrace the cooperative ideal, about how individuals embraced commonality and collectivity in order to satisfy religious and psychic needs. More important, we can see (by looking at a few communities in detail) the process of community formation and charismatic leadership.[46]

Writing in 1956, the anthropologist Anthony Wallace analyzed what he called "revitalization movements." Such movements (here the charismatic and perfectionist communities are particularly important) were "a special kind of culture change phenomenon: the persons involved in the process must perceive their culture, or some major area of it, as a system (whether accurately or not); they must

20

feel that this cultural system is unsatisfactory; and they must innovate not merely discrete items, but a new cultural system, specifying new relationships as well as, in some cases, new traits."[47]

Although Wallace ties such movements closely to cultural stress and the need to reduce such societal and personal stress by finding new mazeways, he does see that such prophets have several choices open to them in formulating new communities for stressful times. Such prophetic figures may, according to Wallace, more toward a revival of traditional culture, import a foreign cultural system, or create utopia. Many of the secular cooperators tried to turn back the clock and recreate the American village, but a surprising number included "manufactories" in their list of activities planned for colonies. On the other hand, religious leaders did create spiritual utopias that sheltered their members from the world. Both patterns utilized an essentially "foreign" system—namely, communal life— as a response to the pattern of American life that was corporate and individualistic.

Although these secular utopians no longer believed that the world could be made right by simple exhortation, they did believe that "the world could be made over for the better if only the right elements of human nature could be put to work and if a suitable environment—whether a small community or a cooperative colony"—could be found.[48] These "postassociationists," as L. L. and Jessie Bernard called then, had not given up on the Fourierist dream but believed that they had to be more scientific and practical in their efforts.[49] In 1865, the Social Science Association was founded in Boston, with many of the old associationists and reformers prominent in its organization. Later, in 1887, the journal *Social Science* emphasized cooperative schemes as a new method for revolutionary change. Between 1865 and 1887, much had happened; however, there were still reformers who placed their faith in the communal way.

Generalizations about correlations between economic distress and religious millenarianism are clearly false when one considers the colonies born during this period. God spoke to the prophets of this period—or at least they heard his voice—in times of both boom and bust.[50] Even though there were structural strains in the society throughout the post–Civil War era, it was often personal and private crises that led individuals into a colony.[51] Some joined because of the potent and compelling leadership, or assumed holiness, of extraordinary men and women. Charismatic leaders dominated the history of such groups, and in addition, there were entrepreneurial colony builders who mixed cooperation and self-interest in order to compound a community. Many joined colonies in search of that simple and elusive quality freedom. For socialists, it was often freedom from the oppressive trusts, from social injustice, from the isolation of old age. For the religiously minded, the community became a place where doubts were stilled, where "I" became "we," and where inner peace and freedom were possible.

In this period, one does see the emergence of new groups, of new strategies for communal organization that distinguish these postassociationists from the Owenites, the Fourierites, and Practical Christians of the 1840s. Clearly, they were a more diverse group, and there was an absence of any single ideology or great figure dominating the era. Bryan Wilson points out than contemporary sects do appear more diverse than their predecessors. For him, "contemporary sectarianism is perhaps more diverse in its teachings and orientations than have sects of the past, at least as sects are found in any one given cultural milieu."[52] Much the same can be said about the groups that flourished between 1860 to 1914 when compared with those that appeared between 1830 and 1860. The post–Civil War utopians were both geographically and ideologically more diverse.

Wilson's approach to the question of communal life history is much more complex than Smelser's instrumental approach. For Wilson, a particular sect or cult must first be both available to and known by a potential member. Second, there has to be something in an individual's background that "renders him in some measure sensitive to the message, style, promises or prospects of a movement, or he must be attracted by the example of the members, by the appeal of the association, or the atmosphere as he perceives it." Wilson believes that individuals join sects (within his definition, communal groups are sects) because they believe that the sects' teachings are "uniquely true." Conversion is a process whereby an individual resocialization is achieved by means of several forces, not just one, and certainly not brainwashing. Wilson affirms, and this study bears out, the contention that such groups are "in a very high degree voluntary movements, and that those who belong to them generally chose to commit themselves to a distinctive way of life."[53]

Communal groups have been characterized as "anti-institutional institutions," and that key idea is important if we are to understand their continuation into the age of "incorporation," to use Alan Trachtenberg's phrase. Arthur Bestor has outlined their qualities in a telling manner: "The importance of these movements to modern society . . . lies in the fact that sects represent a more serious commitment than do any mass leisure activities. They are more emphatically voluntary organizations than are trade unions, membership of which is often obligatory. They offer a wide range of possibilities and a more abiding and penetrating commitment than do political parties. They mobilize more completely the energies, devotion and competence of men than do any of the unremunerated forms, or spheres of activity. In all of these ways, sects have much to tell us about things in which, but for the opportunity for this type of voluntary involvement, the wider society would be deficient." Like Bryan Wilson, Bestor believes that individuals who joined such groups are, in fact, risk takers in risky ages.[54]

Freedom might be gained through unity, through cooperative planning and decision making: freedom for the women at Belton, Texas, under Martha McWhirter's dream rule; freedom for the displaced young Englishmen at Rugby; freedom for the spiritualists on Dawn Valcour Island, Vermont, and the socialists at Equality in Washington State whose paper was *Industrial Freedom*. Today, Americans seek freedom in such different enclaves as Sun City, the Castro, Rajneeshpuram, and the Thomas Road Church; they are continuing the race. The pattern of American life has been varied, and one varied aspect of it has been the communal tradition. These "enclaves of difference" reflected American life in their stress on freedom; they absorbed some of its contradictions in their playing off of individualism and community; they served as a rebuff to the notion that there was an "American way"; they affirmed the pluralist tradition and carried on a pattern first observed among the Labadists who had come to America in 1683.

2 "Behold a White Horse": Visions and Journeys

And I saw heaven opened, and behold a white horse; and he that sat upon him was called Faithful and True, and in righteousness doth judge and make war.

Rev. 19:11

And he who sat upon the throne said, Behold, I make all things new. And he said unto me, Write, for these words are true and faithful.

Rev. 21:5

Writing in his diary in August 1842, Thoreau noted that "there is much to console the wayward traveller upon the dustiest and dullest road" because the "path his feet travel is so perfectly typical of human life." As a lifelong journeyer and seeker, he often used the metaphor embedded in his diary notation for that summer day: "Now climbing the highest mountains, now descending into the lowest vales. From the summits we see the heavens and the horizon, from the vales we look up to the heights again." Thoreau sought utopia in nature and in himself at Walden by journeying westward a short distance from Concord to establish a community of one. There he found a piece of sacred earth and anchored himself in order to confront some practical problems having to do with economy, nature, and society.[1]

Journeying further westward, but within the same seeker tradition, two reformers came to the Miami Valley and the growing village of Yellow Springs, Ohio, to found a community in 1856. They had come north through the valley from Cincinnati, where they had organized a Hydropathic Institute devoted to the practice of medicine using the water-cure techniques. Prior to their arrival in Yellow Springs, Mary Gove Nichols and Thomas Low Nichols had been involved in every reform movement of the day, with vegetarianism, phrenology, women's rights, free love, and Fourierism all engaging their attention.

Yellow Springs attracted the Nicholses not because of any reputation for liberality but because the Yellow Springs Water

Cure establishment was available for lease and because the Nicholses had long harbored a dream that they could establish a center to serve as the nucleus of a movement to reconstruct society along co-operative lines. Horace Mann had come to Yellow Springs just a few years earlier with his own dream and some practical plans for establishing a college. Mann was struggling to place that college on some sound footing and viewed the arrival of the Nicholses with some suspicion. When they turned the Yellow Springs Water Cure into the Memnonia Institute (named after the Egyptian God of Waters), Mann knew that he had a problem. He began to counter the Nicholses when some Antioch students showed interest in a different venture for social improvement. Thomas Nichols promised to "establish, by the side of Antioch, a better, more thorough, and more comprehensive school that it is, or is likely to be."[2] Mann succeeded in driving them out of town by 1857. Before leaving, however, they expanded their utopian dream by converting to Catholicism after a visit from a spirit (named Gonzales) during a spiritualist circle meeting. The spirit appeared to Mary Gove Nichols and exclaimed, "Justice, justice, to the Society of Jesus." Later Ignatius Loyola—himself, as the Irish would say—appeared, as did St. Francis Xavier.

If Horace Mann had had any doubts about the dubious nature of the Nicholses, they were now confirmed. Free love was bad enough, but Catholicism was worse, particularly in an age when newspaper ads appeared indicating a preference for black maids over Irish-Catholic ones. Mann died in 1863, broken by Antioch's erratic finances; however, the Nicholses moved to England, where they continued to work in the health field, promoting hydropathy. Mann had, of course, won the day concerning the institutional basis of reform in Yellow Springs. The Nicholses were not as practical as Mann; they were more spiritual, more catholic in their interests. Their search for community took them over some wilder territory.[3]

Was there anything about the Nicholses, in their quest for a perfected community based on cooperative principles, that was "typically utopian"? In numerous ways, they were like other reformers of the period influenced by Fourier and Swedenborg. Brook Farm, for example, was so influenced. The Nicholses had about them a profoundly religious drive based on their belief that spiritualism was the religion of humanity. It embraced all men and women, offered the possibility of a higher law in the Emersonian sense, and was rooted in mystical and transcendental experience. They were typical in that their community did not last and that they failed to establish a permanent base for their philosophy. In many ways, England was a more congenial place for them, and they found in the Roman church a community that their own amalgam of interests and philosophies had been unable to sustain. Their leadership was a coequal one, whereas the leadership pattern of most American groups was that of the dominant male. Their philosophy was in large measure directed toward purely spiritual ends, whereas most American communal groups at that time stressed the practical rewards of cooperation. They had more in common with such mystical eighteenth-century German sects as Ephrata and the Women in the Wilderness than with Brook Farm or the North American Phalanx, both strongly influenced by Fourierism. The Nicholses' conversion to Catholicism was also unique among utopian and communal leaders, but it parallels the conversion process of Orestes Brownson, the spokesman for urban mechanics.

What was central to the Nicholses' career and has been central to the communal and utopian tradition is the act of journeying. Travelers going from one land to another, voyages undertaken to explore new territory, and fights of mind from "here to there" fill the pages of utopian fiction and romance. More's *Utopia*, Bunyan's *Pilgrim's Progress*, Dante's *Inferno*, Howells's *A Traveller from Altruria*, and Vonnegut's *Slaughterhouse Five* are but a few books that have used the journey theme to fathom other worlds, to describe their contours, and to marvel at their inhabitants.

Recent interest in journeying has ranged from Jonathan Rabin's fascination with the Mississippi in *Old Glory;* to William Least Heat Moon's *Blue Highways,* a circular trip around the United States on secondary roads by a young writer who is part Indian; to Richard Reeves's *American Journey,* wherein he retraced Alexis de Tocqueville's celebrated tour of America, which resulted in *Democracy in America.* Reeves had wanted to see what had changed in America since 1831 and what had remained the same. Predictably, he found both that enormous changes had occurred and that there were still some settled patterns about American life. Clearly, this renewed interest in mobility, movement, and migration—what George Pierson called the "m-factor" in American history—comes at a time when our population is shifting in terms of both geography and ethnic composition.[4] We are, according to the columnist Ellen Goodman, a nation of "leavers."

American communal groups and individuals such as the Nicholses were part of this leaving tradition when they created new places or redefined themselves. An almost archetypal pattern can be found in the history of the best-known American group, Oneida, and its leader, John H. Noyes. Celebrated for its economic achievements, social patterns, and unique sexual arrangements, Oneida—and its membership—mirrored shifting patterns of social and religious life in nineteenth-century New England and the "burned-over" district of New York. Noyes's own personal hegira took him from the developing commercial town of Brattleboro, Vermont, to Dartmouth College, where he had gone rather than to Yale because his mother believed that it "would be a better place for his morals."[5] After an intense revival experience, he went to the Yale Divinity School for his ministerial training and considerable emotional and technological turmoil. By going away to Yale, he was thrust into a world that forced self-examination and self-definition.

While in New Haven, he embraced a radical form of perfectionism, lost his license to preach, journeyed to Boston to pronounce his own importance as a religious figure to such abolitionists as Garrison, and then went to New York, where he "talked familiarly" with prostitutes in the Five Points district and downed stimulants (cayenne pepper, rum, tobacco) in order to test his ability to endure such fleshy attractions. While at Yale, he fell under the tutelage of the liberal theologian Nathaniel Taylor, whose motto was, "Follow the Truth if it carries you over Niagara."[6] Noyes took that injunction seriously. He triumphed over sin in New York, established himself as a serious perfectionist leader, and emerged in 1841 as the leader of a small communal group in Putney, Vermont. Noyes had come only a short distance geographically, yet he had broken with his past and was forging a new identity that involved a redefinition of the family, of sexual relationships, and of community. That redefenition was inaugurated in 1841 when he established the Putney Community, instituted "Bible communism," and began the "complex marriage" system that marked his career as being both radical and conservative.

Noyes and his community of believers settled in Putney until charges of adultery and lascivious behavior broke over their heads and forced them to journey—actually flee—to central New York, where they were taken in by some sympathetic perfectionists and where he established the Oneida Community. His travels did not end there, for he preferred to live in a cooperative household in Brooklyn, New York, for a time and practice "complex marriage" while his upstate group led either celibate or monogamous lives. From 1854 until 1863, he spent much of his time at Oneida, taking frequent trips, however, to a satellite community at Wallingford, Connecticut, to get away from the pressures of community life. His vision was that the Oneida Community would consist of a network of communities held together by communal faith and love, with a mobile population moving from community to community. The Shaker confederation was clearly his ideal extended family. That dream never materialized, and it was supplanted by one that took the community on another tack that had within it the seeds of its own destruction.

Noyes instituted his stirpiculture plan when he was fifty-seven years old and with it sought to regenerate the community and, I suspect, himself. That regeneration process led to the birth of sixty-nine children, eleven fathered by Noyes. He left Oneida in 1877 in the midst of an internal crisis and some external pressure from local religious leaders, who were intent on ridding the area of the community's noxious presence. Noyes spent his declining years at Niagara Falls, Canada, where he reportedly took up with a sixteen-year-old girl. According to one source, he had never been happier, now freed from the burdens and responsibilities of colony life and leadership. Noyes had journeyed continuously westward and in the process had explored the limits of community, the edges of his own psyche, and his own sexuality. That exploration led him to define himself in continuous fashion, to make self and community fluid so as to serve the core needs of faith and security.[7]

On 22 May 1855, another band of travelers set out on a journey from Bethel, Missouri, to Oregon. They were but a part of an enormous overland migration that had begun in the early 1840s and continued unabated for two decades after that. Most travelers were drawn westward by tales of gold or fertile land, and, although they had heard stories about the hardships that they might have to endure—hostile Indian attacks and fierce mountain storms that trapped parties—or about the loneliness that engulfed trains on the two-thousand-mile trek, they still went West.[8] This particular group had faced hardships before and survived: they were bound together by faith and communal dedication, and their trip was reminiscent of the 1847 journey taken by the Mormons under the watchful eye of Brigham Young.

Unlike the Mormons, they had not known persecution for their faith and had moved westward because of a call heard by a man who thought himself touched by God. They were followers of William Keil, an Austrian-born mystic, who arrived in the United States in 1831 on the ship that brought the bridge builder John Roebling. Keil's career had led him out of the Methodist church to found a sect of his own based on the belief that he was one of the witnesses mentioned in Revelation 11:3.[9] The core members of his sect originally had been associated with the Harmony Society and had joined his Methodist church at Phillipsburg, Pennsylvania, in 1839. In the spring of 1844, Keil's entire congregation moved from Phillipsburg to a twenty-five-hundred-acre site in northern Missouri. They named it Bethel after the ancient city near Jerusalem, and by 1847 the colony had grown to six hundred. Some members came to consider Keil an autocrat (with good reason), and in one year over two hundred fifty left rather than serve under such a severe prophet. One of his devoted followers described him benevolently as a man of "upright bearing, a most open countenance, but with positive features."[10] Those upright features were substantial and enabled Keil to lead his communal group from Pennsylvania to Missouri and then ultimately to Oregon.

In 1854, on the basis of sheer inspiration, Keil decided to abandon the Missouri site for one further west. During the preparation for the westward journey, his son, Willie, fell ill. Keil promised Willie that he would go west with the rest of the society because "he had for over two years taken great interest in the plans and was now engrossed with the preparations for the start; talked of it in his wakeful hours, dreamed about it at night." Four days before the planned departure, Willie Keil died. Rather than bury him at Bethel, the elder Keil ordered that a coffin be prepared, lined with lead, and then filled with alcohol and that the boy's body be placed in it. Beyond that, he ordered that the hearse would lead the wagon train and should be the first "to arrive in the land by the sundown sea."[11]

The first large contingent contained thirty-five wagons transporting two hundred fifty men, women, and children. At one juncture, the colonists were fearful of moving further westward since reports of Indian raids had reached them. Keil spoke to the group, saying that they must go forward because he had read a passage from Numbers that had comforted him and given him confidence in their progress: "Be strong and of good courage, fear not, nor be afraid of them, for the Lord thy God, he it is that doth go with thee: he will not fail thee, nor forsake thee."

A bugle order was given to break camp, and the wagon train moved on with the hearse in the lead and the colonists heroically and symbolically singing Luther's "How Mighty Is My Fortress," accompanied by all the available instruments in their possession.[12] They sang as they went west. Reportedly, they met a group of Sioux just after crossing the Platte River, and their singing and funeral procession made a powerful impression on the Indians.[13] Six months after leaving Missouri, the colonists entered Oregon, and their first act after taking up land along the Willapa River was to dedicate a new cemetery and bury Willie Keil after his transcontinental funeral march. The colony prospered in Oregon, lasting as a cooperative enterprise until 1881, four years after prophet Keil's death.

The trail to Oregon had begun in Austria and had led to Pennsylvania, to Missouri and then to the Willamette Valley—with a few diversions along the way. Some of the early members, having left the Harmony Society, the Rappit colony at Economy, to join Keil's congregation at Phillipsburg, had known three prophets—Keil, Rapp, and Count Leon. Count Leon—Bernard Muller—had visited the Rappites in 1831 and announced that he was "Archduke Maximilian of the Stem of David and the Root of David." His prophetic utterances and personality were vital enough to split some Harmonists away from the parent body, establish a church of his own at Phillipsburg, and in 1833 move that group southward to settle a colony on the exact latitude as the original Jerusalem. The group's 1834 settlement at Grand Ecore, Louisiana, was short lived as the climate proved too harsh. Muller (Count Leon) died there, and his followers renamed the site Gethsemane, some drifting back to Pennsylvania and becoming involved with Keil.

This constant search for a Holy Land, for a New Jerusalem, has characterized the history of many groups. This wandering, this overland journeying, this ability to start anew and consecrate new ground with conviction and settlers (and, in the instance of Aurora, with a new body), suggests that communal settlers shared the American passage of restlessness. Yet there was a paradoxical quality about such a quest. Although they sought new land and in some cases new leaders, the settlers always believed that their next stopping place was the final one and that the spot chosen would act as a beacon for others. Their journeys always presumed an end—a resting place—and they remained there as long as the vision sustained them. If it failed, then another prophet could renew them with a new vision or a dream of a new land.

One prophet who renewed himself and his followers with visions and journeys was Thomas Lake Harris, whose career as a communal leader began during the spiritualist upheavals of the 1850s. Harris studied for the Baptist ministry but converted to Universalism in 1843 and then fell under the influence of Andrew Jackson Davis, the spiritualist. After breaking with Davis, Harris organized the Independent Church Congregation in New York City and rejected spiritualism in favor of Christianity. From 1843 to 1851, Harris was in religious turmoil as his faith encompassed Jesus, Davis, and Swedenborg.

Eighteen fifty-one was a pivotal year for Harris as he went to Mountain Cove, Fayette County, Virginia, with about a hundred followers to establish a cooperative agricultural colony. He and his co-leader, James Scott, acted as spiritualist mediums and received "Divine Instructions" about the direction that the colony should take. Their retreat at Mountain Cove was a "gathering-in" place where they waited to see the Messiah. During 1852 and 1853, it floundered, and Harris, according to his biographers, "resumed his wanderings, lecturing on spiritualism throughout the East and South and making several small groups of friends, especially in Georgia and New Orleans."[14]

Late in 1853, Harris published his "proem" *Epic of the Starry Heavens*, written under spirit direction, and for the next forty years (he died in 1906) he moved about the United States and England, preaching a mystical doctrine of "Two-in-One" and asserting his role as the "pivotal man" mediating between the forces of heaven and hell and between body and spirit. His career as a prophet and seer led him to upstate New York. There in 1861 he founded the Brotherhood of the New Life, which he then transported to a second site in New York before moving his dream westward to California in 1875 and establishing the Fountain Grove community. At Fountain Grove (near Santa Rosa and on seven hundred acres), he came to believe in his own immortality and was bedeviled by rumors that he ran a free-love colony. Those rumors drove him back to England, where he ended his journey.

Like the colonist from Bethel, Harris moved west with his congregation, and they remained faithful (with one major exception) throughout his career. None of his colonies ever gained a substantial membership; however, at Fountain Grove he did bring seventeen hundred acres under cultivation and ran a prosperous wine business. His spiritualist message appealed to different audiences in the 1850s and 1890s, and he was always able to temper his mysticism to suit the times. Mr. and Mrs. Horace Greeley were members of his Independent Church in the 1850s, and in the 1890s Harris was a Bellamy supporter, even sending Bellamy a "proem" "not for publication but to strengthen him."[15] Always a reformer, always a prophet, Harris presumed a pivotal role for over fifty years while he turned and moved westward in search of new land, new converts, new opportunities.

Whereas Harris was a successful prophet with a half-century career, not all the groups launched in the 1850s found such a hospitable reception or such dedicated followers. For example, the Vegetarian Settlement Company and Octagon Settlement Company failed to achieve any success in Kansas before the Civil War. Their efforts were duplicated numerous times (particularly in Kansas) during the next two decades. During the 1870s and 1880s, Kansas became a prime target for colony ventures and harbored more settlements than any other state.

This mania for Kansas colonization began in 1855 at a meeting in New York City of the Vegetarian Settlement Company, an outgrowth of the American Vegetarian Society founded in 1850. Henry S. Clubb, an Englishman and a reporter for the *New York Tribune*, was inspired by the work of the New England Emigrant Aid Society in starting free state settlements in Kansas. He viewed with horror the "slide toward meat eating" that was engulfing the United States. Club believed that vegetarianism promoted health and longevity, helped immunize against disease, was economical, and encouraged temperance.[16] According to Clubb, vegetarianism was based on biblical authority, and the early Christians were vegetarians. His ascetic philosophy favored nondenominational schools, colleges, and settlements located in suburban areas "away from the contamination of flesh, alcohol and social vices."[17]

The Vegetarian Kansas Emigration Society could provide a haven for believers who, without such a community, would be "solitary and alone in their vegetarian practice" and "might sink into flesh-eating habits." Prospective members had to be of good moral character and not slaveholders. Fifty-seven prospective members attended the first meeting, and inquiries were received from an additional sixty-one vegetarians, which suggests that the colony might have had over a hundred members. Land was sold at the government rate of $1.75 an acre and held in a joint-stock company with each member paying $5.00 (in either cash or labor) to purchase shares. Each acre carried with it a voting share. Funds generated by the land sale went into a common fund earmarked for street and school construction. The town was platted in an octagonal pattern containing four villages of four square miles each. The colony treasurer, Dr. John McLauren, an eclectic physician, made a visit to southeastern Kansas in 1855 and picked out a site on the Neosho River. Next, a constitution was drawn up proclaiming, "It is desireable that those persons who believe in the vegetarian principle should have every opportunity to live in accordance therewith, and should unite in the formation of a company for the permanent establishment, in some portion of this country, of a home where the slaughter of animals shall be prohibited, and where the principle of the vegetarian diet be fairly and fully tested, so as to demonstrate its advantages."[18]

The advantages of such a plan lay in the ability of each settler "to live in a village where and at the same time they would have pasture land in front and arable land at the rear of his home; that they would enjoy mutual aid and the advantages of cooperation in stores, machinery purchase; that there were educational advantages to be gained for children with the establishment of schools; that certain intellectual advantages would accrue by frequent assemblies in a central building to discuss agricultural, physiological, mechanical and other sciences to avoid the dullness of country life; that living in community would elevate the social arts, mental and moral cultivation." The cooperative features were intended to "promote, and not to supersede, individual enterprise."[19]

Clubb proposed—probably for speculative reasons—that a second company be formed to complement the vegetarian settlement and that it be located on the other side of the Neosha River. The octagon plan of housing and land settlement had aroused interest among nonvegetarians, and Clubb proposed that a large area could be set aside for such meat eaters who were enamored by the octagon features of the colony. In March 1856, the first group of settlers moved westward with sixty-three in the vegetarian contingent and fourteen in sympathy with the octagon principle. Miriam Davis Colt, recording her journey in *West to Kansas*, found that her fellow travelers were "families who have come from North, East, South and West to this *farther* West to make pleasant homes."[20] What they found was that little had been done to prepare the site.

Colt's hopes for the colony had been family centered, not communal and moral. She saw it as a place that had "the advantages to families of having their children educated away from the ordinary incentives to vice, vicious company, vicious habits, of eating and drinking, and other contaminations of old cities." The Vegetarian Settlement was a "most desireable place of residence to all whose tastes are averse to those habits of gross indulgence which are degrading to mankind."[21]

Antiurban sentiment permeated the philosophy undergirding both groups. Images of dark and degrading cities spill forth from their statements, and one finds a profound wish to start over again in a clean place. It was not to be. The advantages of the site (Kansas), ideology (vegetables and octagons), and system (cooperation) were insufficient to stay the hand of disaster. Badly organized and containing too many members with too few skills, the colony was further hampered by Clubb's lackluster personality. He lacked not only charisma but also, as one settler later wrote, the "practical ability to manage the affair of the colony successfully."[22]

Interest in Kansas continued for thirty more years, and reformers eager to abandon cities, shape new settlements, or test some vital moral or aesthetic principle would pioneer towns in Kansas and further west just as long as new ideas abounded and cooperation remained a potent force in the lexicon of American ideas.

The movement of Americans to California or Texas had had several strands. One of them came from Europe in search of political or religious utopia. Plockhoy's Colony, Ephrata, the Shakers, Communia, and New Harmony were all founded by visionaries from abroad. One French visionary continued that tradition in the 1840s and 1850s. Etienne Cabet, and then his followers, organized colonies at Red River, Texas (1848); Nauvoo, Illinois (1849–60); Cheltenham, Missouri (1858–64); Adams County, Iowa (1878–86); and Icaria Speranza, California (1881–86). Cabet's philosophy has been described as "non-Jacobin republicanism with a humanitarian desire to better the conditions of the working class."[23] Through political pamphlets, journals, and books, and most clearly in his utopian fantasy *Voyage en Icarie*, he outlined a program and attracted a following. From 1839 (when *Voyage en Icarie* was published) to 1847, he was a major spokesman for workers' rights in France, and in the pages of his journal, *Le Populaire*, he issued a call to his readers. It was a simple one: "Workers, let us go to Icarie."

One of his followers, Emile Vallet, gives some of the reasons for the forcefulness of that cry and the appeal that it had to young idealists like himself: "He [Cabet] could talk the language of the people and acquired a strong influence and reverence. Many called him 'Father' and a second Christ. . . . As soon as he was satisfied that his theory was well understood, he resolved to wait no longer to put it into practice; asked the French government the privilege to try the experiment in France. The government most respectfully declined, being afraid of contagion." Cabet then proposed that they put his plan into action in America, "where freedom reigned supreme." A land grant was obtained from a Texas company and an appeal put forward in *Le Populaire* for volunteers. In February 1848, sixty-nine men swore allegiance to Cabet and the Texas adventure. According to Vallet, "the enthusiasm was great when they embarked at the city of Le Havre. The Pioneers of Humanity (as they called themselves) looked splendid in their black velvet suits."[24]

The first contingent, however, found malaria and harsh weather on their arrival in Texas, and they abandoned the site when news reached them that the Revolution had broken out in France and that they would be needed on the barricades. On their way to Shreveport, Louisiana, they met up with a second, smaller party (twenty-eight) and then came on a larger group of ninety in New Orleans. Indecision now gripped this substantial body of Frenchmen, and they wrote Cabet, asking his advice about the course that they should take at this pivotal point in French history. Was the future in America or in France? Since the fortunes of the revolutionary party were waning, Cabet decided to join his followers in America, arriving in January 1849. He decided that a new site was essential, and in the spring a group was sent to explore the Mississippi Valley, eventually reaching Nauvoo, just recently vacated by the fleeing Mormons. Where other utopians had failed, Cabet and his followers thought that they could succeed.

On 1 March 1849, 281 Icarians boarded first the steamer *Marshall Ney* (Ney was famous for having covered Napoleon's retreat from Moscow) and then—appropriately enough—the *American Eagle* at St. Louis. They reached Nauvoo on 15 March, and Vallet waxed eloquently about the meaning of their journey:"Our pioneers were not rich, but they inhaled the air of pure freedom. Uncle Sam left them perfectly free to try their experiment. I doubt if the president of the United States at that time ever noticed their presence on this continent. . . . They had nothing to struggle against but human nature, their own human nature. They had the will power, the skill as mechanics, a new and rich country and complete freedom."[25]

Freedom. Freedom to start a new society, to move about at will, to be divorced from their past, to take destiny in their own hands and try to secure a new future. Pioneers of civilization in that most uncivilized and complacent land where the president did not care where they went or who they were, they could call themselves Icarians, or Shakers, or Perfectionists, and, for the most part, they would be left to their own destinies.

Freedom did not, however, guarantee success, and, after a difficult three years at Nauvoo, a decision was reached to start a colony in Iowa. Dissatisfaction with Cabet's leadership caused his ouster in 1855, and a new colony organized by his backers was begun in St. Louis in 1856. For two years, the group had been wracked by turmoil, and the once messiah-like Cabet now looked a devil to some. Cabet was erratic and autocratic and failed to give the colony any positive leadership. But they had survived the difficult first years, and, although there were conflicts over Cabet, the Icarians remained firm in their faith in cooperation. Cabet died in 1856, and a year later the anti-Cabet faction left for Adams County, Iowa. This pattern of splitting, regrouping, and splitting again characterized the history of the Icarians. What began as a coherent, cohesive group under the leadership of a charismatic leader changed over time. Yet their collective determination was to sustain community life in the face of shifting political events in France, Cabet's erratic personality, and financial hard times on the American frontier.

On the one hand, when we look at the Icarians, we can see their weaknesses, their fragmentation; still, they started impressive towns wherever they went and, as Robert Hine has shown, accomplished much in Iowa and California.[26] The last Icarian group settled in California in the 1870s, and by that time numerous other foreign communards had passed through Texas and Kansas to continue the tradition inaugurated by Jacob Plockhoy in 1662.

Considerably less well known than the Icarians were another foreign-born group—the St. Nazianz colony—who settled further north in the 1850s. This group of Catholic immigrants from Freiburg, Germany, came to Eaton Township, Manitowoc County, Wisconsin, under the leadership of Father Ambrose Oschwald.[27] Oschwald was a mystic and a herbalist physician who ministered to both the spiritual and the economic needs of his congregation. Oschwald attended the University of Freiburg, was ordained in 1833, and in 1848 published *Mystischen Schriften,* predicting that the New Jerusalem would come before 1900.[28] The archbishop of Baden condemned him and the work, relieving him of his parish in 1849. In that same year, he organized some followers into the Spiritual Magnetic Association under the spiritual guidance of St. Gregory Nazianz, the third-century church father and poet who had praised the monastic life. Between 1852 and 1854, Oschwald studied medicine and botany at Munich and laid plans to start a community. Deeply influenced by the Book of Revelation, he believed in the eventual appearance of Jesus Christ: "But it will happen, what has to happen. We preach only to those who listen. He who does not want to hear, let him in the end find out for themselves." In 1854, he urged his followers to take the necessary steps to prepare themselves for the coming of Jesus: "In imitation of Gregory the members were urged to flee the corrupt world, enter into themselves, and observe evangelical counsels." [29]

Counseling celibacy for his flock, Oschwald took as his example of community the first Christian community of early converts: "Our example is the first Christian community in which all members were of one heart and soul, and no one said that anything was his." [30] Members wore a distinctive uniform consisting of a white habit with red cincture and blue mantle. Although he had problems with local bishops over his apocalyptic teachings and occult medical views, it was an economic depression in the 1850s in the Black Forest region that forced the congregation to leave. One hundred thirteen members of the St. Nazianz Association purchased thirty-eight hundred acres in Wisconsin and set up the first Catholic utopian group in America, one similar to the Ephrata Colony. There were celibate orders for men and women in addition to nuclear families. All shared in common. Nonaffiliated families held land in their own names, farmed as individual proprietors, and participated in the colony's religious life. The total property of the association extended seven miles from east to west, three miles north to south. By 1866 (the only date for which exact figures are available), there were eighty brothers, 150 sisters, and about 170 others in the village living in over sixty dwellings.

The parish church dominated St. Nazianz, with Oschwald's residence and dispensary located on the ground floor. Worship services were held on the upper floor. Between 1854 and 1873, a brother house (the Loretto Monastery) and a sister house (Holy Ghost) were constructed, and both brothers and sisters maintained a monastic life, the sisters making hats, shoes, and woven objects, the brothers working the land. All observed the common rule. Morning prayers were at 5:00 A.M., at 5:30 domestic tasks were begun, at 6:05 all assembled to recite the "little hours" in German, and at 6:30 Mass was held. Breakfast in common (and in silence) followed at 7:00. After breakfast, there was work till 11:30, then lunch accompanied by a spiritual reading; at 12:30 P.M. Divine Office was read; at 1:30 the brothers and sisters returned to work until 6:30. After the evening meal (again in silence), there was a rosary, and the final half hour of the day between 9:00 and 9:30 was spent in the chapel. Frank Beck reports that, "during at least the earliest years, the lay members of the association who lived a normal family life in the village also followed a rigid schedule and performed the spiritual exercises in the little frame church of St. Gregory." [31]

In sum, St. Nazianz was a monastic community under the spiritual guidance of its abbott, Ambrose Oschwald. All this took place within the context of a German village where the brothers and sisters mixed freely with the other villagers. The convent garden marketed its surplus in Manitowoc, both the male and the female orders took in orphans, and the sisters began a school as early as 1858. Until 1890, the colony school ranked as one of the largest in the county, and, in 1871, a seminary was established with Oschwald and a layman as the first professors. Within the settlement, German village life was carried on in much the same fashion as it had been in the Black Forest except that no one questioned the inhabitants' religious or social practices. Local pageants, feast days, and rural ceremonies were celebrated by villager and colonist. With Oschwald's death in 1873, colony life declined, and by 1877 it had begun to lose its communal features.

This rather extraordinary group reminds one of Ephrata, of Zoar, of Amana—all German in origin, all led by singular men, all close readers of the Book of Revelation. Amana lasted as a corporate entity until the 1930s even though it was considerably altered by the turn of the century; Zoar struggled on until 1898, though much of its community life had gone by the 1870s. Both remained part of larger communities well after their end as cooperative colonies. All of them tried to create village life with a communal core, and all three had remarkably little conflict with their neighbors or state authorities.

Although during the 1850s there was a decline in cooperative colonies and the cooperative ideal among American laborers, there still existed a powerful thrust toward establishing landed communities. The demise of the phalanxes and the failure of Fourierism did not signal the end of utopian settlements in America. Twenty-two separate groups were organized as compared with the sixty started in the aftermath of Brisbane's campaign to convert America to Fourierism. It is a mistake to equate Fourierism with communalism in the antebellum period. The tradition is richer and more varied than the North American Phalanx or Brook Farm.

In 1850, Nils Thun, a wealthy Norwegian convert to Moravianism, started a colony at Green Bay, Wisconsin, modeled after Count Zinzendorf's at Saxony. In 1851, a group of German Swedenborgians tried their hand at communal life on a thousand acres in Iowa; the Oneida Community started a branch family at Wallingford, Connecticut, that lasted almost as long as the main colony at Kenwood, New York; the anarchist Josiah Warren started Modern Times;

and Thomas Lake Harris began Mountain Cove. In 1852, another Norwegian, Ole Bull, the famous violinist, financed a colony in Pennsylvania. In 1853, spiritualists organized in Chatauqua County, New York, and in Warren County, Indiana, while Fourierists continued to start colonies (at Raritan Bay); a group of free lovers invaded Darke County, Ohio, with a colony; schismatic Mormons settled in Iowa; and a spin-off group from the 1851 Moravian settlement moved from Green Bay to Door County.

Eighteen fifty-four saw bloomer-wearing free lovers of the Rising Star Association move into northern Ohio and take up residence in the village of Berlin Heights.[32] At the same time, the celibate Catholics of St. Nazianz were breaking ground in Wisconsin. The Society of True Inspiration (Amana) made its move to Iowa, and French Fourierists settled near Dallas in 1855. Moving from Buffalo to Iowa was an important switch for the Inspirationists, and they prospered with the move. Victor Considerrant, a French reformer, started the Reunionist Colony in Texas after reading accounts of American colonies, and two reformers from Cincinnati, Thomas Low and Mary Gove Nichols, came to the quiet village of Yellow Springs, Ohio, in 1856 to establish a School of Life. While William Keil was moving westward with his coffin to a new site in Oregon, a splinter group from Adin Ballou's Hopedale Community went to Minnesota. In the same year, a Millerite group took deep root in Wisconsin, and the Icarians loyal to Cabet traveled from Nauvoo, Illinois, to Cheltenham, Missouri.[33] In 1858, Alcander Longley continued to community hop by founding a Fourierist phalanx—an Integral School of Science and Art—in Indiana. His father had been a member of the Clermont Phalanx, and young Longley had himself resided at the North American Phalanx for several years in the early 1850s. Longley was both a fickle and a constant utopian; he abandoned the Indiana Fourierist experiment for one in Christian communism shortly after 1858.

Taken collectively, the communities founded in the 1850s displayed a variety of ideologies and leadership patterns and were settled in varied locations. Such diversity characterized groups founded in the next half century, except that many were located in the West and South. Some of the groups started before the Civil War lasted, and they represented—with the Shakers, Oneida, and the Harmonists—standing models for other groups to emulate. Repeatedly, one finds in the community literature of colonies begun after 1860 references to the success of the Shakers, the Oneida community, and the Harmonists. During the 1860s and 1870s, all three were at the height of their material prosperity, housed in impressive buildings, owners of large tracts of land. They conducted their business affairs in an orderly and Christian fashion and represented the maturity of cooperative enterprise. Fledgling groups could take heart not only in their existence but also in their obvious economic success, apparent social stability, and longevity. Writing to Ignatius Donnelly in 1862, Frans Widstrand reflected on the success that the older groups had achieved, and it gave him heart: "There is no reason to doubt that property in common (nearly as the Shakers have it) is the best state of society. Money is the root of much evil. Many such associations have existed long and exist now."[34] Widstrand started a colony in Minnesota in the 1870s. What he could not have known was that the Shakers were beginning their long decline in numbers and wealth and that they had reached their peak just a few years earlier.

The cooperative-store movement, which had faltered with the economic crisis of 1857, received a new boost in 1863 as news about the success of the Rochdale movement in England gained attention. Between 1863 and 1865, Rochdale stores were set up all over the East, and the Massachusetts legislature passed a special act for their incorporation in 1866. As Edwin Rozwenc has noted, "The hundreds of stores established by the Sovereigns of Industry and Patrons of Husbandry in the next decade spread the method to wider areas, never reached by Protective Unionism. The Protective Unionism yielded place to the new cooperatives."[35] What such cooperative stores did was keep alive the ideal of cooperation, particularly within the laboring class. The Rochdale plan and the communal idea were, of course, radically different, but one could lead to the other, and in the hard times of the 1880s some labor leaders did turn to a new commonwealth idea based on collective living.[36]

Although American cooperators would turn to England for guidance and example, there was little that the more advanced English laborers could learn from America in the 1860s. In the "News from the United States" column of the Cooperator, there are few mentions of communal efforts except for Alcander Longley's failed community at Black Lake, Michigan, and the reprinting (from Longley's Communist) of T. Wharton Collins's attacks on the churches and his call for "true Christians to gather round the expunders of Communism."[37] As always, Greeley was optimistic and looked to England for example and support: "To show how successful, and even popular, cooperation has become, we will note that within two or three years the middle and even some of the higher classes in

England, have established themselves among them [the coopera-tors]. . . . Perhaps after a time business men and others of standing and means in the cities of the United States may think it worthwhile to avail themselves of cooperation."[38] It would not be until the visits of George Jacob Holyoake and Thomas Hughes in the 1870s that the British cooperative and benevolent example would interest Ameri-can men and women of wealth.

The Civil War did retard the development of communal groups. Whether because of the intensity of the war effort or because ac-counts about the war published in European papers discouraged em-igration, the effect was the same; there were only eleven such groups started in the 1860s. Of course, Amana, Bethel-Aurora, Oneida, the Shakers, and the Harmonists all continued. Groups begun in the pe-riod represented both the charismatic and perfectionist traditions and the cooperative colonizers. In addition, there were some whose ideas had been generated by the ferment of the 1830s and 1840s; it would not be until the late 1860s that westward expansion once again forced Americans to think about cooperation.[39]

Of the charismatic and perfectionist groups founded in this decade, Thomas Lake Harris's Brocton Community, or Salem-on-Erie, was the most prominent, though another group, the Davisite Kingdom of Heaven in Walla Walla, Washington, was as striking as the Harris colony. Harris's career and philosophy make him the very model of the charismatic/perfectionist leader that one sees through-out history. Someone who heard him preach in 1859 described him: "There seemed nothing remarkable in person, face or feature, except his eyes, which have a depth so spiritual that one might imagine him in communion with the Invisible. . . . He looked steadily above his audience." In looking at a photograph of Harris, one is immediately drawn toward his eyes and then to his handsome face and flowing beard. The eyes are deep set and penetrating. Laurence Oliphant, his disciple, gave this picture in his novel *Masallam:* "His voice seemed pitched on two different keys. . . . When he talked with what I would term his 'near' voice, he was generally rapid and vivacious; when he exchanged it for his 'far-off' one, he was solemn and impressive. His hair which had once been raven black, was now streaked with gray, but it was still thick, and fell in massive waves over his ears, and nearly to his shoulder, giving him something of a lionine aspect. His brow was overhanging and bushy, and his eyes were like revolving lights in two dark caverns, so fitfully did they emit dark flashes, and then lose all expression. Like his voice, they too had a near and far-off expression, which could be adjusted to the required focus like a

41

telescope, growing smaller and smaller as though in an effort to project the sight beyond the limits of natural vision." [40]

Within the dual nature of Harris's voice, eyes, and personality, Oliphant saw a Hebraic prophet, a seer, one chosen by God to lead his people out of the wilderness: "The general cast of his countenance, the upper part of which, were it not for the depth of the eye sockets, would have been strikingly handsome, was decidedly Semitic; and in repose the general effect was almost statuesque in its calm fixedness. The mouth was partially concealed by a heavy moustache and a long iron-grey beard; but the transition from repose to animation revealed an extraordinary flexibility in those muscles which had a moment before appeared so rigid, and the whole character of the countenance was altered as suddenly as the whole expression of the eye." [41]

The prophetic face was both intense and profound. In 1900, when he was seventy-one, a woman remarked that "he had the most beautiful head I have ever seen." [42] That head with the changing eyes, the unkempt hair, the strength of character and will evident in every move, had a magnetic power that both disciples and outsiders noted. His look and manner are what we have come to recognize as that of the guru, the master teacher, the leader who by his presence and spiritual authority demands that others listen and look. In this century, we have seen Eastern mystics hold sway, and they have the look of Madras about them. Thomas Lake Harris, born at Fenny Stratford, England, became a prophet despite his place of birth.

During the late 1850s, Harris had turned away from spiritualism and the influence of Andrew Jackson Davis and toward Swedenborgianism. Soon, however, he developed his own variant on the New Church creed and by so doing placed himself at odds with Swedenborgian church leaders. In a series of poems composed in 1857 and 1858, he wrote that God had revealed to him (as he had done to Swedenborg) certain truths about the spiritual world. During March 1857, he was beset by terrible demons: "Remaining sometimes for hours in prayer to the Lord for strength to combat, while the physical frame was subject to unheard of tortures, I knew what it was to die daily. Realizing full well, however, that it was needful, for Divine ends, that I should thus suffer, and that my agonies were continually mitigated by an interposing influence from the Lord, I sought silent and with entire resignation to bear the heavy load" (italics mine). [43] Having gone through his own Gesthsemane and struggle with the devil, he now emerged as the long-suffering Jesus carrying on his shoulders the weight of human pain and suffering.

Throughout his career, Harris would gladly bear the cross of prophethood and suffer the torments of the flesh and the malice of the world. His stoic pose and his dual character seemed mysterious to his followers. He seemed both near and far, close and distant like a star.

After this struggle with Satan, he became, in his own words, a "pivotal man," between the forces of heaven and hell, and one not only to whom God spoke but who also received—like Jesus—additional help during periods of spiritual crises. In the *Arcana of Christianity* ("An Unfolding of the Celestial Sense of the Divine Word through T. L. Harris"), he outlined a progressive philosophy emphasizing the "unfolding" of spiritual messages through him. As his biographers note, this made it "easy for Harris to publish fresh revelations rapidly, spontaneously and almost endlessly, with little regard to their internal coherence or their consistency with previous revelations." The revelations—simply put—stated that God is infinite and made manifest on this earth in Jesus Christ, that regeneration will restore man to an angelic state, and that there is an eternal conjugal union of counterparts. His theory of celestial counterparts presumed that a spiritual being (a counterpart) existed for men and women in the spiritual realm and that by throwing off the physical world an individual could get in touch with one's spiritual bride. "Eternal" marriages between a husband and wife on earth were "made the means of qualifying the spirit for its final entrance into eternal conjugal love."[44] Love on the spiritual level was the highest form, and Harris's followers sought to deny the flesh in order to achieve a purer state.

In 1859, God appeared to Harris again and told him, "My son, go thou to England, and here I will show thee further what thou must do." By this time, his reputation had grown, and he had a small body of followers within his Church of the Good Shepherd and within spiritualistic Swedenborgian congregations in Georgia and New Orleans. Harris saw himself as a spiritualist priest on a special mission from God and ordained to spread the gospel (both God's and Harris's) abroad. As he moved away from Swedenborgianism (which he considered a sect), he began to think of himself ministering to the world at large about a "New Age" that was dawning.

His trip to England produced several results. One, the British were impressed by his "eloquence and prophetic" assurance but put off (at least the liberal Swedenborgians were) by his vague spiritualism. England also impressed itself on Harris. While there he developed a new sense that the social order was in chaos and that greed

43

gripped the industrial world. Beyond that, he came to the conclusion that through both community and isolation men could restore themselves. By *community* he meant a select group of believers who aspired to become "celestial-natural, that is to breathe by influx from the Lord, through the Celestial Heaven." These men and women— like the monastic orders before them—"must be isolated from all ties which have their origin and action in the principle of self-love." For Harris, a community would consist of a group of regenerate men "breathing in harmony with the pivotal man," who became a "vortex of human power." Thus socially fortified, he and his family became "pivotal radiactive." Harris recognized twelve types of respiration: the celestial, spiritual, and ultimate heavens; the earth of spirits; the world of spirits; the life world; the love world; two form worlds; and the essence world of each of the three heavens.[45]

In the *Apocalypse,* he wrote, "There will arise on earth a society called the 'Brotherhood of the New Life,' internal respiration being the bond of union in the Lord. In Christian and Pagan nations, among Jews and Gentiles, both band and free, this fraternity will exist."[46] This brotherhood was to be international in scope and not just the name of a particular sect, as it actually became. In England, Harris saw the possibility for the creation of an organization that would appeal to believers in universal brotherhood and would also work toward alleviating poverty and greed. Both problems, he later asserted, could be addressed through the creation of a community of believers centered in one place near the "pivotal man."

Probably the most important outcome of Harris's English journey was his meeting with Laurence Oliphant. Born into a distinguished family, Oliphant chose to travel with his mother and sister rather than attend Cambridge. He became a practicing attorney in Ceylon (his father was chief justice), took terms at Lincolns Inn in 1851, and studied at Edinburgh in 1852. Between 1854 and 1863, he was a war correspondent and traveled to Japan and Poland. By the time he met Harris, he had developed an international reputation as a writer. He and his mother met Harris in 1860 through a mutual friend who had an interest in spiritualism. With that meeting began a tortuous relationship between the Oliphants (both mother and son) and their spiritual mentor, Thomas Lake Harris.

Harris returned to the United States in mid-1861, establishing the Brotherhood of the New Life at Wassaic, Dutchess County, New York. There he was joined by members of his immediate family and his New York City congregation. In 1863, they pooled all their resources and purchased some land, a grist mill, and a bank. Harris was now president of the First National Bank of Amenia. The Oliphants joined them in 1865 at the height of Laurence's career. Oliphant had just been elected to Parliament and had written two best-selling novels. But he felt a certain spiritual emptiness in his life, and, after Harris had made a return trip to London in 1865, Oliphant made a decision to go to America: "At that period under a pressure that was irresistible, I felt myself compelled, much against my natural inclinations, to abandon the pursuits and ambitions of the life I had hitherto been leading, and decided to devote myself to prosecute my researches into the more hidden laws of nature, which I felt convinced, concealed Divine truths that had as yet been hidden from man. . . . It appeared, for many reasons, that the seclusion and opportunities I sought would be most fitly found in the United States." [47] Thus, young Oliphant—the seeker after agnostic truths—came to sit at the hand of the prophet, Thomas Lake Harris.

Numerous other stories circulated concerning Laurence Oliphant's decision to join the Harris community. Some believed that Harris had mesmerized him or promised to cure him of his reported syphilis, or that his mother had entreated him to join her, or that he was in hot pursuit of a young woman, Lee Waring, who had come to London with Harris. All these stories had a plausible ring about them, yet equal credence must be given to Harris's supporters, who said that Oliphant came in search of some inner peace after years of traveling and dissipation. He hoped that his journey to America would be his last and that he would find that hidden law of nature best suited for himself.

Oliphant's biographers believed that he "suffered from a number of acute needs and was more than ready to offer his allegiance to a leader, spiritual or otherwise, who promised to satisfy them. First, he required a clean break with the past, an entirely new regimen. And secondly, he needed punishment and suffering that would symbolize purification and atonement." In a marginal note in a letter, Oliphant later wrote, "My maker made it quite clear to me, at least, in answer to a deep supplication for guidance, that in order to be a man one must be in control of one's own organism; for if one is not the master of powerful passions, one is bound to be their slave." [48]

Although he sought release from slavery, Oliphant found that Harris demanded abject servility. At first, Harris was slow to admit him to the community; once admitted, Oliphant was made to live in isolation: "I am therefore not allowed to hold intercourse with anyone, except one or two persons, for ends of use—and I live in the sort of temporary encampment which I built myself of vine bores."

45

Oliphant was given a spiritual or "Use" name, "Woodbine" (each brotherhood center—such as Amenia—was called a "Use"). Here was Laurence Oliphant, world traveler, cosmopolite, and sybarite, purging himself of the world, the flesh, and that self that he wished to lose by working with a hoe in a vineyard in the wilds of America. This self-abnegation, this going to hard labor after the pleasures of London, has, in addition, a Thoreauvian ring about it. It is also Jesus fasting in the desert; it is the adept following the commands of the prophet. It is the active man throwing off the pleasures of the world so that he can know himself and, by knowing himself, enter a community of other perfected persons: "I have found that in doing this kind of work that we must trust Divine guidance in every step. Success is certain if we do, but if we venture upon a single move in the selfhood, failure is inevitable."[49]

In a letter to an English friend, Oliphant outlined his new status: he was a pilgrim. "A pilgrim to the land of love," he wrote, "I cross the stormy sea, and still in voices from above, my Lord is leading me."[50] At that time, the only authority that he recognized was in "Faithful" (Harris's Use name). He was not the only pilgrim to come under that authority, but his discipleship was certainly dramatic and represented the powerful bond that can be created between master and follower. Whatever drove Oliphant to the New World (and it was probably the same demon that drove him back) also urged others to place themselves within the orbit of the "pivotal man." The Oliphant/Harris relationship highlights a continuous pattern in the history of communal groups—that of the unswerving faith that the prophet demands and receives from his or her followers. It is an area where rationality does not enter, where the demands of the prophet are the only demands that one may hear and where the entreaties of friends and the common sense of the world have no authority.

With financial help from Lady Oliphant, Harris purchased, in 1867, two thousand acres at Brocton, on Lake Erie, near Buffalo. It was an area well suited for grape cultivation, and Harris had grandiose ideas about establishing it as the center of his international brotherhood. The community at Brocton consisted of between sixty and seventy adults, including a group of Japanese. All the membership (except the Japanese) had been Christians, two couples had lived with the Shakers, and one was a former Quaker. Several had experience in wine making and horticulture, and their skills were put to use in the large Brotherhood Winery that they established. A substantial number came from Swedenborgian churches in the South, and several brought considerable fortunes for the Use.

All accepted unquestioningly the leadership of Thomas Lake Harris, and they turned their possessions over to him on entry. Jane Lee Waring—"Dovie"—brought in a fortune estimated at between $250,000 and $500,000. A beautiful and talented woman, she worshiped Harris and acted as his confidante in all matters. The membership lived a common life in the sense that they were all reduced to the same social level and owed complete loyalty and fealty to Harris. They did not, however, eat in common or live in a communal household; rather, they settled in cottages around the property. Harris, like many a prophet and charismatic leader, exempted himself from physical labor and lived in more comfortable surroundings. His critics said that he lived in splendor, was waited on by Japanese servants, and enjoyed pleasures (such as tobacco) denied his followers. Mrs. Harris lived in another part of their house and appears to have been mentally unbalanced. Their two children both proved troublesome and bridled at their father's interference in their private lives. Apparently, they were often unsettled by Harris, who rearranged the household from time to time to maintain the proper spiritual balance; "consequently no member knew at what time of the day or night he might be transferred to another part of the grounds."[51] The members' children lived by themselves in a house called the "Garden" and called Harris "Papa Faithful." Married couples did live together, though they kept celibate.

In addition to the wine business, the community maintained a grist mill, a general store, and a restaurant and bar and sold their excess produce to the surrounding communities. Harris often spoke of himself as a socialist, though there was clear evidence that he believed that the spiritual millennium was at hand. All members at the colony were working toward a "pivotal" goal of self-purification, presumably in advance of the millennium. Although there was no formal or proscribed worship (Sunday was not observed), they did hold services on occasion, with Harris preaching. One member later wrote that his sermons were "most searching and quickening, and brought us into states of humiliation and penitence."[52]

Sexual abstinence was the rule at Brocton as members prepared themselves to evolve into "structural, bisexual completeness above the plane of sin, of disease, or of natural mortality." One's spiritual counterpart might be revealed on earth, but only as a fay or a fairy or in a dream. One of Harris's great strengths as a leader lay in his ability to understand personal problems and suggest simple solutions. One woman gave up her home, her family, and her husband because "Father John had touched just the chord in her nature that was wanting to vibrate; he had shown her that she loved herself more than God, that she loved her children more than God's children."[53] A chord wanting to vibrate or a chord wanting to stop vibrating: Harris had an answer for all.

Although the colony received enormous sums of money from the Oliphants and Miss Waring, it was always, seemingly, in need of funds. Laurence Oliphant was allowed to go to England in 1870 to resume a journalistic career because his wages would help support the community. While in England, however, he fell in love with and married Alice Lee Strange, who accepted his religious philosophy, Thomas Lake Harris's prophetic leadership, a celibate life, and the need for her to turn over her considerable fortune to sustain the Use. Her love for Oliphant and his obedience to Harris came into conflict, and the brotherhood proved a stronger bond at this time. The colony held its most celebrated member for another five years. The New York phase of the brotherhood came to an end in 1876 when Harris decided to find a warmer climate for himself and his vineyards. The California phase will be treated later. It must be acknowledged that Harris was a remarkably successful prophet and that his ability to plant, sustain, and then replant a colony based on his inspiring message was impressive. He promised his followers that if they joined him at Brocton they would find the perfected life, a spiritual center devoted to purification and self-knowledge. Harris had achieved what he set out to do: he had a faithful membership, a reasonably secure financial base in industry and contributions, and a continuing career as a seer with a message. Most of all, he had prophetic belief in his own destiny. During the 1860s, he achieved what many others would try to do, and try in vain.

Sources for the Brotherhood of the New Life are as plentiful as sources about Celesta are scarce. What we do know about Peter and Hannah Armstrong is that on 14 June 1864 they made a formal declaration before a justice of the peace in Sullivan County, Pennsylvania, that they were to "grant, deed and convey to the said Creator and God of Heaven and to His heirs in Jesus Messiah" six hundred acres of land. The Armstrongs believed that "His children should not claim to own property of any kind as individuals, but that they should bear and consecrate unto God all things that they possess for the common good of His people who are waiting for His Son from Heaven, and who are willing to live together in holy fellowship."[54]

Armstrong was a peddler from Philadelphia who had prospered enough to establish a communal gather-in site, and it included a public park surrounded by nine blocks each containing forty lots.[55]

This 360-lot site was evidently copied from the street plan for Philadelphia, and Armstrong issued an appeal for settlers in his paper the *Day Star of Zion and Banner of Life of Philadelphia and Celesta*. Apparently, he issued the paper for a considerable period of time, but the only extant copy is dated May 1880. In that issue, he set out (and presumably had been setting out) the "Objectives of the Paper: First, to build a House for the God of Israel, not only of earthly material—but as a place of refuge against impending judgements. Second, to organize a bond of perfectness—and thus hasten the coming of the world's Redeemer. Third, to show how we may enter into life without seeing death and corruption etc. Fourth, the nature of man, what he loses through Adam and gains through Christ—shall be the mission of the *Day Star*."[56] Approximately twenty persons resided in the community. Armstrong maintained a combined store and printing office on the first floor and the second housed an auditorium for religious services. Names of some of the members have come down to us, but little more.

Contemporary accounts depict him as a "very good looking man, [who] wore no beard and had a very pleasant address." He is remembered as quoting profusely from the Bible and being "entirely sincere in the religious convictions."[57] Those convictions led him to deed over the property to God, clear a hundred acres for cultivation, and proselytize from Philadelphia and the mountain retreat. All we know is that a handful gathered in, that the *Day Star* printed three thousand copies, and that Armstrong died in 1892—a meager history to be sure and one that lacks the memoir accounts, the novels, and the photographs that surround Harris's colonies. One might ask the question, as did William Hinds, "How many societies have been based on the doctrine of Christ's second advent?"[58] During the 1860s, Celesta and Adonai-Shomo are the only ones on record, though I suspect that there were other gathering-in communities, or at least churches, devoted to that vital doctrine and operating within the shadow of William Miller's 1844 crusade. The House of David, started later in the century, and its predecessor, the Michael Mills colony in Detroit, were both part of the tradition. Possibly Armstrong was not charismatic enough to attract a substantial following and his religious sheet insufficient to generate anything other than a ripple.

One of the elements of prophetic leadership involves the ability to make manifest a message. Successful charismatics have been able to combine their message (usually in pamphlet or periodical form) with a personal and visible ministry. That ministry gives flesh to the word, gives the prophecy a human face. One sees this in the prophetic styles of Thomas Lake Harris, Eric Jansson, and John Humphrey Noyes.[59] In all cases, the word became flesh through the personal qualities of the leader. Members were able both to hear and to feel that message in convincing fashion.

Another community where the word of God became flesh in the eyes of the believers was the Kingdom of Heaven Colony at Walla Walla, Washington, which started in 1867 and lasted until 1881. Whereas Harris asserted his Christhood in a metaphoric and elliptical fashion, the central figure of the Kingdom of Heaven had his thrust on him. This colony's leader was William W. Davies, who was born in Wales in 1833 and who, at age thirteen, converted to Mormonism. He became a preacher and followed the path taken by many of his countrymen when, in 1854, he emigrated to America, settling in Utah in 1855. On his arrival, he was unsettled by the worldly quality of Mormon leadership and the events surrounding the Mountain Meadows Massacre, where Mormon militia attacked and killed their Gentile opponents. Davies then followed James Morris, the Mormon schismatic, who announced his prophetic mission in 1859 and gathered a group about him. "Praying Joe," as some called him, received visions that placed him at odds with the Mormon leadership. One of his basic tenets was reincarnation, and he broke with the Mormon hierarchy when he declared that Brigham Young was not Joseph Smith's spiritual successor, though he was a legitimate temporal one. Smith's spiritual successor was, of course, James Morris.

By the early 1860s, the Morrisites numbered in the hundreds and encamped near South Weaver, Utah. The Mormons laid siege to the settlement till the Morrisites surrendered. Morris and his chief lieutenant were shot. Davies fled the area, moving first to Soda Springs, Utah, and then to Montana. While in Montana, he had a series of revelations, one of which directed him to set up the Kingdom of Heaven in Walla Walla. With forty of his followers in tow, he arrived in Washington and in 1866 established a colony on eighty acres. Davies reportedly declared, "This is the place"—echoing Brigham Young's famous declaration as he saw the Salt Lake flats after a journey across a wilderness.[60]

In February 1868, Mrs. Davies gave birth to Arthur Davies, who his father had announced was the reincarnation of Jesus Christ. When another son was born the following year, he declared that child the "Spirit of God the Father," and William Davies became the "Holy Ghost." This holy family—Mrs. Davies received no special recognition—was accepted by the Daviesite followers. It was not a

50

closely guarded secret that they believed in their own divinity, and it was common knowledge among their neighbors. All property in the kingdom was held in common, with land title remaining with the elder Davies. Resources were pooled, a common storehouse established, and a campaign begun to spread the Daviesite gospel based on the doctrines of reincarnation and the godly nature of the male members of the Davies family. According to Russell Blankenship, "They believed implicitly that he [William Davies] was the voice of God and the reincarnation of the Holy Ghost and they accepted his statements concerning his sons with few reservations."[61] Some believed that he could perform miracles. His right-hand man, Grover Andrews, was an unusual figure who was the community disciplinarian and had a penchant for fighting. Popularly known in the area as the "Destroying Angel," Andrews kept his reddish-brown hair in curls that hung to his waist. One story about him alleges that he lost a thumb to a biting opponent in a fight and that he felled the local marshal with a single blow after the hapless marshal interrupted him while telling a story.

The colony came to an end in 1880 when both the "Walla Walla Jesus" and the "Daviesite God the Father" died of diphtheria. In traditional communal fashion, a lawsuit precipitated the breakup of the group as three members filed suit for back wages and monies presented on entry to the community. The court allowed the plaintiffs $3,200 in order to satisfy the judgment property, including the Davies home; personal belongings and livestock were sold. The suit effectively destroyed the economic base of the colony, though it seems doubtful that it could have survived the deaths of two of the three resident gods. At the time of its breakup, there were forty-three people in the community. In 1881, Davies married a local schoolteacher, declaring that she was the reincarnation of his first wife. They later moved to California.

The Kingdom of God, the Brotherhood of Man, the Celesta Colony, and Adonai-Shomo all operated within a perfectionist tradition. Promising a perfected life to their members, they all had unique qualities that held them together. For one it was the leader, for another the children of the leader, for another a particular place within the Adventist tradition. All sought and found a degree of separation from the world, all presumed that the membership could and would move from one holy place to another, and all demanded collectivity and commitment from their members. When compared with the Shakers or Amana, they were not as successful, yet they did secure a foothold for themselves and provided a place (a secure place) for their members to consort with a prophet, to be closer to God, and to continue that religious odyssey so characteristic of utopian settlers.[62]

Religious enthusiasts and voyagers were not the only communal settlers in the 1860s, as groups of utopians made efforts to found cooperative colonies in New Jersey, Minnesota, Ohio, Missouri, and Colorado. Again one is struck by the variety of these efforts, by their contending philosophies that had a single common thread: the presumption that a better environment for social progress and growth was both desirable and possible; that members could, by sharing land, resources, and labor, shape a community and be responsive to individual and collective needs; that a community of "social interests" did exist in contrast to the growing and seemingly pervasive philosophy of individualism permeating American urban life and threatening family life.

Writing in 1867 in the *New York Weekly Tribune* on the "Moral Aspects of Cooperation," Horace Greeley commented on the life led by urban mechanics: "The vital cause of the workman's ill success is usually as follows: As an apprentice or minor his means are scanty, and he spent them on his own needs and appetites as fast as he received them. At length he became a journeyman, when his income was suddenly swelled to double or treble its former sum. He had already expensive appetites; he has now the means of securing their gratification. . . . He is single; he is in the heyday of youthful passion; thus he is drawn irresistibly and gradually into a career of dissipation and debauchery. Ballgames, saloons, grogshops, gaming houses and we have even more shameful haunts." For Greeley, the solution to this downward slide into debauchery and corruption was that "a cooperative store, judiciously and honestly managed, will prove a true business college to its stockholders and a perpetual excitement to thrift and economy."[63]

Cooperation would release the working class from "dependence, dissipation, prodigality and need" while at the same time providing for a sound basis for "forecast, calculation, sobriety and thrift, conducive at once to mental comfort, its intellectual culture and moral elevation."[64] While Greeley was touting the cooperative way in the *Weekly Tribune*, the first of several cooperative and communal ventures was launched in Colorado. Between 1869 and 1872, Colorado became an important site for such projects. The term *colony* was widely used to describe "any group, large or small, organized or unorganized, that entered the territory."[65] For example, ten families who had joined forces to move westward were called the

Illinois Colony, and a group of emigrants from a Kansas town was called the Wyandotte Colony. A more common practice—one encouraged by the railroads—was for a group to travel on special tickets and then settle in one area, an area usually owned by the rail company that had sold the discounted tickets.

Three groups, however, did come to Colorado with more than this minimal sharing of resources. They joined together as a matter of social policy and out of economic necessity. They were the Union Colony, the German Colonization Colony of Colfax, and the Chicago/Colorado Company. Of these groups, the German Colonization party had the most in common and, in terms of organization, was the first.

What attracted all these groups was the promise that the Colorado Territory held out for them. After 1858, Colorado had become a mecca for gold hunters and had a few settlers, but by 1863 the fever had subsided because of the difficulties surrounding gold mining, and a six-year depression set in. Mines were abandoned, mills stopped, and the territorial population actually decreased. Problems with Indians and an inadequate transportation system hampered the growth of the area and made the movement of goods and services into Colorado difficult. Although the Indians were eventually subdued (some in the infamous Sand Creek Massacre), the key to change in Colorado's prosperity came in 1868–69, when the railroad arrived in the territory. The Union Pacific reached Cheyenne, Wyoming, in 1867, and the Denver Pacific Railroad connected Denver with Cheyenne. In August 1870, another connection was made to Kansas City, and freight and passenger traffic reached Colorado Springs in late 1871. The railroads opened up the state in those years, and they made a concerted effort to populate it.

Although some settlers had come to farm during the early 1860s, Colorado was essentially virgin territory for agricultural development. In particular, lands owned by the Denver Pacific were prime locations since they crossed the South Platte River. The Denver Pacific, in conjunction with the National Land Company, sold land on a partial payment basis, arranged transportation at reduced rates, and had a network of offices in Chicago, St. Louis, and Topeka. The general agent for the company, C. N. Pratt, played an important role in placing these cooperative colonies in Colorado during this period.

The National Land Company launched an aggressive campaign to entice settlers westward. James Willard has succinctly described their depiction of the West: "In its most complete form, attained in 1870, this picture was one of Arcadian simplicity and prosperity."[66]

They sketched a land of abundant crops and enormous yields, all fed by an extensive irrigation system. One of the problems that the promoters faced was the popular image that Easterners had of the "Great American Desert" stretching from Kansas to California. To counteract the image of sterility, the land company put on exhibit in Chicago gigantic cabbages, beets, and potatoes all grown in Colorado and purported to be of average size. A prospective settler confronted with a sixty-pound cabbage must have booked passage at once.

The first effort to organize along cooperative lines came in August 1869, when Carl Wulsten, an editor of Chicago's *Stats Zeitung* and a Union Army veteran, proposed to settle a colony of poor Germans from Chicago. Propelled by "a desire to ameliorate the physical condition of the poor class of Germans, who were condemned by a cruel fate to work in greasy, ill ventilated and nerve destroying factories of the great city of Chicago," he "formed a band of about a hundred into a colony, took them and their families out of the nauseous back alleys and cellars of the over crowded Garden City and brought them to El Mojuda."[67]

The conditions for membership in the colony, outlined in the constitution, were liberal: good moral character, twenty-one to forty-five years of age, sound health, and $250. These "pioneers of civilization," as the *Chicago Tribune* called them, took off in a blaze of publicity. Their railroad car was festooned with a banner: "Westward the Star of Empire takes its Course—the German Colonization of Colfax, Fremont County, Colorado Territory." A special freight train was employed to carry the livestock and household goods. The *Tribune* described the colonists in the most glowing terms: "They were a splendid looking set of people middle aged, sober and matrons with their numerous families; muscular athletic young fellows, with rifles strapped across their backs; and there too, a spice of romance in the intensely practical party—twenty, fair-haired, clear skinned German girls, all young and good looking, and all capable, seemingly of taking good care of themselves and making excellent wives for those same gallant rifle bearers"—A romantic scene for a romantic adventure despite the puffery in the reporter's tableau.[68]

Wulsten believed that the only way that the colonists would survive the rigors of frontier life was to cooperate—at least initially. His communism was a means toward achieving economic and social independence for the settlers. Each member was credited with two dollars a day for labor (both skilled and unskilled) and charged for food, transportation, clothes, and other supplies. All industries (including agriculture) were to be carried on cooperatively for five

years, with the proceeds divided at that point. Individuals were prohibited from carrying out any business independent of the colony.
The site that they selected (outside a railroad grant area) was in West
Mountain Valley, south of Canon City. The valley had agricultural,
commercial, and mining possibilities. In order to secure their land
grant, they petitioned Congress to modify the Homestead Act so as
to allow cooperative ownership of the land. The colony town was to
be called Colfax, after Schuyler Colfax, then vice president.

For the settlers, the westward journey was an unusual one in
that they had been sent first class and avoided all the trepidation
associated with overland trips. When contrasted with the journey of
the Bethel-Aurora group in 1855 to Oregon, it was luxurious. Not
only did they travel west by train, but at every point federal officials
made their passage easier. At Fort Wallace, Kansas, they were delayed for two weeks awaiting the arrival of ox teams; then they spent
the next two weeks leisurely learning how to drive and handle them.
The secretary of war had authorized the use of government wagons
to transport the colonists and provided a military escort and tents.
The governor of Colorado was not to be outdone and shipped them
three boxes of rifles and two thousand cartridges.

The Germans arrived in March 1870 at Pueblo, Colorado, and
Wulsten gave them an address at the Court House. In the party were
ninety-two families, a total of 337 members. Six births had taken
place en route. In his address, Wulsten emphasized that the new
settlers were fleeing the crime and congestion of Eastern cities: "At
one period of my life, while officially engaged in enumerating the
inhabitants of the region known as the Five Points in the City of New
York, I was daily brought into contact with the disgusting filth, misery, want and crime of that locality. I became satisfied that the want
of food and necessaries of life were the principal causes of the crime
of that great city. I then formed the idea that the overcrowded cities
should send their surplus inhabitants to the broad acres of the West,
where their miserable condition would be changed to a state of comparative comfort and happiness." [69]

Wulsten was clearly aware that his journey was the first of
many, for he alluded to other colonies being organized under the
auspices of Greeley and Meeker. He ended his address by asserting
that they would vote the straight Republican ticket and that their
new neighbors were invited to join them in a housewarming in the
fall at which lager beer, Dutch pies, and dumplings would be served.
Wulsten sounded like a politician on the hustings, for his speech
was peppered with fulsome projections about the future of the col-

ony and the West. That future was clouded, however, by a group of squatters who settled on colony land and demanded a fee before they would leave.

After paying off the squatters, the colonists immediately went to work erecting temporary cabins and putting in a community garden on thirty acres. Their petition to Congress had failed to receive approval, and, until they each filed individual claims, they, too, were squatters. After July, conditions grew worse. Dissatisfaction with Wulsten's leadership caused some families to leave, and they were forced to send a petition to the governor asking for rations because the first crop was not yet in and the colony store had burned in December. Several reasons contributed to this sudden failure of the German Colonization Company. Inexperienced as farmers, the colonists had delayed getting the crop in, and an early frost had spoiled their efforts. One critic later charged that it failed because "there was too much Kommunismus." [70] Wulsten, an optimist, saw it as a success because all those who stayed in the area had, in fact, gained their independence from Chicago and were able to homestead land—on their own, of course, and without cooperative features.

In many ways, the German Colonization project was like New Harmony. Both began on high notes with praise and publicity surrounding their inauguration, both had articulate and competent spokesmen who turned out to be inadequate leaders, both presumed to be consistent with emerging egalitarian and democratic aspirations, and both lasted for very short periods.

The second Colorado project was organized under even more auspicious leadership: Nathaniel Meeker and Horace Greeley were its founders. Meeker had been a Fourierist lecturer before joining the Trumbull Phalanx in 1846, and as a member he stayed for three years before moving to Euclid, Ohio, where he went into business. In 1865, he joined the staff of the *New York Tribune* as agricultural editor. From that vantage point, he began to write about the necessity of cooperatives, and, in December 1869, he issued a call in the *Tribune*: "I propose to unite with the proper persons in the establishment of a colony in Colorado Territory." Meeker believed (in Fourierist tradition) that cooperation had its advantages but that land should be held by individuals and that the family unit (contrary to Fourierism) should be maintained. He wrote, "Happiness, wealth and the glory of a state spring from the family." [71] The *Tribune's* various editions had a combined circulation of 300,000, and Meeker's call was answered in the first month by twelve hundred inquiries.

Meeker then called a meeting of interested parties for late December at the Cooper Institute. The *Tribune* covered the event. Greeley opened the meeting with an address that stressed the large response that Meeker's call had evoked in the readers, the practical problems that had to be faced (land division, irrigation), and the need to view it as an experiment that other colonies could learn from.[72] At the meeting, a provisional committee was formed, a name agreed to—the Union Colony—and fifty-nine would-be pioneers paid an initiation fee of five dollars. At a second meeting, a locating committee was established to go West, authorized to purchase land. The genesis of Meeker's own interest in Colorado lay in an 1869 trip to the Utah Territory. On that journey, he visited Colorado with two railroad land agents and returned to New York with a clear idea about where a colony should be located. The colony vice president was General Robert A. Cameron, an Indiana Republican and early Lincoln supporter who had lost his eyesight in the war and since that time had acted as agent for several colony ventures. After a trip to Colorado in May 1870, the locating committee announced that it had purchased almost twelve thousand acres for $60,000 on a site near the Platte River at Greeley, Weld County.

Between April and June 1870, almost a hundred families went to Greeley to take up residence at the Union Colony. Four hundred forty-two members paid an initial fee of $155 for membership. Even though the first organizational meetings had taken place in New York City, few members came from there. In a circular prepared by Ralph Meeker, the leader's son, Colorado was described thus: "The scenery is grand beyond description, and the land in the vicinity unsurpassed for agricultural purposes. . . . The climate is said to be spectacularly favorable for persons troubled with weak lungs." Residents were encouraged to bring complete households, including "servant girls and other hired help," because such help was scarce and demanded high wages. The majority of the settlers came from New York, Pennsylvania, Ohio, Michigan, Illinois, Connecticut, New Hampshire, and Massachusetts, with a few from Colorado and California. What distinguished the members and their town was its emphasis on temperance. Greeley was the third temperance town in the United States (after Vineland, N.J., and Evanston, Ill.), and there was local support for the idea of a dry town. The *Rocky Mountain News* acknowledged that drinking often led people toward "destructive recklessness" and that an example of the other "extreme by a whole community may prove a wholesome example and restraint to the rest of us."[73]

Meeker's experience at the Trumbull Phalanx had convinced him that unitary housing would not work; thus, the only substantial cooperative venture (aside from the creation of the colony) was a cooperative irrigation project. Greeley itself was thrown up in great haste to accommodate the settlers, and some marveled at the "instant city" quality of it all and the speed with which churches, schools, and other institutions began to operate. Within a month after their arrival, seventy homes were built and numerous businesses established. Yet there was dissatisfaction. About 10 percent of the first group left early and sold their interests. Wood and coal had to be transported long distances, and arid land discouraged farmers who had been accustomed to green pastures and ready water.

In October 1870, Greeley visited the colony and in a speech gave some advice about the colony's management, "especially in the matter of labor pursuits; advised the organization of a farmers club and other societies for mutual and beneficial intercourse, information and amusement." When interviewed by the *Rocky Mountain News,* Greeley expressed the belief that the colony would prosper and saw no reason for its demise "unless its members should take to drink, or gambling, or some kindred folly, and so squander their magnificent opportunities."[74] The key question facing the colony had to do not with the whiskey question but rather with the corollary water question.

Irrigation was essential to survival, so in the spring of 1870 a nine-mile ditch had been begun to bring water to the fifty thousand acres held by the colonists. Fencing the land had been a cooperative venture, and a fifteen-mile fence had been erected in short order. Irrigation proved much more difficult. Ditches were inadequately graded or too small, and, although wealthier farmers were able to raise enough cash to build proper ditches, the poorer ones were to suffer from a lack of water for their crops. By 1871, the colonists voted to replace their officers with an elected town government. Greeley ceased to be a colony and became a town. Meeker left and became a government agent on the White River Reservation in Wyoming. Never known for his tact, he succeeded in outraging the Utes by plowing up some pasture land and a corral. They shot and then mutilated him.

Dolores Hayden has summed up the Union "experiment" (to use Greeley's phrase) in admirable fashion: "The Union Colony advertised collective religion, industries, irrigation, fencing and housekeeping, but members were unwilling to give up existing faiths, personal capitol or Eden myths for these collective ideals. The town developed a hodge-podge of symbolic religious architecture, a rambling business district, and hundreds of homes and shacks before everyone recognized that the colony had been successfully 'boomed' and 'puffed' into a city that was not in any way a commune."[75]

Greeley and the Union Colony were the products of several visions held by old-time utopians, Meeker and Greeley. Their previous experience with phalanxes had taught them that one had to go slow, had to compromise, and that too much collectivity could destroy a colony. So they emphasized the moral benefits from cooperative labor and industry. They were reacting to their own unsuccessful experiences and adopted a conservative ideal in contrast to the cooperative and participatory ideal that had burned in both their breasts thirty years earlier.

In contrast to this limited cooperative experiment in Colorado, there was a commune in Kansas that came into being while Union languished. This colony was to succeed because of its patron and the leadership that he exerted over a decade. The patron for Silkville or the Prairie Home Community was Ernest de Boissiere. Born into an aristocratic Bordeaux family, he was educated at the Polytechnical School of Paris and granted a commission in the French Army Engineer Corps. After serving for several years, he resigned his commission to take charge of the family estate, Chateau de Certes. Part of the estate bordered on several thousand acres of sea marsh where channels had been cut in several places. At high tide, fish came into the marshland area, and by building a sea wall de Boissiere was able to harvest them. Under his direction, the family estate grew profitable from both the fisheries and the pine forests that he had planted.

During the late 1840s, he became involved in politics, aligning himself with the radical Republican forces in opposition to Louis Napoleon. When Napoleon seized power in December 1851 and crushed the opposition, de Boissiere left for America. After traveling in the United States for a time, he settled in New Orleans, where he purchased several merchant ships and engaged in mercantile trade. He seems to have moved back and forth between his estate in Bordeaux and his New Orleans home during the 1850s, resettling in France on the eve of the American Civil War. When the war ended, he returned to New Orleans, where his philanthropy got him into trouble. He donated $10,000 to the Freedman's Aid Society of the Methodist Episcopal Church because he "wanted to do something for that part of the human family that is most needy." This generous act brought to his doorstep irate citizens, who told him that he could not spend money in New Orleans for Negroes. De Boissiere left New Orleans in 1868. His interest in helping the "human family" had been evident as early as 1856, when he had met the Fourierist Charles Sears and indicated a desire to start an educational and industrial institute run along cooperative lines. De Boissiere visited Sears, who was then president of the North American Phalanx, again in 1861 in New Jersey, where the idea of a colony was born.[76]

The architects of the colony plan were de Boissiere, Sears, Albert Brisbane, and E. P. Grant. Brisbane was the most distinguished American Fourierist of his day, having single-handedly introduced and then popularized Fourier's ideas in America. As a young man, he had met Fourier in 1832 and studied with the great universal genius. On his return to the United States in 1834, Brisbane established a society to promote Fourier and published *The Social System of Charles Fourier* (1838) and his own *Social Destiny of Man; or Association and Reorganization of Society*.[77] The turning point in his campaign to make Fourier's works known came when he purchased some space in Greeley's *Tribune* in order to publish a weekly article on Fourierism. Through the *Tribune*, he reached an enormous audience, and that exposure was profoundly instrumental in launching the phalanxes of the 1840s. During the 1860s, Brisbane continued his crusade through the American Social Science Association and its efforts to promote rational and scientific approaches to social problems.

E. P. Grant was another Fourierist who participated in the planning of Silkville. A graduate of Yale and an attorney, he founded the short-lived Ohio Phalanx and was considered the leading Fourierist in the West. After the colony's failure, he went into business at Canton, Ohio. It was de Boissiere who reunited these old Fourierists (Grant was sixty, Brisbane fifty-nine), and in 1867 he traveled throughout the Mississippi Valley in search of a site for a colony. By January 1868, negotiations were underway with an agent of the Kansas Educational Association of the Methodist Episcopal church to purchase twenty-four hundred acres of land in Franklin County. Initially, the plan called for the cultivation of a thousand acres and the settling on the land of thirty families to manufacture silk. De Boissiere and his cothinkers had an arcadian vision, one that coincided with the Fourierist emphasis on handicraft labor. The environment was one that de Boissiere recognized because he "found the climate of Kansas similar to that part of France where silkraising was the most prosperous."[78]

Early in 1869, the land purchase deal went through, and the Kansas Cooperative Farm came into existence on thirty-five hundred acres of undeveloped prairie land, twenty miles south of the county seat of Ottawa. Grant, Brisbane, and de Boissiere drew up the articles of association, probably modeled after the articles of the North American Phalanx. Together they subscribed a total of $29,000 to the new community. By April, de Boissiere had settled there: "I am living on the wide prairies on which I hope to see the germ of a phalanstery built. I sleep in a small garret at the top of a rough farm house, as cold as the outside atmosphere. We are fifteen crowded together and our cottage is situated near the road. Sometimes immigrants come and ask for shelter. It is a severe life for me, used to the mild climate and comforts of Southern France, but I think that the sufferings of the flesh are nothing and preserve the predominancy of the spirit. . . . My European income is five times my yearly wants."[79]

Such hardships forced Brisbane and Grant to leave; de Boissiere (also fifty-nine) remained. In 1870, Grant published the pamphlet *Cooperation: or a Sketch of the Conditions of Labor, with a Notice of the Kansas Cooperative Farm of M. Ernest V. de Boissiere*, and he maintained a lively interest in the farm colony, though he never returned to Kansas.[80] Brisbane seems to have lost interest, and it is unclear just how much money he actually put into the venture; de Boissiere had hoped to put the farm on some firm financial footing, then induce other socialists to join him in supporting it. In an interview with a reporter for the *Topeka Commonwealth*, he indicated that he wanted to found a colony where workers could receive a just return on their labor and escape the grinding consequences of industrial poverty. His plan was to build a large unitary building (a phalanstery), a common dining hall with optional living arrangements for those who preferred cottage or family life. In short, it was to be a phalanx. His approach was cautious, and that caution must have been urged on him by the experienced Grant and Brisbane.

The manufacture of silk was begun in 1869 and broad goods woven from fabric in 1870. Also in 1870, the colony planted seventy acres of Russian mulberry trees. Silk worms were imported from California. During 1870, two families returned from France with de Boissiere, and over the next several years forty French immigrants came to the colony. Few American families joined, and de Boissiere recruited workers during periodic trips to France. There silk production had been stimulated by the invention of new machinery, and silk societies were promoting its growth and use. De Boissiere calculated that with his French laborers he could develop silk culture profitably in Kansas. Soon after their arrival, his imported labor discovered that higher wages could be obtained in nearby towns, and he was forced to replace them with local workers. Plans to construct a phalanstery proceeded and were inspired by the factory works of Pierre Godin at Guise: "A preference is shown for a parallelogram of the dimensions of 72 by 120 feet, with a covered court and tenements on four sides," according to a report in the *New York Herald* about the colony.[81]

A three-story frame building was used for housing. There is no evidence to suggest that the more substantial Godin-inspired "palace" was ever constructed. During a visit in 1871, Charles Riley, state entomologist for Missouri, observed that 150 acres were under cultivation, that cattle raising was being considered, and that there was a stone silk factory on the premises. Eight thousand mulberry trees had been planted, and an additional twenty-five hundred were to be set out. Viticulture was under way, and de Boissiere envisaged additional business ventures, including broom making, meat canning, and the processing of agricultural goods. According to Fourierist philosophy, a varied range of industries was necessary for a well-rounded community since job rotation was a key element in the scheme of passional labor. Yet Riley found that the silk operation had been rationalized because the French handicraft workers had left and the process had to be automated. Keeping the silk works in running order was a constant problem because of the turnover of labor and the constant need to train an unskilled labor force.

Over the next two years, the physical plant grew. Additional buildings, including a twelve-hundred-volume library, were added, and De Boissiere thought his foundation secure enough to issue a call to other cooperators to join him. E. P. Grant, now resettled in Canton, Ohio, agreed to publish a colony prospectus: *The Prairie Home Association and Corporation Based on Attractive Industry*.[82] Garrett Carpenter believes that the pamphlet is the work of de Boissiere, not Grant.[83] However, it was issued under both names, announcing "that it is now thought expedient to inform those who wish to take part in the Associative enterprise . . . [that] its proprietors, will be prepared to receive persons the ensuing spring." It described the preliminary accomplishments of their "Farm" (since named Silkville) and stated that one of the leading features of the project was a large single residence for all the associates—a "Combined Household."

The principal aim was to "ORGANIZE LABOR, the source of all

wealth on the basis of remuneration proportionate to production" in such a way "to make it both efficient and attractive." Accommodations for between eighty and one hundred residents would be available soon, with one caveat: that the ensuing year designated as a "preparative" one was limited to "collecting a few persons to form a nucleus." Clearly, de Boissiere was moving slowly to draw out the true believers from the large number that he knew would respond. The document was less a prospectus than a statement of ideology designed to appeal to individuals with Fourieristic leanings. Offered were "opportunities to engage, on liberal terms, in as many varieties as possible of productive industries" and a combination of agricultural and mechanical pursuits. But Fourierism was to be the working context: "Having provided associates and candidates with these facilities for industry, and made them responsible each for his own support the projectors propose to form themselves into organizations for industrial operations, and select and invent their own kinds and modes of cultivation and other practical processes, under regulations prescribed by themselves."

Although there is no specific mention of "groups" or "series"— the industrial language of Fourier—or of "passional attraction," it is clear that the Fourierist notion of self-guided and life-enhancing labor would be carried out at Silkville under both benevolent and scientific auspices. During a period when labor was increasingly coming under the regimen of industrial production, these old Fourierist must have thought that they could appeal to discontented workers, particularly since the manifesto came out in the wake of the 1873 depression.

No effort was made to select individuals of similar views or beliefs or "to mold them afterward to any uniform pattern." Since unanimity was not expected in practical matters (industry and labor), there was even less regimentation expected in social life: "All that will be required is that each shall accord to others as much freedom of thought and action as he enjoys himself." Paupers or destitute people were discouraged and two months rent for room and board required in advance, plus a $100 deposit per person, which was refundable. The best class of associates for Silkville were those who had an income independent of earnings (the word *wages* does not appear in the document) and who were able to devote themselves to "attractive occupations which are not remunerative." Without specifying the kinds of individuals that he wanted, de Boissiere expressed a clear preference for those with aesthetic (not remunerative) interests and those whose presence would inspire others to attractive industry, particularly music, a Fourierist favorite. There is a certain genteel ring about the community as "neatness and good taste, and even modest elegance," would be approved of and "superfluous personal decorations" disapproved. References and photographs were requested from prospective members. Alienated workers and refined gentlepersons were supposed to mix on this Kansas silk farm.

Freedom was the key word in the prospectus: freedom to labor, freedom to choose the mode of production, freedom to be oneself. De Boissiere and Grant expected that the colony would be—at a minimum—self-sustaining, with contributions, community industries, and a cooperative spirit providing the mix conducive to balancing a budget. A letter written to the Chicago Monthly Dagslyset by Marcus Thane tells of a visit he made in 1872 to Silkville. The colony was still in its infancy, and no effort had been made to secure additional members, yet he had serious doubts about its ability to survive. His reservations lay in doubts about the desirability of having all the colonists reside in a central building: "In town we have to put up with that kind of thing, but in the country it seemed uncalled for. I cannot understand why they should not build a number of small houses with spaces between them"—in short, the kind of suburban worker's cottages that were beginning to emerge on the outskirts of many industrial centers in America. Thane was kindly disposed toward de Boissiere: "It was a great pleasure to watch the old count, tired of the narrow mindedness and trivialities of modern life, now working with a pitchfork and sitting down to his meal with the working men. Freethinker, internationalist, socialist."[84]

Rather than attracting laborers and associates, the Panic of 1873 set back the colony. It slowed development in Kansas, restricted markets for colony goods, and put out of work individuals who might have been attracted to the scheme but who could not now pay the stiff entrance fees. Building did continue, and de Boissiere's hopes remained high. A three-story residence containing sixty rooms, parlors, and dining rooms adequate for one hundred was constructed. Silkworm eggs were imported from Japan and seemed to take well to Kansas. Charles Sears and his son came to take an active interest in the colony. In 1876, they exhibited silk goods at the Centennial Exposition in Philadelphia, and praise lavished on them encouraged de Boissiere to think that Silkville could become the center of an American silk culture industry.

The years from 1876 to 1880 were prosperous ones for the community, with about fifty residents renting rooms at the phalanstery.

Accounts by members are scarce; on balance, such reports indicate that normal family life existed, that marriages took place, and that de Boissiere was a benevolent patron. His own annual income from properties in France was $25,000, and his own needs were few; it was always possible for him to make additional improvements to the physical plant. Around 1880, a cheese and butter factory was started, but it proved to be an unprofitable business. By 1882, de Boissiere had come to the conclusion that he could not make Silkville profitable. Competition from foreign markets, high-priced labor, and the death of Charles Sears in 1883 hastened his decision to abandon the colony. In 1883, he returned to his estate in Bordeaux and sponsored an industrial school on the estate. The Silkville property continued to be managed by Sear's son. De Boissiere returned to the United States for one last time in 1892.

At that time, de Boissiere announced his desire to bequeath the property to the state or some educational institution. After studying several proposals, he presented the Odd Fellows Lodge with the land, now valued at $125,000. He died at his Bordeaux estate in 1894. What had begun with the failure of the Revolution of 1848 in France ended on the Kansas frontier forty years later. De Boissiere's social sympathies had been stirred by the exploitative nature of industrial labor, and in the American Fourierists he found warm companions and soul mates. Their practical experiences at community building had been modestly successful, and Silkville has to be placed alongside the North American Phalanx as the longest-lived Fourierist effort in America.

It was successful, however, only in the number of years that it lasted. Workers were not drawn to this vision of utopia. They might be organized into colonies for the journey westward to Greeley, but "attractive labor" in Kansas failed to draw them. De Boissiere's vision was idealistic in the best sense, and it was sustained by his wealth. Silkville may have failed because he was too little the entrepreneur. The colony had not been promoted the same way the railroads had touted their lands, he had not opened offices in cities, and he had relied on a single prospectus to sell the colony idea. Brisbane and Grant had been able to promote Fourierism in the 1840s; by the 1860s and 1870s, those ideas had faded, and their proponents had aged. It seems doubtful that workers would have responded to boarding-house cooperation, and what is most remarkable about Silkville is that it lasted as long as it did.

The Fourierist appeal was too abstract and failed to convey any excitement about the plan. By all reports, de Boissiere was kindly, but such kindness is not the sort of charisma that draws people into an active relationship with a colony. His wealth and benevolence made it last but could not make it succeed. The Brotherhood of the New Life lasted on the basis of its members' wealth and the magnetism of Harris; Greeley survived by turning away from cooperation. The lure of the West and what it might offer was still a potent one, and colonies begun in the 1860s—these pioneers of civilization—hinted at the attraction that open land had for disgruntled city people, for laborers wanting more room, and for immigrants for whom the United States meant land, bread, and freedom.

As a rule, communities often start out by brashly announcing their intention to remake the world. Soon afterward, they rush about trying to gain converts by issuing a glowing prospectus. Silkville had begun cautiously, with de Boissiere slow to make the grand announcement until he and his advisers felt on secure ground because they, better than others, knew that heroic gestures were insufficient to see a colony through a hard winter. Secular groups were in particular quick to proclaim their vision on the presumption that others would quickly accept their plan and join. Religiously inclined groups often had the revealed word to guide them, and they expected converts to marvel at their revelations, accept the gospel, and join. One group, however, that was formed in the 1870s was slow to define itself, slow to make its presence known in the world, and yet among the most remarkable of all the charismatic and perfectionist groups. It shaped its cooperative ideology and way of life over three decades and made a distinct success of it along the way.

The Women's Commonwealth, or the Sanctified Sisters of Belton, conformed to few rules about colony organizations or the processes of Texas life at mid-century. First, it grew slowly and organically, with that growth dictated by the economic and social conditions of small-town affairs in central Texas. Second, it crystallized its cooperative life at some point, but that point is less important than its accomplishments. It was the first feminist collective in the United States.

The members' coming together first began in 1866 under the guidance and leadership of Martha McWhirter. Born in Jackson County, Tennessee, in 1827, McWhirter joined the Methodist church at age sixteen and remained a believing member till the 1860s. Married in 1845, she came with her husband and family (she was to have twelve children) to Belton, Texas, in 1855. In 1866, she suffered a double tragedy when two of her children and her brother died. She interpreted those events as a sign from God that she should lead a better life. A revival meeting at Belton failed to allay her anxieties about the state of her spiritual life; in fact, after one of the sessions a voice asked her if the revival was not the work of the devil. Hearing such a voice threw her into a state of great confusion, which was not relieved until the next day; "while she was in her kitchen and busy about breakfast," she experienced a pentecostal baptism (or the second blessing) and realized that the voice that she had heard had been the voice of God."[85] From that day forward, she believed that she was "sanctified" in the Wesleyan tradition and over the next few months began to discuss her blessing and the theological implications of sanctification.

Like Anne Hutchinson, she encountered difficulties because she began to assume a leadership role in theological discussions. Her Methodist minister questioned her about holding a Sunday School meeting separate from the regular church group. Over his objections, she continued to hold such meetings in the church building. Even after being locked out of the church, she and her followers entered via a window to hold their meetings in defiance of the minister's leadership. When a Union church was constructed in 1874 for interdenominational use, the prayer group used it for their meetings.

There seem to have been two elements in McWhirter's developing belief system: Wesleyan sanctification and dream interpretation. Years later, Robert McWhirter stated that "the doctrines taught by the sanctified band are the same as taught by John Wesley. . . . We believe in dreams and they are generally given to us to make us have more trust and confidence in God. To let us know that he knows what we are doing and sometimes we act on them literally."[86] God came to the believers in their dreams, and they met to talk about them. The key element in their faith was sanctification and McWhirter's insistence that the women separate themselves from their unregenerate husbands. One husband seeking divorce and custody of his children stated that "this band teach and enforce the doctrine, that it is sinful for a wife, who is a member, to live with a husband who does not believe the doctrine, that such a husband is a serpent in the house and the wife should separate and depart from him."[87]

McWhirter first denied that such separation was an essential principle of the religion; however, women who received the second blessing did leave their husbands. During the 1870s, the women— they numbered about twenty—met in both the Union church and each others' homes. McWhirter's own relationship with her husband was an unusual one. According to George Garrison, he was an extraordinarily tolerant man: "A man of culture, of clear perception, and strong character, he appears to have had the confidence of all." Though he disagreed with his wife, he made no effort to stop her, even when humiliated by her actions. On one occasion, he guarded her against a physical attack. In the two years before his death, he lived apart from her, but he never instituted divorce proceedings and appointed her executrix of his will. Her only known comment about him came after his death: "Major McWhirter and I became estranged some years before his death. The cause was this: I observed some things in him towards a hired girl which I thought unbecoming in a man of his age and a husband and when I reproached him for it he said I was unjust. . . . Our married life had never been a happy one. He was fond of wasting time reading novels to which I objected."[88]

Whatever the source of the McWhirters' difficulties, it does appear that many of the women who joined with Martha had problems with their husbands. One complained that her husband was habitually drunk and brutal, and another stated that her spouse kept her without any money.

During the 1870s, McWhirter refused to accept any money from her husband for household expenses because he demanded an accounting. She sold butter and eggs to maintain the household, and several of the fellowship followed her example. Early in 1879, the women discussed the idea of living together and whether the faith demanded it. One member had been teaching school and offered twenty dollars toward a common fund. After a while, the fund (with McWhirter as its treasurer) grew from the sale of butter, eggs, and weavings. From the sale of the woven goods, they purchased an additional loom. Later, a young woman was hired out to do housework for McWhirter, and that money went into the common fund. During 1880, the nascent colony created a furor by accepting two men as Sanctificationists. Both men were subsequently whipped by local townspeople and ordered to leave Belton. When they refused, they were judged insane ("for their own protection") and sent to the state asylum at Austin. There the officials declared them competent and then discharged them with the understanding that they would not return to Bell County. A county grand jury investigated the affair and indicted the husband of one of the sisters; he was, however, acquitted.

The sisters' communal sharing obviously took shape when they created a common fund, and their living in common occurred over time during the 1880s. As the women came into property through either the death of a husband or a family inheritance, they began to take one another in, as Martha McWhirter had done with the young girl servant in 1879. In 1882, according to one source, a local home was converted to a hotel, and the community began in earnest. The most reliable account of their life together comes from George P. Garrison, a history professor at the University of Texas who wrote about them in 1893. Garrison asserts that the women began taking in washing at the McWhirter home in 1882 and over the years turned it into a profitable business. They rotated the laundering from one home to another, and, when it came to one household, there was trouble. The husband objected, drove the group away, and beat his own wife. Undaunted, they regrouped at the home. Four members were arrested and subsequently paid a fine of $41.00 that came out of the common fund. After this fray, the women hired a builder to put up a home on a lot owned by McWhirter.

After the structure was completed, it was occupied by the woman who had been assaulted by her husband. It may have been the first battered wife shelter in the United States. Their common fund was exhausted by construction of the home; they continued to replenish it. They sold wood and, in 1883, began to expand their domestic services, acting as nurses, cooks, and general housekeepers, such services providing a bedrock of financial support until 1887. Many of the women had been raised in genteel homes and had servants of their own before breaking with their husbands over the faith. But their wages as servants were good (a dollar a day), and money was needed to restore the communal kitty. Yet it was not easy labor for these women, as Garrison reported: "Whenever an application for a servant came, most of them would fall at once into a great fit of weeping, for no one wished to go; but go they did." [89]

At one point they were able to help out at a hotel in Temple (nine miles away) and gained some invaluable experience that served them well in their next business venture. In May 1886, they opened a hotel in the home that they had unsuccessfully tried to do their communal laundry in several years before. After the death of the woman's husband, she had tried to run it as a boarding house for two years before the sisters decided to run it as a hotel. Earlier that year, they had purchased the machinery for a laundry. Thus, by the late 1880s they had launched several self-sustaining businesses. With the death of McWhirter's husband in 1887 the group came into $10,000. The Central Hotel (incorporated in 1891) was an enormous success, and in addition to it they acquired town lots and farmlands that they rented out to tenants. During 1893, the group had thirty-two members, including four men. Some members worked a farm about two miles from town, others in the laundry and hotel. No one worked for more than four hours a day. Of the four male members, one worked as a clerk, another as an engineer in the laundry, the third as a carpenter, and the fourth selling pianos in New York City as part of an experiment in economic diversification.

Garrison noted that the members' cultural interests were varied; Bellamy and Tolstoy were their favorite authors, and they took subscriptions to the *North American Review, Arena*, the *Women's Journal*, and Cyrus Teed's *Flaming Sword* (published from another cooperative colony). As a group, they enjoyed traveling, visiting New York in 1890, where three separate parties spent six weeks each. In 1893, they attended the Chicago World's Fair under a similar arrangement. They maintained their own school for members' children since McWhirter believed that they should be sent away to boarding school only if God revealed it to them. No formal worship service was held; they met in common to discuss their "religious experiences which they try to interpret so that it will serve to guide them." Guidance came from dreams and, as McWhirter said, "from a delicate sense which belongs to the entire community rather than to any individual, and which enables them to detect any mistake they have made or false step they have taken, by causing an unpleasant reaction in the whole body."[90]

By the mid-1890s, the women had won grudging admiration from their neighbors in Belton. They had avoided any scandals since the early years and had made the hotel a success by sheer hard work, mutual support, and faith. In addition, they had reached out to establish two hotels in Waco. Having achieved this success, they decided (it is not recorded how) in 1899 to move to Washington, D.C. According to an article in *Ainslee's Magazine*, the "older members felt they had earned the right to rest from hard work, the young women who had grown up with them demanded a broader outlook in life than they felt they could have in the town in which they always lived."[91] Appropriately enough, the home that they purchased in Washington had earlier belonged to Major Willard Saxton, who as a young man had lived at Brook Farm. The 1900 census lists twenty-three residents in the household, including a Negro male servant. Martha McWhirter was listed as "landlady"—true, but certainly an understatement. Their new home was viewed not as a retreat but rather as an expansion of their Texas home. Domestic labor was done in rotation, and the women maintained a certain self-sufficiency about the enterprise by keeping a garden, some livestock, and "doing for themselves whatever they could." Children were still educated at a home school, and the young women took night classes since they were (by their own admission) "unlettered women and are trying to learn."[92]

Clearly, the women had come to Washington to improve themselves, and they indulged their interests by continuing to travel as a group to places like California and Mexico. Newspaper accounts of their life in Washington stress McWhirter's continuing leadership role, her outspoken statements about their faith, and the inevitable question, "Can men be members?" Her answer: "Oh, yes, we have had men among us. . . . they are welcome if they are willing to live the life as we do. But they never stay too long. Yes, see it is in the nature of men to want to boss—and, well, they find they can't."[93] Her death in 1906 appears to have brought the group to a close, though there is evidence to suggest that their membership peaked in the 1880s when it reached fifty. Shortly after their arrival in Washington, McWhirter had purchased a 119-acre farm in Montgomery County, and it was to the Coleville Community Farm that they switched the focus of their lives. Some of the members continued to live at the farm into the 1930s.

There is no convenient decade within which to place the colony: their perfectionist beliefs had their origins with the primitive Methodists and enjoyed a great vogue in the 1840s, and such perfectionist sentiment continued to be a wellspring for the holiness movement after the Civil War. McWhirter worked within that tradition and was forced by her religious convictions to find a practical solution to her domestic situation. Throughout her life, she thought of her faith as a practical alternative, and one reporter noted that "belief with her is action."[94] One does get a sense in reading the history of the group that it could have taken hold in any town in the United States. For the conditions that led to the formulation of the colony, McWhirter's revelations, the precarious financial situation of the women, and their subservient economic and social roles all came together at Belton in 1869, but they could just as well have surfaced at Cambridge, Massachusetts, at Santa Cruz, California, or at Salina, Kansas. As Dolores Hayden has demonstrated, there was a cooperative housekeeping group in Cambridge in the 1870s. Secular in inspiration, it led a group of women to abandon the domestic sphere in search of freedom rather than intensifying and building on those abilities as did the Sanctified Sisters.[95] What has to be noted about McWhirter's group is, first, its success and, second, its ability—over time—to transform their isolated domestic skills (however hateful) into cooperative work designed to sustain a common faith and a common vision.

Martha McWhirter's dreams and her insistence on following the promptings of the Lord led her away from one home to found another. Elizabeth Thompson's wealth and her concern for urban castaways led her to support a vision of a community in which children rather than men or women would be the focus of the future. The distances between McWhirter and Thompson were considerable, yet both saw their belief in a collective life take hold and blossom for a time in the arid Southwest. They and all the other varied colony promoters made the work community a vital one in the years after the Civil War. With Thompson, we again have an instance of holiness leading religiously inclined individuals to join together—in part out of self-defense—to sustain themselves. The Women's Commonwealth had known violence and persecution because of their faith, and the Lord's Farm in New Jersey was seen to be corrupters of morals. Led by inspired figures; these last two groups wandered, tried unsuccessfully to set down roots. They failed, whereas the women of Belton were able to secure a home and achieve respectability.

Whereas the founders of both Topolobampo and the American Colony had visions that made them believe that utopia lay outside the geographic confines of the United States, the Koreshan Unity, founded by Cyrus Teed, was based on a vision that looked inward. Communal settlements have been organized around a wide variety of social, economic, and educational philosophies. The eighteenth-century Pietist community at Ephrata, Pennsylvania, ordered itself around the sainted celibate Conrad Beissel and his mystical preachings; the nineteenth-century Pilgrims followed Isaac Bullard and his command to fast, to abstain from washing, and to chant as they sought the promised land by heading Southwest; the twentieth century saw Isaac Rumford's Holy City sustain itself on a diet of celibacy, racial superiority, and divine inspiration. There were, of course, steadier philosophies, like Robert Owen's moral cooperation, John H. Noyes's Bible communism, and Job Harriman's economic socialism, but numerous communities have been founded on exotic principles.

Certainly, then, Cyrus Teed's community should surprise no one because of its exotic philosophy, yet it, of all the communal enterprises, is the most puzzling and, if one needs a standard, the most outlandish. Located first in Chicago, then at Estero, Florida, it was organized around the theory of cellular cosmogony. For Teed, the earth was a hollow concave sphere, and we live on its inner edge. The story of Teed and his followers is easy to dismiss on the presumption that some people will believe anything, the cynical view that it is the gullible who inhabit the earth, not the meek. There is more than that, however, to the Koreshan Unity since it represents a curious nineteenth-century response to changing social and scientific conditions. To be sure, Teed and his followers stand on the fringes of the social world and touch mainstream forces only at varied points, deflecting away from major movements as if pulled by gravitational forces that are mystical and otherworldly. They saw a world in chaos with force and greed central elements in that universe, and they constructed a static world that closed in on itself, denied progress, and affirmed man's place in that world.

Cyrus Reed Teed may have been a lunatic, a fraud, and a swindler; however, to his followers he was "Koresh," the prophet whose philosophy was not only divine but a mandate to cultivate the earth and save it for future generations.[96] Born in 1839 into a farm family at Moravia, New York, he began medical studies at age twenty with an uncle at Utica after working on the Erie Canal for nine years. He moved to New York City in 1862 with his family and then enlisted in the Union Army Medical Corps, serving fifteen months. After the war, he attended the Eclectic Medical College in New York and graduated in 1868. A move to Deerfield, New York (near Utica), started him in the practice of eclectic medicine, the smallest and weakest of the three major medical sects in mid-nineteenth-century America. Eclectic physicians were less educated than regular physicians, their practice combined a variety of methods derived from regular and homeopathic medicine, and their practices were located mainly in smaller communities. Some eclectics were disreputable charlatans, but others worked in the botanical drug tradition and served their communities as well as the other sects did.[97]

Teed turned early to "electro-chemical" experimentation on the relation between matter and energy and worked in a laboratory with batteries. According to Teed, it was in that laboratory—in the autumn of 1869—that he discovered that the universe was all one substance: limited, integral, balanced, and emanating from one source, God. He further discovered that the Copernican theory of an illimitable universe was false because the earth had a limited form: it was concave. After discovering that the earth had limits, he had a vision and a visitation from the "Divine Motherhood," who told him that he was destined to redeem the human race and carry on the work of Jesus Christ. Teed was to devote the rest of his life to elaborating on that 1869 vision, which, he thought, brought science and religion together. Word about his vision spread, with the result that his wife left him and a few believers accepted his prophetic role. During the 1870s, he moved from Utica to Sandy Creek, on the shores of Lake Erie, to practice medicine. His theories drove patients away, and he returned to Moravia in 1880 to establish a small communal household and publish a periodical, the *Herald of the New Covenant*. Earlier, he had begun a correspondence with the Harmonist Society in the hope of getting some money, and he visited Economy in 1878. John Duss, the Harmonist leader, thought well of Teed but gave him only $100 from the fading Harmonist millions.[98]

An exchange between Teed and D. M. Bennett, the freethinker and editor, appeared in the columns of Bennett's paper, the *Truth Seeker*, in 1877 and 1878.[99] Teed affirmed the proposition that "Jesus Christ is not only Divine, but is the Lord God Creator of Heaven and Earth," which Bennett denied. Teed had issued a challenge to "infidels, unbelievers and spiritualists" to debate him for seven days at Moravia, beginning on 12 October 1877. The *Truth Seeker* ("A Weekly Journal of Radicalism and Reform") opened its pages to the debate, and Teed outlined his views derived from two sources, the Bible and those who "collate facts and make scientific deductions." He said that he might be "styled a clergyman, though not dependent upon any recognized sect for my authority to declare the truth against all opposition."[100] Teed propounded a cyclical theory of history involving cycles of twenty-four thousand years, and he emphasized man's capacity to know Jesus and the world. At one point, Bennett discontinued the debate because he found Teed's style too "metaphorical, ethereal, or vapory to meet the appreciation of most of the readers of this paper." It did continue until 1878, however, only to have Bennett regret the extension because Teed's philosophy was a sophomoric compound of metaphysics and gnosticism. Teed's contribution to the debate consisted of his saying that chemistry, astronomy, and evolution, as taught, were all false and that the new gods (Train, Andrews, Davis, Manchard, Ingersoll, and D. M. Bennett) were all freethinkers or spiritualists. His ideas were an amalgam of pseudoscience and Christian uplift that failed to gain much notice during the 1870s despite his efforts to promote himself.

During the 1880s he practiced eclectic medicine with his brother, Oliver, in Syracuse and did gain notoriety in 1884 by being sued by Mrs. Charles Cobb. She charged him with obtaining money from her and her mother "under plea that he is the second Christ." According to the *New York Times* story, Teed had an office in a fashionable area, and he told reporters that he would be translated to heaven when he was forty-six years old (he was then forty-five) and would return fifty days later to found a kingdom where "all would be love." The news story about the charges against him also indicated that while he had been in Moravia he had eloped with the wife of a local liveryman. After the Syracuse episode, Teed and his small band of disciples—four women, including his sister—moved to New York City. From 1868 to 1886, he had moved about the burned-over district, plying his eclectic profession and trying to win converts to his scientific theories. From town to town he moved, always with the same results. One of his early supporters, A. W. K. Andrews, a graduate of Ann Arbor Medical School who practiced at Binghamton, New York, wrote that he "would come to our house and stay for months at a time. Despite the fact that his clothes were sometimes worn and shiny in appearance, he was always immaculately neat in his attire."[101] Andrews also found that Teed "had an answer to all his questions." Andrews became one of Teed's coworkers in 1888 and subsequently moved to Chicago with his wife and four children to help in the grand work.

Teed was to find his audience at a convention of the National Association of Mental Science that he addressed in September 1886 in Chicago. His speech "electrified" the group, and he was asked to become president of the association. Teed moved to Chicago in the spring of 1888 and established himself in a second-floor location on Wabash Avenue. He had his general offices in the front, a lecture hall, a dining room, and a printing office on the premises. The lunch room was for not only seekers who came to hear him lecture but also the general public. Those who waited on tables were members of the group, and the offices served as a distribution center for his speeches and written pronouncements.

Shortly after arriving in Chicago, he organized a communal household centered at two homes on College Place, near the site of the old Chicago University. A doorway was cut through the wall of these two attached houses so that members could move freely throughout this combined printing shop, church, and communal residence. Many of the first members were elderly and presumably came to Teed because of his faith-healing reputation. It was at College Place and from a third household on Thirty-fifth Street that the nucleus for the Koreshanity Unity in Florida was formed. Annie G. Ordway, a Theosophist, joined at this time and took the title of "Preeminent" when she assumed leadership over the women in the group. She took a new name and would be called Victoria Gratia henceforth. Other early members were Professor O. F. Lamoreaux, who had taught Latin and Greek for over thirty years at Wheaton College in Illinois, and Teed's sister, Mrs. Emma Evans, who continued to follow his lead.

Chicago was his reaping ground as converts came quickly into the church, the Assembly of the Covenant. He began to publish a journal, the *Guiding Star*, in which he laid down the outlines of a proposed city for the "United Life." He believed that united labor and capital could work within a cooperative framework and produce an environment free from the defects of civilization: "The slums of Chicago, New York and large cities will never create anything else but filth, in the minds of the people which [sic] live in them. They must lower, and will never raise the people. . . . In our poverty where so many people are homeless, without an inch of ground to rest their foot permanently the question is, how to build cheap cities and homes."[102]

Instead of smoke, dust, sewer gas, and horse manure, these united cities would be saturated with the "fragrance of flowers, roses, plants, grass and desireable trees, cool and sprinkled with fountains of spring water." Teed's vision, like A. K. Owens's, was grandiose. He imagined agricultural cooperation on a large scale, industrial production ("a thousand horse-power locomotive is demanded in our times"), and a hothouse environment where the sweet smell of flowers would invade daily life. Teed asked, "Why should the American laborer with his wife and children not live as well as an emperor."[103] If he were well fed and well tended, the American worker would be a much improved "machine" capable of accomplishing three times as much labor. His social plan thus announced, Teed went on to describe the heart of his mission, his religious principles. They included celibacy, the gathering in of the elect 144,000, a common sharing of goods and fellowship, Christ's Second Coming in the form of the Koresh, reincarnation, alchemy, and cellular cosmogony. Teed offered a cure for social problems in the form of his united city, a cure for religious ills with his philosophy, and a cure for physical ailments with his treatments. What those treatments consisted of is unclear except that they were a mixture of faith healing, positive thinking, and electric shock: "It does not matter what the disease or what stage it has reached. Everything is curable under this treatment if the patient will get into a condition of response to the action of our Psych-pneumic battery."[104] The treatment fee was five dollars a week, yet supposedly no one was denied care because he or she lacked the necessary funds.

Koreshanity spread rapidly, with converts grouping at centers in Denver, Baltimore, Portland, Lynn, and Springfield, Massachusetts. A cooperative business organization, the Bureau of Equitable Commerce, was organized in 1891 and directed its efforts at winning over the laboring classes. While on a tour in California in 1890, Teed organized a church in San Francisco (on Noe Street) where a printing plant and a store called the Bureau of Equitable Commerce were operating. In its literature, the bureau emphasized the cooperative and antimonopolistic character of the society and highlighted socialistic theory and practice. In a series of theological pamphlets published over the next ten years, Teed set forth a creed that promised security for those who would follow.[105]

Throughout his writings, one finds assertions like one that appeared in *The Messianic Appearing and Personality:* "We are offering to the world a system of universal science from which every problematic and doubtful question has been eliminated, because of the final revelation of the mysterious in which it is no longer occult or hidden"[106] When one looks at a picture of Koresh, it is hard to detect any charisma. There is, instead, an austere man wearing a starched collar, wire-rimmed glasses, and a minister's black coat. There is a certain firmness about the face, a certain resolve that suggests the surety of a Presbyterian minister confident in the meaning of the Westminster Confession rather than an eclectic physician peddling an inside-the-earth theory. Teed's appeal lay in his ability to convey his message with absolute certainty, with sufficient scientific emphasis and religious fervor so as to convince his followers that his theories were grounded both in fact and in divine revelation.

Since the Divine Motherhood had announced her vision to him in 1869, and because he believed in a dual godhead (male and female) residing in one presence (God), women played a vital role in his organization. Teed believed that sexual drives could be channeled into other areas and that, once women were allowed to escape the domination of men, true equality would take place: "The wild, lustful, and dissipating pleasures of sexuality had blinded the human mind to the sanctity of the potencies of proliferation and higher uses to which the hidden energies of being should be devoted."[107] The community at Chicago grew in numbers so that by 1894 the Koreshan Unity had three hundred members in the city and another 150 living in a mansion in Washington Heights.

Like Owen, Teed believed that the colony had to have both a spiritual and a commercial center. As a spiritual center, it was a gathering-in place, a refuge for the elect 144,000, a site for the New Jerusalem. At the same time, it would have to gear into the world's economic system. That system operated on greed and led to individual self-aggrandizement rather than social unity. Only in these new cities—these hives of spiritual activity—could true fellowship grow. According to Teed, the Bureau of Equitable Commerce had to develop a commercial center with access to the "great water thoroughfares": "It is our purpose to place streamers and flatboats on the Mississippi and its tributaries and to ply larger ships from New Orleans across the Gulf to New Jerusalem to be owned and controlled by the Koreshan Unity. We will plant a city which for beauty of location, magnificence in architectural construction, municipal government, educational facilities, and liberality of sentiment, cannot be surpassed." [108]

By placing themselves on this grand waterway, the Koreshan people would be in contact with all the peoples of the world: "Ours is not merely a colony. It is the beginning of a universal system of industrial exchange on the basis of equity." Paradoxically, of course, this approach was being taken by a group that had rejected an expansive view of the universe and held that the natural world had limits. Their expansionist commercial views coincided with the views of American imperialists. However, such entrepreneurial views were based on individualism and led to social chaos, according to Teed, whereas his vision was unified and corresponded to natural laws. Whiskey, beer, tobacco, and opium were excluded from the Koresham commercial centers: "New Jerusalem, therefore, as a central and Holy City, a religious and moral power, must be exempt from the control of vice." [109]

People of good moral character could enter the society as full members, or they could support Teed's efforts by joining a lower order of association. These were married people who wished to enjoy the educational and financial benefits of association yet who wished to retain their conventional marital status. There was a second order—the marital order—consisting of couples who would not prostitute the marital act "by having relations for any purpose other than propagation" but who wished to retain family property. [110] The third and highest order, the ecclesia or home center, was celibate and devoted to the communal life. Members of this order were committed to the principle that one had to throw off the body's demands and lead a noncarnal life in order to conserve vital sexual energies. All these orders were intended to complement each other in a harmonious balance.

On joining the group, members signed articles of agreement turning over all property to the "Society Arch-Triumphant," agreed to follow the colony rules, and agreed to accept whatever the colony wished to convey to them if they left. In return, the "Ecclesia, or Home," of the Koreshan Unity promised to deal "justly with the new member and be Slow to condemn, always cognizant of the fact that the spirit is often unwilling where the flesh is weak."[111]

During 1892, there were some questions raised about Annie Ordway's leadership; however, Teed admonished other sect members to follow her lead "until the final Victoria should be manifest."[112] The San Francisco group was consolidated with the Chicago group in 1892, and the addition of new members forced Teed to expand once again, this time to the suburb of Washington Heights. There he found an old mansion on several acres. It was rented, called Beth-Ophrah, and became the focal point of his messianic mission to Chicago. The two houses in Chicago were retained as a communal household. At Beth-Ophrah, he held Sunday services on the lawn and ministered to his flock but found that he still needed additional space. The group's next acquisition was located in another suburb, Normal Park, where they purchased an apartment complex known as "Sunlight Flats." The apartments were three hundred feet in length but only fourteen feet wide on a six hundred by fourteen-foot lot. Again, passages were created to make it a single dwelling space for Koreshan believers. Now they were located in four Chicago-area locations and by 1894 had put down some roots in the city.

Yet it was in that year that Teed decided to shift the focus of his activities away from Chicago to the South. He visited the west coast of Florida and convinced a local landlord, Gustave Damkohler, of his vision. Damkohler owned 320 acres on Estero Creek, south of Fort Myers, and agreed to cede the land to Teed in return for lifetime care. It was at this location that Teed saw the erection of his world capitol of Koreshanity since, as he wrote, the site was at the "vitellus of the Great Cosmogonic Egg."[113]

Although the land came to Teed as part of a gift rather than as part of a conscious design, it was also a likely spot for his dream, particularly for a city that was to be located in a flower grove. On 31 January 1894, a party of seventeen believers, including Koresh, boarded the Rock Island Train at Washington Heights for a trip South. A. W. H. Andrews, one of the members of the party, remembers the journey as one into a forbidden territory, an almost magical land: "The place was as wild as tropical nature had made it; saw palmettoes as high as ones head and scrub oak bushes still taller."[114] They cleared the land, built a log house for shelter and then a building to house a dining room, a kitchen, and a women's dormitory. A large dining room made it possible to hold musical and theatrical performances since they were now forced to entertain themselves. The colony was located on a site bordering the Estero River, and they held land at the southern end of Estero Island in the bay. They took lumber from the island and milled it at the colony site using a sawmill purchased in 1895. A colony-owned sloop enabled them to ship lumber out and bring supplies in from Fort Myers. Later, they purchased additional land on Big Hickory Islands plus additional acreage at Estero.

All in all, the colony accumulated two thousand acres by 1901. Teed's dream city contained elements taken from L'Enfant's plan for Washington, D.C., and Albert K. Owen's "Pacific City" plus some unique ideas about transporting sewage to other areas for cultivation purposes. During 1896 and 1897, Teed and A. E. Morrow conducted a number of experiments at Estero and Chicago that resulted in the publication of *Cellular Cosmogony* in 1898. Their experiments proved to the satisfaction of the Koreshan group that the earth curved upward at a rate of eight inches to a mile and that such data confirmed their concave earth theory. "The survey was completed on May 5, 1897, corroborating the discovery of Koresh in the winter of 1869–70."[115]

For Teed, the earth had a diameter of eight thousand miles and a circumference of twenty-five thousand miles. The sun was an invisible electromagnetic battery revolving in the sphere's center. Inside the earth there were three separate atmospheres: the first composed of oxygen and nitrogen and closest to the earth; the second a hydrogen atmosphere above the first; and the third an aboron atmosphere at the center. The earth's shell was one hundred miles thick and had seventeen layers. The outer seven layers were metallic with a gold rind on the outermost layer, the middle five were mineral, and the five inward layers were geological strata. Inside this sphere there was life, outside a void. One can understand why the Koreshan believers were reported to have sported badges that proclaimed "We live on the inside" and to have erected a sign over the entrance to their Estero colony proclaiming that truth. By 1901, there were fifty members in residence belonging to only two orders of membership: the ecclesia and the marital order.

The Florida community grew in 1903 when the Chicago sites were closed and one hundred journeyed south. That move was prompted both by the belief that the home center at Estero should be the center of their activity and by a suit brought against Teed in

Chicago for fraud. From 1904 to 1907, the community enjoyed what one writer has called the "golden days." The physical plant grew to include a large three-story dining hall and dormitory, a residence for female leaders, a home for Teed and Victoria Gratia, a bakery, a laundry, a print shop, a greenhouse, and a school.

Life in the community was under Teed's complete domination, and the membership accepted his regal authority. There was an elaborate hierarchy within the association, and the leaders carried metaphysical titles. In fact, however, Teed and his "Pre-Eminent" partner, Victoria, ruled. Within the colony, considerable emphasis was placed on education and cultural affairs, with music having a special role through an orchestra and a band. A College for Life had been established as early as 1886 in Chicago with a curriculum that featured mental science and Koreshan metaphysics. It was continued in Florida under the grand title of Pioneer University of Koreshan Universology. At Estero, informal religious services were conducted on Sundays consisting of hymns, prayers, and a sermon by Teed. Life seemed to move serenely enough within the colony as the membership cultivated fields, ran a large quality printing business, and periodically celebrated their unique religious theories at lunar and solar festivals.

Teed was clearly influenced by Swedenborgian theories of correspondence and saw himself as walking in Emmanuel Swedenborg's steps: "The Immanuel of his age, must descend to the natural plane, and through and in the divinely appointed Cyrus, consummate the fullness of the world. Emmanuel Swedenborg constituted the terminus, or line of demarcation between the old and the new in the spiritual world. His mission was messianic to the world, to introduce judgment, or to cause separation between the elect and the non-elect. In the consumption of that judgment the new spiritual heaven is established called the New Jerusalem."[116] According to Teed, Swedenborg saw the earth as a concave sphere and believed that immortality of the body was a possibility. The first step in gaining that immortality was to embrace celibacy: "The greatest of all the causes of mental depletion; premature mental decay and degeneracy is sexual excess."[117] Through celibacy, through community, through belief, and through Koresh ("every esoteric manifestation of the present time is but the reflex of the presence of the Messiah now in the world since 1839") immortality could be attained.[118]

Although such lofty goals were the ultimate end of the colony, there were some proximate problems that had to be faced immediately. Relations with the surrounding area were peaceable until

1906, when the community became embroiled in a controversy with the Lee County Democratic Party. The Koreshan people had always block voted for Democratic candidates but failed to support the party's presidential candidate, Alton Parker, in 1904. An effort to disenfranchise the Koreshan voters followed, and they retaliated by supporting the socialist organization in Lee County in 1906. The colony paper, the *American Eagle,* became the vehicle for their own anti-Democratic party vendetta, and Teed organized a "Progressive Liberty" ticket to run a slate for county officers. They offered a platform that emphasized public ownership of utilities, free schools, equalization of wealth, protection of the environment, and conservation of natural resources. Though the party won no elections, the results were close in several contests and indicated that they were willing to put up a fight when their vital interests were threatened.

Teed's sudden death in December 1908, in a boating accident, came as a shock to the colony. Some members believed that Teed was immortal and now thought that he was simply in a trance. Believing that he would soon rise from the trance, they had not embalmed him. Pressure from local health authorities, however, forced his burial in a stone vault that carried the inscription "Cyrus Shepherd Stone of Israel." After his death, there was dissension in the colony, with some members following Victoria Gratia and others moving out and incorporating themselves into the Order of Theocracy at Fort Meyers.

How is one to assess this bizarre and yet quite successful community? We may conjecture that the members sought shelter from an increasingly open-ended and conflict-ridden world. Teed had told them that the forces of Gog and Magog were mobilizing for final battle, that greed gripped millionaires and workers alike, and that the commercial trusts and labor trusts were assuming greater domination over American life. His vision was not unlike that of Ignatius Donnelly's *Caesar's Column.*[119] He gave firm answers to all these troubling tendencies and buttressed them with his own science and religion. A large number of the members were women.

Did the Koreshan Unity fit the pattern described by Donald Meyers of women seeking truth and social security in organizations like Christian Science that spoke directly to their needs?[120] Or was Teed merely aping John Cleve Symmes, whose theory of concentric spheres was brought before Congress in 1822–23? Or had he simply taken his notion from Jules Verne's *The Voyage to the Center of the Earth* or W. F. Lyon's *The Hollow Globe?* Or did he speak to a new conservative cosmogony that was attempting to reestablish man at the earth's center just as Darwin had removed him from there? Teed believed in spiritual evolution, the possibility of physical perfection over time if only one would eliminate impure sexual drives. There is no simple explanation for the Koreshan Unity except that it worked for a small band whose eyes were always on a horizon that eventually tilted upward.

Topolobampo, the American Colony, and the Koreshan Unity were all shaped by singular personalities whose vision took them onto new ground. Owen was, in the end, just a pawn in the transcontinental railroad race. His vision, his persistence, and his failures mark him as a man like the railroad tycoons of his day. Anna Spafford's American Colony took members from several countries to the one "Holy City" that could satisfy them all, and Cyrus Teed both closed and opened the universe for his flock. All three demanded that their followers travel with them to new lands, to lush tropical climates, where they would be rejuvenated in the sun, kept fruitful, and multiply. Eden was on the west coast of Florida, the west coast of Mexico, and the west bank of the Jordan. Each journey brought them closer to God, closer to paradise.

For some colonists, the bedrock of their faith lay not in an idea or in a personality but in a place. Whereas Owen was able to make Topolobampo shine in the pages of his periodicals, another place, much more rooted in history and tradition, began once again to exert a hold over the minds and hearts of utopians. The place was the Holy Land, Jerusalem in particular. Three groups were drawn to it, and they all operated within a context that emphasized the special spiritual quality that they associated with that holy place. The first group—the Jaffa Colonists—was led by George Adams, who was described by Mark Twain as "prophet Adams—once an actor, then several other things, afterwards a Mormon and a missionary, always an adventurer." [121]

A second and long-lived effort was the American Colony, started by Horatio and Bertha Spafford in the aftermath of a personal tragedy that altered their lives. He was a prominent lawyer in Chicago, and both were members of the Presbyterian church. During the summer of 1873, she took their four children to France on the liner *Ville de Havre*, which collided with another vessel. In the confusion following the accident, the four Spafford children were lost and drowned. On her return to Chicago, Bertha and Horatio began to hold prayer meetings in their home in Lincoln Park. "They gave up all form and ritual and organized themselves into an assembly founded on the old Apostolic faith." [122] That faith demanded that they hold things in common and go to Jerusalem to prepare for the Second Coming. A group of eighteen left Chicago in August 1881 and on their arrival in Jerusalem took up residence in a house close to the Damascus Gate.

Another view of why the Spaffords went to the Holy Land is revealed by a suit against Bertha in Chicago in 1896. At that time, one member of the church stated that they had gone to Jerusalem to avoid arrest for mismanagement of a trust fund. It was alleged that Spafford (as an attorney for a client) had taken $8,000 from a trust fund in order to cover some financial losses. As his financial problems increased in 1881, so did his religious zeal, according to T. C. Rounds, a colony member. Whatever the origins of their faith and the motivation behind their journey to Jerusalem, there is little doubt that it was carried off with intense religious fervor. One neighbor described their religious meetings at the Spaffords' Lake View home in Chicago: "I used to hear 'em holler'n over at the chapel. I guess Miss Rounds had'em harder than any of them. Miss Spafford and Miss Lee had 'em easy. Just kinds 'o turned white and lay still."[123] Their excited religious meetings were noticed, but there is no evidence that they were thought unusual. During the summer of 1881, the community learned that they would be leaving, but it was not until August that Anna Spafford had a vision directing her where and when to go. It was later charged that the revelation was timed to avoid a public scandal about her husband's financial dealings.

Writing to Hannah Whitehall Smith, author of *The Christian's Secret of a Happy Life*, in 1883 after arriving in Jerusalem, Anna Spafford gave her version of her religious transformation: "God came to us seven years ago and spoke supernaturally to us, giving us truth and telling us that this coming to us was the coming of Elias, or Christ coming as a thief. Many things we did not understand, but we believed it was God's voice speaking to us and if it was God's voice to us, He should not fail to find willing instruments in us. We saw plainly enough that to obey these teachings was to kill us in every sense of the word and brand us as fools and devils by the church." In 1880, Spafford said that she had her struggle with Satan and that with God's help "Satan was cast down." God's hand became evident in everything that they did and had continued to be there since coming to Jerusalem: "We often sat up whole nights wrestling with God in prayer until suddenly more than two hundred Gadites arrived in Jerusalem. The Lord said that this was the 'going in the mulberry trees.' The Lord tells us that this time is over—the time of preparation before he comes with his power. . . . God is working wonderful with us and the day will soon declare it to the world."[124]

Until that day, the American Colony, or the "Overcomers," as they were sometimes called, led a simple life in Jerusalem, ministering to the sick, living the Christian life, and listening for God's voice. They had brought substantial funds with them; eventually, they established a photographic business that produced postcards for a tourist shop that they ran. In addition, they sold baked goods and weavings. According to a reporter for the *Westminster Gazette,* "They have no priests, these theocratic communists, no method of government save the promptings of brotherly love."[125] A visitor to the colony in 1889 attended their service (attended also by a few Jews) and reported that chapters from the Gospel of St. John were read, two or three hymns sung, and the impression left that it was a "reverent, thoughtful and fervent" service. The original party from Chicago had been supplemented by several Englishmen, "the widow of a colonel of the United States Regular Army, an accomplished Chicago lady, a teacher from England, a Spanish Jew who serves as interpreter, a carpenter from Lynn, Massachusetts, a shoemaker from Chicago, a devoted German Jew, a blind Arab full of enthusiasm in this Christian work." At that point, the group consisted of nineteen individuals under the leadership of Bertha Spafford—as her husband had died in 1888. When they first arrived, the American consul had been against them and distrustful of their celibate ways, but their good works won the respect and admiration of locals: "The colony is full of good works. They care for the blind, minister to the insane, feed beggars, watch the sick, turn their quarters into a hospital when occasion requires, entertain tourists, keep no record of their work and publish nothing to the world."[126]

Their quarters were in a compound just off the Nablus Road that had been built by a pasha. The Moorish-style buildings were surrounded by carefully tended gardens and ample space for both the colonists and visitors. Their services were open to the public, and an 1890 account emphasizes the simple character not only of the services but also of the members: "There was nothing dramatic. The brothers and sisters stood with closed eyes, absorbed in the prayer, and uttered frequent murmurs or assent as an expression suited them. 'Yes, Yes; Our God, Our Dear God.' " Beginning in 1889, they began to take in a few boarders free of charge. They made no attempt at proselytizing and for that reason "are much beloved by the Mohammedans. They aim to demonstrate their faith by their life that all may see, and seeing, ask to know the secret of their happiness and goodness. They go much among the poor, the sick and the afflicted, teach in the schools and open their house to all who will come to it."[127]

They read the Scriptures daily and led a simple life, sharing everything in common and relying on donations from America to sustain them since the sale of souvenir goods was an inadequate source of income. In 1895, Anna Spafford returned to Chicago to try and settle a property dispute and to recruit some new members.[128] She had great success recruiting among Swedish evangelicals. She was able to convert several from a Chicago church because one of its members had a dream: "I dreamed that some people who had lived in Jerusalem for fourteen years, came to see us. They seemed to have much in common with us, but that they had a higher light, and we were able to be one with them." That dream was confirmed when she went to a service at which Spafford spoke of Christian love, of meekness, and of the need for people to overlook each others' weaknesses and forgive as Christ had forgiven. It was from this philosophy of overlooking faults that the name *Overcomers* was derived. Spafford was invited to the Swedish Evangelical church, and, when she saw the church, she murmured—in Christ-like fashion—"This is it; a large upper room furnished." She told these Swedish "Larsonists" (after Olof Larson, their pastor) that she had received a message on arrival in Chicago that said, "I will show you a large upper room furnished."[129] That furnished room became the center of her activity during her stay, and, by 7 March 1896, she had converted a considerable number, with a party of seventy-two leaving with her that day for the Holy Land. On their arrival in Jerusalem, the group moved into larger quarters, and Larson wrote to his congregation at Nas, Sweden, telling them about the relocation. There was interest and excitement in Sweden when the news came, and they, too, wanted to "witness the fulfillment of prophecies in Jerusalem and to await the coming of the Lord on Mount Zion."[130] Larson and Jacob Elihau then went to Sweden to bring the new colonists and on arrival found that they had already sold their farms and were ready to migrate.

On 14 July 1896, thirty-seven pilgrims left Nas by carriage for the railroad station at Vansboro, then on to Gothenburg, then by boat to Antwerp, and then by rail again to Jaffa and Jerusalem. With the addition of the colonists from Sweden, the group had grown to over a hundred. Previously, the tone and character of the settlement had been passive, with the Overcomers simply watching and waiting for the end. With the addition of the Swedes, however, a new vital element had been added. Looms were built and used, vineyards planted, and crops harvested from rented lands. Cakes and jams were now sold aggressively to tourists and the photographic shop expanded to meet the demand for views of the Holy Land. A startling change occurred in 1904, when Bertha Spafford married. Before that, she had preached about the necessity for rooting out sin before realizing the perfect marriage with Christ. Her advocacy of celibacy had been an accepted fact of community life. She married Frederick Vester, an Englishman, and, when their first child was born, there was a physician in attendance, whereas in the past the art of self-healing had been the rule.

The colony's fortunes changed again in the 1920s. Mrs. Spafford had a stroke in 1922 and died in April 1923. With her death, the group found itself in a difficult legal position since they had neither a constitution nor any written procedures. "Mother" Spafford had been the central figure in the colony for forty years and ruled as the "bride of Christ." There could not be a successor in the spiritual sense, but her husband moved quickly to put the group on a secure legal foundation. According to former members, it had become—by 1923—a wealthy enterprise with several businesses (including the American Colony Store) and large land holdings. A struggle for control began that year, with Spafford's daughters and their respective husbands, Frederick Vester and John Whiting, joining forces against some older colonists, most notably Joseph Larson.

The American Colony's history shows just how far the reach of utopia could extend and how people were willing to undertake long journeys to fulfill their needs. The Spaffords' religious life had quickened after the death of their children, and they wanted to push beyond the faith of Presbyterianism into personal holiness. In the process, they brought a small group along with them on their personal journey to Jerusalem, where, in perfect patience, they were willing to wait for the Lord to lead them and come to them. They needed to be at the center of the Christian world, and they needed to be witnesses to the Second Coming. They were genuine pilgrims except that their pilgrimage never took them home again, unless it was to bring another boatload of pilgrims back to Jerusalem. From Chicago, from Sweden, from England, they all came in the wake of Anna Spafford's calm and comforting visions. They went to the Holy of Holies but stayed to make their faith visible.

Theories of charismatic leadership, conflicts between contending leaders, all form a certain drama inherent in the developing tensions of communal life. Those tensions and the resolution of them are central to both the groups' survival and our own understanding of utopianism. The Holy Ghost and Us Society began simply enough, with a man and his inspiration, but in this case ended in both personal and social tragedy. For all their eccentricities and, in some cases blatant illegalities, few communal leaders have been jailed, though there were almost always brushes with the law along the way. Frank Weston Sandford was a major exception. His case was one in which the limits of American religious pluralism were tested. Here was a prophet who not only failed but who suffered the consequences of his faith. That faith and his history were rooted in Maine, where he was born on Ridge Road in Bowdoinham on 2 October 1862. At eighteen, he experienced a religious conversion that started him on his religious pilgrimage. After attending Bates College (where he was a standout baseball player), he entered the Cobb Divinity School, was ordained, and took a pastorate at the Baptist Church at Topsham, Maine. In 1890–91, he took a trip around the world to assess Protestant missionary activities and, in 1893, resigned his pastorate to begin a religious crusade that eventually took him to the Holy Land and jail. What started him on this new evangelical career was the voice of God speaking to him in a simple and direct manner. It was not the last time that God would speak to him, but this first message was certainly brief. God told him, "Go!"

It was on the subject of that received word that he preached to his congregation on 1 January 1893. He announced that he was resigning his pastorate to take up an independent career as an evangelist. His 1891 trip had awakened in him the need to spread the gospel, and he began a series of tent meetings with some students from the Gordon Missionary Training School in Boston and, with Charles E. Holland, the Holy Ghost and Us Bible School. Three years later, he broke ground for a center at Durham, Maine, and by the fall of 1896 had begun construction on a remarkable structure, the Temple of Truth, which cost $100,000. Free-will gifts and the voluntary labor of two hundred believers went toward the construction of a center intended to house missionaries trained by Sandford to revolutionize the world for Christ. The buildings were dedicated on 18 August 1896 and were described by one paper in the most glowing terms: "There are four fine buildings that surround a large court. Over each flies a flag. On the center cupola, which is surmounted by a gilded crown is a big banner inscribed 'Victory.' On another floats the Stars and Stripes while the British flag floats over a third. The fourth building flaunts a curious affair supposed to represent the flag of Israel. In the usual star corner is a shield traced in white. In the centre is a big white star called the star of David and around it twelve small stars to represent the disciples of Christ. Outside the shield and all over the rest of the flag is a milky way of small stars which Mr. Sandford says represented the Gentile world. These stars are made of pieces cut from Mrs. Sandford's wedding gown."[131]

At the dedication service, Sandford said that America and Britain were destined to rule the world, and he hinted at the eventual subjugation of other planets. He alluded to royal lineage everywhere: "Americans . . . are descended from Manasseh, while Queen Victoria herself is a descendant of King David." After dinner, thirty-two people were baptized in the Androscoggin River, among them a woman from Michigan who gave all her money and a blind man who expected to be cured by Sandford.

Cures were to be effected by prayer. Sandford believed that he could not only cure the sick but change the course of history. In the cupola of the Temple of Truth, prayers were offered on a continuous basis. Beginning in 1895, Sandford's followers prayed for healing, prayed for money, prayed for the success of their missionary efforts, prayed that their sins would be forgiven. Sandford gained a reputation as a faith healer, and several miracle cures were attributed to him. He did not believe in medicine, and his followers simply trusted in the Lord to guide them in all their actions.

Messages came to Sandford from God, and he interpreted those messages in a literal manner. In 1893 he had received a message to "Go!" in 1896 the words "Let us arise and build" came to him, and by 1900 he had a believing congregation of over two hundred settled on top of Beulah Hill. In 1900, in his autobiographical "Seven Years with God," Sandford summed up his career up to that point: "The seven years from that date [1893] to this [1900] may be divided into two great divisions—country evangelizing, covering about three and a half years, and the erection of buildings in the interest of worldwide evangelization, covering the remaining three and a half years. During the first period the son of God by fiery trials, tribulations and tests of nearly every conceivable kind, was preparing me personally to represent Himself among men. In the second, He was preparing a place where I might teach others the lessons I had learned and thus fit them to reproduce the same to the ends of the earth."[132]

He had a helpmate throughout those seven years in Helen Kinney, who had spent two years prior to their meeting as a missionary in Japan. Sandford believed that, throughout this whole period, "his soul was reaching out for wider territory." The community of

Shiloh was, by 1900, impressive, and Sandford had, almost single-handedly, brought it into existence by sheer dint of his hard work, prayer, and faith. Money had poured in; families had come to offer their labor and test their faith.

The colony sent out missionaries and by 1902 had groups in Ithaca, New York; Liverpool; Jamaica, New York; and Jerusalem. In Ithaca, they were known as the Church of the Living God. This group ran into trouble when one of their members refused medical attention and his fellow believers tried to pray away his pneumonia. He died. Although threatened with reprisals, the members continued to proselytize. The group in Liverpool had been organized after a visit by Sandford in 1902, and there were twelve members of the church in Jerusalem beginning in the summer of 1901. Those twelve represented to them both the Apostles and the twelve tribes of Israel. In 1902, a party of fifteen came to Shiloh from Scotland. They had but $40 with them, but Sandford's chief deputy, C. E. Holland, took them in. What kind of a colony did these Scottish immigrants come into? It consisted of about five hundred people, all living in common and sharing with one another. There were three substantial buildings: Shiloh, the combined church and residence hall; Bethesda, for the sick; and a children's building, Olivet.

Fortunately, we know a great deal about their internal life from the autobiography of a young man, Arnold White, who was an eyewitness to much of its hair-raising history.[133] By White's account, life at Beulah Hill was hard. Though they received generous gifts from believers over the years (a fact later confirmed by the British consul), the community was always hard pressed for funds to maintain such a large enterprise and to finance Sandford's increasingly grandiose vision. That vision was fueled by his belief that he and Charles E. Holland were the two witnesses mentioned in Revelation, the two "sons of oil" mentioned in Zachariah 4:11. These witnesses—regardless of the cost—were going to lead a restoration of the Kingdom of God throughout the world, but particularly in the Holy Land. Missionary activity among the Jews and in the Holy Land became the focus of Sandford's ministry, and everything became subject to that vision. Trips to Jerusalem, the maintenance of a center there (and one in Alexandria), the purchase of two yachts to make trips, all spoke eloquently to an orientation away from Maine and toward Palestine. Life at Shiloh centered on chapel meetings or on work on the main building plus agricultural work in the fields. There were no community industries such as the Shakers and Oneida maintained since the sole purpose of the community was to further the religious transformation of the world by prayer and example. Food and prayer were enough.

Students attended Bible classes or prayer meetings that lasted into the night. Arnold White reported that their food was simple, with tea and coffee prohibited (presumably because they were stimulants); however, supplies were often short. Fasting was a common fact of life, its purpose to mortify the soul: "A fast of three days was proclaimed. Nobody was to eat or drink for seventy-two hours except the children, for which the abstaining period was thirty-six hours. Pregnant mothers and the sick would break this fast at half time. Babies cried from thirst and hunger while distraught mothers wept or hardened their hearts to maternal feelings, the while beseeching God to turn his anger away."[134]

Sandford periodically harangued his followers at chapel services, and these "blowing up" sessions sometimes involved fits of temper on his part and physical abuse of members. It was this physical abuse and the practice of refusing medical aid to the sick that caused local authorities to move against him in 1904. In January 1903, a fourteen-year-old boy, Leander Bartlett, came down with diphtheria and was, in effect, allowed to die. Young Bartlett had committed a gross sin when he, in league with another boy, planned to run away. Both God and Sandford were angry with him, and he was not only denied medical attention, but no one even "laid hands" on him in the Shiloh tradition. In September 1903, there appeared a story in the *Lewiston Journal* that signaled a growing storm of controversy around Sandford's activities.[135] A former associate of his, the Reverend Harriman of Tacoma, Washington, turned against him and exposed his "fanaticism."

Harriman, a graduate of Harvard and the Bangor Theological Seminary, had congregations in Boston and Malden before moving to Tacoma to head another Baptist parish. There he heard about Sandford's work and decided to join him. Harriman was among the group of twelve who went to Jerusalem in May 1902, and it was from Jerusalem that he defected from Sandford's church. He said that Sandford was now making extraordinary claims: "One would think that Mr. Sandford's mental condition 'acute religious overappreciation of his own greatness', as I have charged, could be apparent from his claims alone. Here they are: Apostle, prophet, overseer of the world's evangelization, baptizer of all God's true sheep, meaning all true Christians; Elijah—the restorer of all things; and forerunner of the Messiah's second advent; David, who is to rule the whole earth and prepare the throne for the Messiah; the 'Branch'; High Priest of the Melchisedech priesthood; and first and chief of the two witnesses, 'with power to command fire and plague upon his enemies whenever he will.' "[136]

Sandford had gone over the top, and Harriman offered as evidence not only his religious megalomania but also his fits of anger (usually directed against those who had questioned his authority), his terrorizing of followers, and his erratic behavior. As an example of his erratic behavior, Harriman described the "cleaning out" times that took place at Shiloh. These were times when the colony members had to pray continuously and empty out their pockets for a special project. During these sessions, Sandford cajoled them, insulted them, tricked them, and did what was necessary to get their funds out of hiding places or from additional revenue sources such as relatives outside the colony. Coercion—both religious and financial—was at the heart of these "cleaning out" sessions. Harriman made no charges concerning social or sexual irregularities, but he drew a sharp portrait of a religious fanatic.

Just after Harriman's renunciation and public denunciation, reports reached Maine of the death of two Shilohites in Jerusalem. The American consul in Jerusalem, Selah Merrill, wrote that an English physician had stated that Frank Templeton's death was caused by malarial fever and by "culpable neglect, as all proper medical treatment was refused."[137] The consul wrote that the members' physical conditions were shameful and that the six or seven members stayed by themselves and seemed "content with tormenting one another." Clearly, their faith healing and praying were insufficient to cope with Middle East health hazards.

In February 1904, manslaughter charges were brought against Sandford for allowing Leander Bartlett to die and for cruelly abusing his own six-year-old son, John. He was acquitted on the manslaughter charge but fined $100 on the cruelty-to-children charge. From 1900 to 1906, the history of the colony is one of accusations, of Sandford's trips abroad to England and Palestine, and of a growing sense of crisis within the group. The purchase of a yacht in 1903 had allowed for some community training in seamanship, and later, when two others—renamed the Coronet and the Kingdom—were purchased, Sandford was prepared for a voyage to Palestine. Both the Coronet and the Kingdom set sail in August 1906. Sandford was taken aboard at Gibraltar with a portion of his baggage consisting of a harp purchased in England. From there they sailed on to the beleaguered colony headquarters in Jerusalem.

The Coronet was a magnificent yacht, over 130 feet long, capable of fourteen knots; it had made a trip around the world in 1893. Handsomely outfitted, she was purchased in October 1905 and had sufficient space for thirty passengers and crew. Speculation suggests that what prompted Sandford to take his final ill-fated journey were the charges leveled against him by Harriman and state officials. By his own account, however, he was motivated by obedience to God's call. This time, the message that came to him was as brief as the earlier ones, but for Sandford as easily comprehended. He was told to "Go Around," and he interpreted that command "to mean that they should sail around this world on a missionary voyage in the interests of all man's souls. They remembered that God had told Abraham to walk the length and breadth of the promised land, with the assurance that all the territory touched by the soles of his feet would become his, under God. They remembered that Joshua and his men had been told to compass the walls of Jericho, and that in response to this strange act of obedience God gave them the city." [138] So from the city of man to the city of God. The age-old journey was being recreated.

In October 1907, Sandford departed from Jerusalem with thirty believers, including his wife and five children (the youngest aged two), on a voyage that took them through the Straits of Gibraltar, to the Canary Islands, to the Caribbean, then south around South America, passing Cape Horn in April 1908, then on to Lima, and a final Atlantic crossing to Maine. Sandford's own account of the journey (without the disasters) reads like Bacon's *New Atlantis*. On the outward leg to the Caribbean, he compares his own trip with Columbus's heroic voyage of exploration. His ship's name—the *Coronet*—was taken from Revelation: "A Coronet was given unto him and he went forth conquering and to conquer." He opened his tale with the announcement that he was "the white horse and his rider set forth upon the career of conquest." [139] For Sandford, it was the continuation of a crusade started seventeen years before when, as a young man, he had taken his first missionary tour.

But it was more than that. He was playing his part in Christian history, taking up where Joshua had left off: "God's forces in Joshua's day marched around Jericho, in our day they sail round the globe." He was John the Evangelist, who had also heard the voice of God and had set out to speak the truth: "That a voice was heard on earth in 1892: it separated a man of God from common Christianity. It was heard seven years later as he addressed the first seventy to be sent forth as evangelists with the message. 'Go! behold I send you forth as lambs among wolves.['] It was heard again, startling in its intensity, at the opening of the twentieth century—'Go!' It was heard at the opening of Exodus—'Go home!' and again upon the Atlantic—'Go around!' referring to this very journey. It was heard at the departure of the 'thirty' from the Holy City—'Go Forth!' But its final and absolute meaning finds expression today as we weigh anchor, as our sails fill, and as the *Coronet*, with the same message, 'Go forth!' sails out upon her long ocean voyage, 'Conquering and to Conquer.' "[140] His ship was riding on the waves of prophecy, on his premillennialist belief that his life, his colony at Shiloh, his voyage, signaled something great to come. And he sailed on his own increasing megalomania.

That megalomania made him see signs everywhere, identify his work with that of earlier prophets (including Columbus—"an instrument in the hand of God"), and demand from his followers in the name of prophecy and Christ their obedience. The Amazon reminded him of the flow of God's grace; the harbor at Rio de Janeiro seemed no longer neglected but a "royal harp in the hand of David's son." As they approached Lima, Sandford was reminded of the conquest of Mexico by Cortez and of Peru by Pizzaro, and he felt an affinity with those men because he too "had stepped out into a life of absolute abandonment to the will, the Word, the spirit and the providences of God."[141]

Just as the *Coronet* approached St. Ambrose Island in the Pacific on its way to Australia (a destination it never reached), the British consul in Manchester, Massachusetts, was transmitting to Lord Bryce a report on the "Fortified Kingdom of Heaven" compiled by the vice consul at Portland, Maine, J. B. Keating. That report grew out of the concerns of the parents of Margaret Neary, who had left her home in Winnipeg, Canada, in 1901 to join the church of the Everlasting Gospel at Shiloh. Money sent by her parents wound up in the colony coffers, and they feared that she was "kept by this man Sandford for immoral purposes, and I beg of you to assist me in saving my child." The British vice consul was met courteously by Sandford's attorney, and they appeared to have worked out an amicable visiting agreement, only to have it shattered by the unannounced visit of other Neary children. They did see their sister, and she chose to remain. Furthermore, Mr. Neary later reported that he was wrong about the alleged immoral character of the place.[142]

Yet the vice consul's report to his superiors did contain some interesting information. Over a million dollars had been raised by the group and, of that amount, $250,000 came from England and $125,000 from British Columbia. He reported the population at seven hundred, with a "large number of British subjects," including an "enthusiastic lady of refinement" who had handed over £2,900 to the group. He reported that men and women were housed separately, that marriages took place on occasion, and that no children had been born out of wedlock. "I was assured that the bitterest enemy to the institution [presumably Harriman] has said that he knew absolutely nothing against the morality of the Institution or its people. . . . The Bible class teacher was a British subject, a native of Maitland, N.S. far from being well versed in Scripture and his strongest point is his being somewhat of a leader and disciplinarian. . . . The main dining room seats 500 . . . the waitresses are dressed in black and white aprons. Of course everybody gives his labor to the cause without pay."[143]

Consul Keating further reported that members believed Sandford to have been chosen and sent by God to prepare the way for the Second Coming. At that point, they had three thousand acres under cultivation, seventy-eight head of cattle, and thirty horses. He said that they prayed three times a day, at nine, noon, and three, and on Sundays held two services and another one on Tuesdays. Miss Neary—the object of all this inquiry—taught kindergarten and was "perfectly well cared for." Despite all this reassuring news, the consul concluded that the "whole structure of Shiloh is false and must eventually fall if left alone" since persecution would only make people sympathetic.[144]

While these inquiries were being made, Sandford and the *Coronet* crew were enduring starvation on the high seas. Violent storms and inadequate provisions wreaked havoc. The *Lewiston Journal* reported her arrival at Portland in October 1911: "From her sides, long sea grass was hanging, barnacles covered her from stem to stern, and convincing evidence of repeated battles with hurricanes was everywhere to be seen on her deck. Members of her crew, gaunt and ill, lined her rail and looked with tears of joy in their eyes upon the first land they had seen in many months. They were so emaciated that it was evident that they had passed through terrible suffering."[145]

The ship was quarantined and Sandford charged with causing the death of Charles Hughey by failing to provide sufficient food for the crew. During the trial, it was learned that while the crew suffered from scurvy the leader had provisions and a special cook. Sandford defended himself before the court and said that he had received a simple set of instructions from the Lord as he set out on the journey. Those instructions were, "Continue!"

The jury found him guilty of the death of six crew members, and he was sentenced to a ten-year prison term at the federal penitentiary in Atlanta. He preached a farewell sermon on 18 December 1911 (throughout the whole day) to his followers and curious onlookers. Several times he broke down and wept. With his two hundred followers surrounding him, he predicted the early coming of Christ and the ultimate triumph of the Shiloh group as other denominations faded away.

Without their leader, the colony sank into despair and poverty but survived. They were still on the millennial trail in 1914 when visited by a black millennialist group from Boley, Oklahoma, led by one "Chief Sam." That group later went on to Liberia and to a disastrous conclusion. When Sandford was released from prison in August 1918, he returned first to Boston and then entered retirement in upstate New York. The Kingdom of Heaven church survived him and still functions atop Beulah Hill, Maine.[146]

Sandford was, of course, a man possessed—possessed by prayer, possessed by a sense of mission, possessed by the power that he could wield over people. He created a community of believers, a colony of followers, and in his zeal caused some of them to die. His and their answer was that it was the will of God. That followers willingly followed him attests to the power of his message, their own belief in the power of prayer and faith healing, and Sandford's charismatic presence. At times he appeared to have harangued them, browbeaten them, and been insensitive (unto death) of their needs. Possessed by a belief that the Lord had laid his hands on him, Sandford thought that he could seize history and cure the world.

Thomas Low Nichols and Mary Gove Nichols began their utopian careers as health practitioners in New York and Ohio and ended them in the south of England; Thomas Lake Harris started in England, moved to western New York, and closed out his days in California; Martha McWhirter went from Tennessee to Texas to suburban Washington, D.C. All were visionaries; all were utopians.

For them the words of Revelation 1:3, which said that they who "hear the words of prophesy" would found the "city of my God, which is new Jerusalem," were a clarion call. Not all visions were inspired by Revelation since there were special insights that came to people like the idiosyncratic Cyrus Teed. In addition, there were secular socialists like Cabet and de Boissiere who took their inspiration from *The Rights of Man*. To seize history and to cure the world are old ambitions that found voice in figures like Giordano Bruno and Gerard Winstanley, who wrote in his *Fire in the Bush* that the "voyce is gone out, freedome, freedome, freedome." John Bunyan had written about a time when it would be "always summer, always sunshine, always pleasant, always green, fruitful and beautiful." [147]

America promised to be that place and was a perfect spot for utopian projections and projects. It had not only space but an ideology that suggested that perfection was possible. These latter-day utopian travelers saw, however, that there were imperfections in the garden. They thought that they could—through community—create a new Eden. The Adamic myth continued to operate in the post–Civil War period in Kansas, Texas, and California. Most followed the sun westward and kept their eyes on the horizon as they journeyed. They thought that it was still possible to be born again, to create a perfected colony, to seize history and cure both themselves and the world.

3 "Hard Times": Common Land and Common Labor

I have not given up on the work of reform, but I have turned my efforts from those of political endeavor to the line of cooperation. This country offers exceptional advantages to colonies. Land is cheap and abundant and productive. The country is less developed than in the "wild west." Winters are extremely short and very mild. . . . I have secured a large tract of land upon which I shall establish a cooperative colony. A portion of it is upon the immediate sea shore, where the scenery is grand and the fishing and oystering superb. On account of the surpassing beauty of the surroundings the future town will be called "Dreamland City."

Coming Nation, 9 July 1898

Henry Villard, of the American Association for the Promotion of Social Sciences, noted in his 1872 report to the English Cooperative Congress the "preliminary" status of the cooperative movement in America. Persons unfamiliar with its history presumed that it was growing and vital, but, in fact, it had so far "only attained to a very little development."[1] He accounted for the lack of development (here he is writing about production or distributive cooperatives) by looking at several factors.

One, there was the fact that wages were higher in America and that American laborers (as distinct from British laborers) were "less impelled to seek improvement of their condition through Cooperation." Two, American workmen would (with greater ease) find the "means and opportunity" to establish themselves independently "owing to the higher wages, the cheap lands and the chance to 'grow up' with the country." Villard believed that it was quite "usual" for both skilled and unskilled workers to save enough money in a few years to settle on cheap lands or in the fast-growing western cities, where they would, in due time, be "materially independent." Three, that independence and a feeling of self-reliance generated by economic prosperity "renders him [the American workman] disinclined to make the sacrifice of individualism which associated labour in a measure demands." Finally, he detailed the "migratory habits" of native American workers and the "promiscuous character" of foreign-born labor. The native-born worker rarely established roots in any locality or community for any length of time, and the foreign born lacked "mutual confidence" because of their "diverse and often antagonistic backgrounds."[2]

Villard saw the fluidity, the individualism, and the expansive nature of American society all working against cooperation. Yet the cooperative life he wrote of in this pessimistic assessment did have an appeal to "associated labor"; it was "in the over-crowded cities and manufacturing districts of the Atlantic States [where] the working classes need relief through it almost as much as in the countries of the old world."[3]

The squalid conditions of urban life and the fluctuating nature of the economy with its periods of boom and bust suggested to some reformers the colony idea as a solution to the "labor problem." A coalition of those interests did come together in the 1870s to promote the idea, not just, as Villard suggested, on the Atlantic coast, but in several midwestern locations. While Horace Greeley was editor of the *Tribune* during the late 1860s and during the promotional campaigns drumming up support for Colorado, one sees a constant effort to encourage men toward cooperation:

> Cooperation, forever! This year there is a cooperative cottage at Long Beach under the sheltering roof which several families are living in great peace, and we hope, harmony.
>
> A cooperative market farm in the Hackensack Meadows conducted with ordinary prudence and skill would be a great success. Are there no workingmen in our midst, among the number of those who are constantly complaining that the city is overstocked with labor, who can take hold of and develop this?
>
> A hundred such [cooperative ventures] may fail to achieve success, without exhausting the infinitely varying conditions under which success may be sought— whereby it may be attained. It would be a miniature New York, and after passing through its crisis, would be constantly reinforced by troops and relatives of the colonists from this city and every quarter.[4]

Not until late in the decade would there be any single body organized to promote cooperation. Villard, in his 1872 report, had commented on the publicity generated by the *Tribune* and how little success it had. There was some modest support within the struggling labor movement located primarily within the Sovereigns of Industry. Independent projects such as the one launched at Philadelphia by H. Haupt in 1872 at Mountain Lake, Giles County, Virginia, were few. Haupt's appeal was to recent immigrants who had come to American cities by the "hundreds of thousands" and to "artizans [sic] and laborers in our cities unable to accumulate sufficient capital to purchase a home." He proposed to establish a colony in southwestern Virginia "to carry on various branches of mechanical industry in connection with agriculture." Through a kind of association practiced by the "Shakers and Economists," he believed that conflict between labor and capital could be avoided. Earlier failures in cooperative colonies had made an impression on him, though he was cheered by the recent successes of the Godin colony at Guise, France.[5]

In Haupt's colony, association was made to appear compatible with individualism and was, in fact, the vehicle for advancing it. Persons would not be grouped by trades or occupations or with reference to their views about marriage or temperance; rather, an effort would be made to "harmonise antagonisms by allowing perfect individual liberty."[6] Land was acquired near Mountain Lake (now West Virginia), and the possibilities, according to Haupt, were limitless. He envisaged not only a farm but also a shoe factory, cattle, swine, and sheep production, and forestry. One special feature of the plan was that prospective members would have their children cared for in the event of their death—the colony was life insurance. His proposal was wide sweeping, intended to reach a wide audience, yet there were sections clearly aimed at urban mechanics dissatisfied with city life and willing to try an experiment in the mountains. Nothing seems to have come of the project, although a similar one did get started in the South in 1871.

Organized at a meeting at the Cooper Institute in New York, the project attracted fifty colonists onto fifteen hundred acres at Warm Spring, Madison County, North Carolina. A mortgage was taken out on a property that included a hotel and mineral springs. Work was begun to cultivate the land, a dam was erected, and a store opened. Three men did build houses, but the majority preferred to live at the hotel. This joint-stock company required each member to contribute $100 for each share, and it drew, according to the Tribune, a mixed group of "active and energetic men" and, unfortunately, "visionary and ne'er do well people who were attracted to it because there was a magic in the word cooperation and the colony was a kind of Providence for their wants."[7] How long it lasted is unclear.

The Virginia area attracted a colony of German socialists from New York into a settlement forty-five miles above Lynchburg. They purchased 264 acres for $3,500 and fixed up some former slave quarters to live in. By May 1873, there were eighty-three people on the site working poor land and mining ochre. The settlement was still in existence in May 1876 but may have failed shortly after that. One member was Eugene L. Fischer, who had wanted to join Nauvoo years earlier, did join Warm Springs in 1871, came to the German socialists' colony during the Panic of 1873, and ended his cooperative life years later at Topolobampo on the west coast of Mexico.[8]

In the late 1870s, Jesse Jones and T. Wharton Collins pressed for a kind of social Christianity that was a precursor to W. D. P. Bliss's emphasis twenty years later. In the pages of *Equity* (1874) and *Labor Balance* (1877), we see a kind of radical Protestantism that had a wider appeal in the 1890s. Writing in response to the depression of 1877, Collins called for the introduction of a "social economy" that included the "formation of communities having all things in common, or the cooperative exchange of labor and its results agreeably to truly equitable and invariable rules."[9] He called for cooperative homes and what can only be described as Christianized Fourierism. Modest efforts to start practical communities were initiated by Samuel Leavitt, editor of the *Eclectic and Peacemaker*, with Collins's blessing: "He is one of the ablest men in the department of true reform, as unfolding under the influence of the spirit of Jesus Christ. With a few friends, he is endeavoring to develop practical beginnings of communistic movement in New York City." A second effort in that direction was also being attempted in 1878 by J. S. Rankin, editor of the *Free Flag*, at Muskoda, Minnesota, who was already "on good land, in a desirable location and ready to welcome Christian people who would join him in cooperative labor. This is a very favorable opportunity for a Christian cooperative colony."[10]

Scattered efforts like Rankin's in Minnesota in 1878 and at the Home near South Frankfort, Michigan, in 1877 appear as brief notes in journals or compilations. Like Warm Springs, they may have lasted for as long as three years or barely survived a winter, but could report, as the twelve-member Home did in 1878, that it was "slowly prospering."[11] There were no national reform associations devoted to communitarianism, no papers like the *Dial* reporting on cooperative ventures, only scattered efforts by reformers in scattered locations. It was a movement without a center.

The only coordinated effort to engage the laboring classes during the decade came in 1879, when R. Heber Newton, Felix Adler, and O. B. Frothingham met at a dinner party in New York and their conversation turned toward the condition of the "unemployed poor." They joined together to form the Cooperative Colonization Aid Society and secured the financial support of Elizabeth Rowell Thompson to plan and purchase land for a colony. It was in her honor that the Kansas-based colony, the Thompson Colony, was named. Earlier in the decade, Thompson had underwritten the Chicago-Colorado Colony at Longmont and would provide extensive support later to the spiritualist Shalam Colony in New Mexico. The main purpose of the Cooperative Colonization Aid Society was to "relieve the unemployed working man at the same time by stimulating and guiding a return to that agricultural life which is the natural life of man." [12]

The broad purpose of the society was resettlement, their specific goal to encourage workers to plant colonies and work in association with one another. Family life and individual effort were to be respected; however, the mode of labor was associated labor. An agency was established in New York City and a campaign undertaken to educate workers (through promotional literature and meetings) about the colony. In June 1879, the society announced that a special committee of businessmen was looking at land on Long Island and that land had been offered (possibly by the German socialists) near Lynchburg in Virginia by twenty-five colonists already there. R. Heber Newton emphasized that the colonies would be nondenominational: "I wish to state that this colonization scheme differs very materially from those of the Hebrews and Catholics. It is entirely independent of race or creed. We aim to plant American townships where all questions of religion shall be free to take care of themselves in accordance with American ideas." [13]

These joint-stock companies were supposed to attract investors: "We hope and believe we can interest our wealthy classes in these corporations as affording a safe and profitable investment, with a philanthropic motive to recommend it." The leaders envisaged a cooperative store, cooperative cooking—in fact, all activities were to be done on the cooperative principle. Bonanza farmers were making it impossible for small farmers to compete. Their major concern was, however, for the city dweller: "We shall thus create a permanent overflow pipe for the surplus population of our larger cities. We feel that this is the true manner in which wealth should extend a helping hand to the needy." [14]

Thompson had also funded the publication of the Worker, "Advocating Cooperative Colonization," which it featured articles by figures like George Jacob Holyoake. Writing in the Worker, Holyoake said that he was heartened by efforts at colonization but that the United States still lagged behind Britain on the question. His trip to the United States had been undertaken with support from the British government and Mrs. Thompson in order to gather material for an emigrant guidebook to the United States. Cooperative societies like the Guild of Cooperators in England and the Cooperative Colony Association could help in the emigration process: "Our aim was always to set up cooperative colonies which should be self-provided, self-directed and self-supported. It is, however, on boundless lands in America where this problem can best be solved. All I hear and see in America convinces me more than heretofore that to this complexion social and industrial efforts has got to come. Crudeness, eccentricity and superstition have done their best to bring these colonies into failure and contempt. The problem of cooperative life has yet to be solved."[15]

Holyoake gave added publicity to the society during his visit to New York in November 1879, when he spoke at the Cooper Union and paid an eloquent tribute to his sponsor, Elizabeth Rowell Thompson. On the same platform sat Felix Adler, who made an "earnest" introductory speech stressing the need for cooperation in order to avoid the development of a "large and wretched class of poor as found in European countries."[16] After all this fanfare, the colony was finally located at Salina, Kansas.

According to Nell Waldron, who studied colonization projects in Kansas, the Thompson Colony members worked the fields in common, held farm machinery and tools in common, but maintained separate homes and gardens. Approximately twenty-five families were thought to constitute the ideal number for such a project, and the colonists were expected to repay (in annual installments) the principal advanced to undertake the settlement. At some point, they would have the choice of either continuing to work in common or reverting to a purely individualistic basis for colony life.[17] If the colony made a success of itself, it would serve a "double purpose, demonstrating the advantages of cooperation in agriculture and opening to the industrious poor who fail of success in overcrowded cities, a method of getting upon the soil and making for themselves new careers of usefulness and prosperity."[18] The Thompson Colony appears to have fallen quick victim to one of the problems faced by those who get on the Kansas soil—drought. The drought of 1880 ended the colony.

Ironically, a great deal more is know about another Kansas experiment that was started at the same time but under less distinguished sponsorship—the Esperanza Community located at Neosha Valley. An offspring of a communal group located at Buffalo, Missouri, led by Alcander Longley and begun in July 1877, it was reported to be a "colony of communists" and to have purchased a hotel building in Urbana, Kansas.[19] Another paper reported that it was an offshoot of Oneida! Esperanza had a brief and volatile history, lasting probably less than a year. In that year, the colony published its members' views and aspirations in a paper, the *Star of Hope*. Liberal communism, as they called their philosophy, was multifaceted and included support for the Socialist Labor party, a demand for the eight-hour day, and the direct popular recall of elected officials. Their fifteen-point platform called for liberal legislation regulating sanitary conditions, child labor, accident insurance, a graduated income tax, a national bank system, and the equalization of wages for men and women. In an address delivered at the opening of the colony, R. E. LaFetra made an attack on the millionaires of the country and the banking system and then forecast an immediate revolution: "Yes, it is plain to be seen that we are upon the eve of the revolution, and the railroad riots of the past six months show conclusively . . . that we are treading upon a magazine or volcano." His vision of what the good life could be reads like a scene out of the *Rubaiyat*, with gardens, large commodious accommodations, Turkish baths, and a first-class library ("no drudgery, no wage slavery, no unrequited toil is here to mar the happiness of this productive and busy life"). In numerous ways, he had described the Oneida Community as it stood in all its communal and material splendor in 1878. Esperanza was to usher in an age in which communism would "cure hard times, panics, starvation and poverty."[20]

Such exalted prose was conventional rhetoric at the outset of many a communal venture. Neosho had little to offer beyond that rhetoric, its platform, and its prospectus. It had a home in Neosho with fourteen rooms, and interested parties were asked to come and visit—for the small fee of $2.50 a week. Response to their periodical announcement was varied.

Under its slogan, "All for each, each for all—United we stand, divided we fall," the *Star of Hope*, under R. T. Romaine's editorship tried to stir up faithful communists with inspirational poetry and dire statements about the condition of American life in 1878:

> We've a Communal Home in the land of the west
> Where the souls of our people are free.
> Where Friendship and Love find a voice in each heart. . . .
> Will you come to our home, then, that's waiting for you

Where each one can reap the rewards of their toil. . . .
Here women no longer shall be crushed in the dust
Shall be queen of her own social realm. . . .
Then say will you come to our home in the west
Where Friendship and Love find a voice in each heart
Like the shell as it sings to the sea.[21]

They realized that their "trip was an experimental one," but, with three million unemployed, class legislation and unequal taxation eating away at local government, and the National Banking Act of 1878 (which demonetized silver) pauperizing the working class, they believed that cooperation was the alternative. The railroad riots of 1877 signaled a spark of rebellion ("we are on the eve of a revolution"), and there did exist a universal panacea for all these troubles, communism: "We have found a center here, a nucleus at Urbana, Kansas, a rallying point for those whose hearts are in the work and who are willing to devote their means and their labors to this immaculate and unselfish end."[22] By April 1878, the colony had received sixty-one applications and established a dialogue in the *Star of Hope* with other socialists struggling against the capitalist system. A. P. Bowman wrote from "The Home" in Gilmore, Michigan, and sent a photograph; Mrs. H. C. Garner of Long Lane, Missouri, sent her philosophy of individualism and some poetry; and negotiations were begun with the Russians at the Cedarville Community. Little was to come of all this.

Bowman wrote again to say that he had been working two years to establish a similar New Order of Hope and might join them. T. Austin of Ancora, New Jersey, had inaugurated a similar movement there, and a few others expressed interest. Their philosophy of liberal communism ("that every subject has two or more sides and shades of belief and opinion should be fully and fairly presented before the formation of our judgment") or rationalism apparently attracted applicants. By August 1878, however, one leader was dead, and the other two (N. T. Roamine and R. E. LaFetra) had moved to another town. Such erratic leadership was not unknown in communal history, and the change at Neosho signaled the effective end of the colony. The area seemed to have an attraction for groups since a temperance colony had been proposed for the Neosho Valley in 1872.[23]

The career of Alcander Longley is an equally instructive one for the decade since it acted as a bridge between the reform worlds of 1840 and 1870. Longley's father was a Universalist minister who had helped start the Clermont Phalanx, east of Cincinnati. At age eighteen, young Longley had proposed a phalanx of his own but deferred that plan while he joined the North American Phalanx for two years. In 1854, he moved to Cincinnati, where he married the first of three wives and owned a printing firm that specialized in publishing reform literature. With his three brothers, he began publishing the *Phalansterian Record* in 1857. From that year until 1865, he promoted phalanxes at Moores Hill, Indiana; Black Lake, Michigan; and Foster's Crossing, Ohio. During 1867, he and his family became probationary members at the Icarian settlement at Corning, Iowa, staying only briefly before moving to St. Louis, where he commenced publishing the *Communist*. By the age of thirty-five, he had been in two communities, had proposed and publicized several more, and was involved with several reform issues, including free love and phonography. He had used his first wife's money to promote his interests and aid the poor. She grew weary of his schemes and divorced him in 1874.[24]

By 1867, Longley was just breaking into full communal stride when he launched the Reunion Colony at Carthage, Missouri, in the pages of the *Communist*. The community lasted from 1868 to 1870 and never had more than twenty-seven members. One visitor found that it contained fifteen adults and ten children in 1870. All members lived in a two-story house. A sitting room served as the children's playroom, and the attic held a printing press, "a box with a plaster skeleton, some books and a large bed, which the guest shared comfortably, with the regular occupant, Stephen Briggs." Briggs called himself a "hygienic physician and surgeon" and advocated several reforms, including women's rights, vegetarianism, hydropathy, and spiritualism. He was a leading member of Reunion and on Sundays lectured on anatomy, using the attic-stored skeleton. One of the community's key tenets was its commitment to women's rights; however, in the summer of 1870, the majority were converted to free love, and a schism developed. According to one member, Longley was a particularly inept leader, and his great ability lay in generating new communities, not sustaining them.[25]

On the heels of his failure at Carthage, Longley proposed the Friendship Community, which began with a small group of five near Buffalo, Dallas County, Missouri. Among those attracted was J. G. Truman, a printer who had graduated from a Universalist seminary in Ohio only to renounce that faith in favor of "spiritualism and pantheism." A student of philosophy and phrenology, he was a Greenbacker and a "theoretical" socialist who had read Comte's *Moral Philosophy* and decided to join a colony. Another member,

William H. Bennett, provided nearly all the funds for the group and insisted that they lease a hotel, open a store, and raise crops. His faith wavered quickly, and he left, taking all that he had donated with him. Longley then purchased a nearby farm and continued the small community. Between 1877 and 1883, he tried, unsuccessfully, to start communes in Polk and Bollinger County, Missouri. Both were undercapitalized, and Longley's own personality was not a winning one. Throughout this whole period, he continued to publish the *Communist* sporadically. In between colony ventures, he worked as a journeyman printer in St. Louis.

Longley's career and the career of William Frey crossed at Reunion, which Frey joined after spending sometime at the Progressive or Cedar Vale Community in Kansas. Frey (Vladimir Konstantinovich Geins) was born at Odessa, Russia, in 1839 into a military family and attended military college only to reject an army career after receiving his commission. He rebelled against his authoritarian upbringing and chose a career in science. The ideas of Fourier, Saint-Simon, Cabet, and Owen interested him, and he may have been a member of the Land and Liberty organization that planned to overthrow the government. When he was twenty-seven he went through a severe mental crisis, possibly because of his realization that the revolution had failed. He then resolved to emigrate.

In a letter to a friend, Frey wrote; "To the devil with this Russia it only smothers everything decent." He was attracted to America after reading about the Oneida Community in a St. Petersburg journal. Before emigrating, he married, and, in February 1868, he left Russia for Germany with his final destination America. On his arrival in the United States, he gave as his name William Frey and, after staying in Jersey City, asked for admission to Oneida. Before the community could act on his request (they probably would have denied him admission since there was little in his background that suggested an interest in "Bible Communism"), he entered into a correspondence with Alcander Longley. Frey then applied for admission to the Reunion Colony, stating that he had left Russia because of persecution, the indifference of the government toward social programs, and his own conviction that communism and love of neighbor were the cornerstones for a new society.

In March 1870, he and his family set out for Reunion and arrived just as it was in the process of breaking up. It had split over the free love question, and Frey was opposed to such individualism because it suggested immoral behavior. Although ten years later he would remember Reunion as "the most discordant and hellish life that could be imagined" (and although he had also lost money at Reunion), he was still eager to continue the cooperative life, moving to a site in Osage County, Kansas, where he and Stephen Briggs took the lead in the Progressive Community. Its capital resources consisted of $231.50, one cow, a wagon, and some farm implements. They staked out land on the newly opened Osage Trust Lands in southern Kansas. Their journey from Missouri to Kansas had been slow and painful since they had encountered a fierce snowstorm that caused both Frey and Briggs to suffer from frostbite. At the end of twelve hard days on the road and with now less than $40 in their common cashbox, they arrived in what Frey recorded in his diary as the "promised land." The men immediately built a shelter against the elements and waited for Frey's family. His wife and sick daughter arrived after twelve days on the prairie, during which they had slept in the open most of the time. They had carried with them a cot, nine hens, a calf, and a cat!

By April 1871, the settlers had erected a three-room shanty and put some land under cultivation. At this point, they could hardly be thought of as a commune, though they saw themselves as the genesis of the Progressive Community. They were, in fact, some idealists wandering about the plains, barely eking out an existence while the idea of the New Jerusalem lured them. A brief notice in Longley's *Communist* about the Cedarvale Community changed things. That notice and the subsequent publication of a constitution brought inquiries to the colony (at this point three adults). Its appeal to "Liberty, Equality, Fraternity" had one caveat to that sweeping declaration: no one would be accepted who was "grossly sensuous, seeking only the gratification of his own senses." A number of queries came from expatriate Russians who, like Frey, had migrated to escape Russian tyranny. During April 1872, the colony's membership rose to seven adults, plus three others on probation. That same year, it was incorporated, and the colonists' physical circumstances improved ever so slightly. Essentially, it was, as Avrahm Yarmolinsky put it, "plain living and high thinking." The Freys abstained from pork and tobacco and used no stimulants (including tea or coffee), though the daily round of life was pleasant. They practiced "mutual criticism" on one another, a technique borrowed from Oneida, and, like at Oneida, members found it a hard discipline to be told their faults. Apparently, at Cedarvale (the names *Cedarvale* and *the Progressive Colony* were both used to describe the group) they met for mutual criticism on a weekly basis. Frey believed in self-discipline and denial as key elements in the transformative process that took individuals from society to community. His motto was; "Break your-self." By 1875, the Freys had grown apart: she had fallen in love with another man, and he practiced male continence, as urged by the Oneida Community. During that period, Mary Frey left the colony with her lover, became pregnant, then begged her husband's forgive-ness, and asked to return to the group.

March 1875 saw the community again reduced to six, a number that was "swelled" when three families joined. In July, the Freys seceded, taking with them a third of the acreage (160 acres) and a few disciples. This new Investigating Community was devoted to mo-nogamy and communism, whereas the Progressive or Cedarvale Community was now controlled by a small band of spiritualists and healers. The splinter colony consisted initially of only two families (the Freys and the Rights), but that arrangement was to be altered when in the fall three Russian men knocked at the door of the Frey house and announced they were the advance guard of a group (fifteen in all) who wished to join them. Led by Alexander Malikov, this group of "God-men" practiced "a synthesis of Quakerism and social-ism, opposed both to the existing order and to revolution."[26]

The "God-men" had all participated in the revolutionary move-ment in Russia in the early 1860s and now rejected violence in favor of a radical perfectionism that asserted that men could achieve spir-itual regeneration and that such "God-men" were incapable of evil. When these religious revolutionaries went to the people with their ideas, the authorities became alarmed, particularly when their talk turned to attacks on private property. Fearful of persecution, they emigrated to the United States, where they heard of Frey and his commune. What they found, of course, were two barely surviving families who—as Malikov put it—were "paupers who were presum-ing to be able to enrich the world by the perfection of their lives." The "God-men" decided to start a community of their own rather than join the Investigating group. To further confuse matters, they called their group the Cedarville Community and located it on 160 acres four miles from the Frey household. Yet they then had difficul-ties getting along with one another and decided to throw their lot in with the unsuccessful, though experienced, Frey.

Frey now had a community of his own, and it had come to him in the most serendipitous and backhanded fashion. He was both dis-ciplinarian and rule maker for these religious zealots, and they chafed under his austere rules. According to Yarmolinsky, life at the new commune "was little short of hellish" and "degenerated into mutual persecution in the name of a moral idea."[27] The Russians were homesick and now yearned for more stimulation than this barren Kansas landscape could offer. In the summer of 1877, the group broke up, with Malikov returning to Russia and the others scattering. One couple joined a Shaker society in New York State.

Frey then entered into correspondence with the Icarians at Corning, Iowa, tried to join Oneida in 1879 (they were in the middle of their breakup), and offered the land to the Bible Community of Plattsburg, Missouri, who rejected it, saying that they wanted to be near a center of civilization and stay at Plattsburg. However, they knew of a group led by "Brothers Romaine and Brother Lafayette [sic]" that might be interested. That was, of course, the Esperanza Community of Urbana, Kansas, that had started a colony in 1877.

With his faith in the communal life undaunted, Frey continued to search for that right combination of persons, site, and philosophy. He now began to mix Comte's positivism with his own brand of socialism, and in 1880 he was heading a "complex family" at Clermont, Iowa, where he had been invited by G. L. Henderson, the editor of the *Positive Thinker*. The *Positive Thinker* carried a brave statement on its masthead: "Freest of the Free, Bravest of the Brave, Purest of the Pure, Destroying Only to Replace." That last phrase could have been used to describe Frey's own career. He had a long life before him, and his communal phase was poised for one final turn. Positivism became Frey's new faith, and by the summer of 1881 he was in New York City, working to reform the world through the "Religion of Humanity."

Before closing out Frey's career, we should look at another group of emigrants who came to Kansas earlier in the 1870s. They came with high hopes and considerable publicity, to survive for only two months. The founder of the Hays Colony was Louis Albert Pio, a Danish radical who became active in the socialist movement and in 1872 was charged with "crimes against public authority" when he called for a mass meeting to support strikes. He served a three-year sentence and on his release edited a socialist newspaper, the *Social-Demokraten*. Dissatisfaction with the Danish socialist movement led him to consider organizing emigrants and establishing a socialist colony to serve the needs of Danish workers. He encouraged the chairman of the Socialist party to visit the United States to look for a colony site. During his visit, the chairman, Geleff, sent back reports about Kansas that Pio published in the journal. Scandinavians had settled in Kansas as early as the 1850s and by 1870 were scattered throughout the state. In 1877, Pio and Geleff left Denmark because Pio "longed more and more for a tangible proof of the theories feasibility or unfeasibility in practice, and my future activity in the party became clearly dependent on this being provided." Actually, Pio and Geleff had engaged in secret discussions with the police aimed at getting them to leave the country. There was an implicit threat that if he did not leave he would be back in prison, a place that had almost killed him before. The police offered to help him get to America if he left by the end of April 1877, if he closed the newspaper, and if he agreed never to return to Denmark. Such was the major driving force behind the establishment of a colony in Kansas.[28]

Pio left for America, and he and Geleff parted company in New York after quarreling over money. Approximately twenty-five members gathered in New York, then moved on to Salina, Kansas, to meet Pio, who had traveled on ahead. Salina appealed to some colonists as a desirable spot because it afforded some of the rudiments of a civilized life, but Pio wanted them to settle in a more isolated area so that they could cement their social relations. He went ahead to Hays, a hundred miles further west, where they acquired land and, according to one colonist, "worked like Hell." There were constant arguments between the Danes and the Germans in the group (all socialists) over ideological questions. According to Kenneth Miller, the Germans had little faith in the Danes' ability to understand political theory. "There was a weaver, a Westphalian, who said that all Danish socialism was completely shallow; only the Germans had a real understanding of Lasalle and Karl Marx."[29] The women argued with one another over who should do what in the kitchen. The colony lasted only six weeks, possibly a record in communal endeavors. Pio apparently left even before that. Both Danes and Germans were unprepared for, and unwilling to accept, frontier conditions. The colonists agreed to sell everything that they had pledged to hold in common, and each one was given $30 from the proceeds. Pio remained in the country, working for a Florida Railroad company and managing their pavillion at the World's Fair in Chicago in 1893. In that year, he tried to promote a "business venture on the east coast of Florida," calling the colony White City. He died in Chicago in late 1893.

There were curious twists to Pio's journey to communal failure. His political idealism had got him into trouble (and into prison) in Denmark; his idealism was rekindled by the plight of workers and the promise of Kansas colonization, only to find that the only way he could sustain that project was to turn his back on the socialist movement in his native land. His journey to the New World began as an alternative to prison, and he received no rewards when he and the other colonizers reached Kansas. There they fell on each other and wrangled about metaphysics. In the end, he turned to real estate speculation in America. This Dane who knew eleven languages and participated in the First International ended his career by selling lots in Florida to his countrymen from Chicago.

Pio's serendipitous career was matched by Longley and Frey. After embracing Positivism, Frey stayed in New York City for two years before getting on the road again for a communal cause. This time he was associated with the Am Olam (Hebrew for "eternal people") movement that in 1881 had sent Jewish refugees to the United States from Russia. The proximate cause for that wave of migration was a wave of anti-Semitism that followed the ascension of Alexander III to the throne following the assassination of Alexander II in March 1881. Pogroms took place in numerous Russian cities, and Jews were forced, once again, to consider emigration as a means of survival. Schemes to encourage Jews to emigrate to the United States went as far back as 1783 and continued throughout the nineteenth century, particularly plans to have them settled in agricultural areas. Mordecai Manuel Noah's plan to establish a colony— Ararat, a City of Refuge—on Grand Island in the Niagara River received considerable publicity, though it never materialized. In 1855, a leaflet was issued, *A Call to Establish a Hebrew Agricultural Society*, in order to promote Jewish interest in agriculture and to provide an alternative to the commercial sector that Jews usually worked in. Renewed interest in agricultural colonies was stirred in 1857 when Isaac Lesser, editor of the *Occident*, wrote; "If we could organize farms and colonies away from the dense masses of large towns, we should have the satisfaction of seeing the industrious engaged in drawing their sustenance from the mother of all-the-living—our native earth."[30]

Most of these pleas and efforts fell on deaf ears as American Jews defended their involvement in commercial affairs and they were fearful that any collective settling would create greater prejudice than already existed. In addition, there were practical problems about financial support, organization, and the ability of former settled dwellers to adjust to frontier life. While American Jews debated the question, European Jews worked through the Alliance Israélite Universelle to set up relief agencies for the refugees fleeing the pogroms in Russia and promoted emigration. Two organizations came into existence at this point, both based on "emigration and the establishment of colonies among the Jews of Eastern Europe." One was the Bilu movement, which settled kibbutzim and moshavat settlements in Palestine. The Am Olam movement hoped to do for America what the Bilu set out to do in Palestine. One succeeded, the other failed—both tried.[31] The Am Olam attracted young intellectuals, university and gymnasium students. They believed that farming was the "noblest occupation for man."[32]

In November 1881, twelve hundred immigrants left for the United States, and American Jewish leaders responded to their needs. They were heartened to hear from Moses Herder and Marya Bahal, Am Olam leaders, that their membership was not encouraged to look toward charities for help but would work cooperatively. A Russian Relief Committee was established, and the Hebrew Emigrant Aid Society began to grapple with such practical problems as how much capital was needed, who would make successful farmers, and which locations in the Northwest were the best. Dr. Julius Goldman went West to examine sites and try to find some answers to these questions. He came to the conclusion that "no colony should be organized on a communistic and cooperative plan, and that the refugees should be disposed of not collectively, but individually."[33] That was easier said than done, for several reasons. There was support within the Jewish community for agricultural colonies, and the American Israelite, a prominent paper, supported that strategy.

By mid-1882, an international strategy had been agreed on to facilitate the emigration. The Alliance Israélite Universelle in Paris agreed to direct the emigration, the Mansion House Committee in London agreed to select and then get emigrants to America, and the Hebrew Emigrant Aid Society would aid them on arrival. Enormous problems arose because of the numbers who needed help, the lack of funds, and difficulties in America about coordinating regional groups. In the 1880s, the Am Olam movement encouraged the founding of twenty-six agricultural colonies in eight states, mostly in the West. There were seven alone in Kansas.[34] The great majority were not communistic or collective but settled like the "commercial" colonies of the 1870s in Colorado. Goldman's advice had been followed.[35]

The first colony settled, the Sicily Island Colony in Louisiana, established a pattern that many others would follow. It consisted of twenty-five families from Kiev and twenty-five from Yelisaretgrad who were recruited from three classes of emigrants—young idealists who wanted to show that Jews could be good farmers, immigrants from southern and southwestern Russia who looked upon agriculture as a means of earning a livelihood . . . the rest of the immigrants

had no definite aim and were largely influenced by the former two."
Louisiana was chosen as a site, and the settlement was financed by
funds from the colonists themselves ($3,000), from the New York
Committee ($1,800), and the Alliance Israélite Universelle ($2,800).
The New Orleans Jewish community was eager to help, approved of
the colony settlement plan, and offered—in the name of the governor—160 acres of land to each family. The land offered by the Governor turned out to be infertile, and another site on Sicily Island was
accepted. The men then left their wives in New Orleans to work the
land and plant the colony. With the onset of summer (1882), their
enthusiasm waned as they missed their families, came down with
malaria, and found that the Mississippi River could be dangerous.
That summer, the river rose and swept away much of what they had
worked on since March. But they were still hopeful: "We left for the
colony with high hopes, but after having spent a few months there,
we found conditions unbearable. The heat affected most of the colonists, and malaria had strickened the women and children. We are,
however, still hopeful and full of expectations for a glorious future."[36] The colonists regrouped and moved on to South Dakota,
where they founded another colony.

The Sicily Island Colony was utopian only in the sense that the
colonists shared a journey from Russia to New York and then from
New York to Louisiana, where their experiences forced them to journey even farther westward. They were not committed to communism
or collectivity and were forced only by necessity to share with one
another. However, the second group to form a colony—the Bethlehem Yehudah—left New York with the idea of founding an agricultural colony based on cooperative principles. In their constitution,
they outlined their intent to act as a model for future groups, to help
liberate Jews from "economic and spiritual" bondage, and to prove
"that Jews, like other groups, are capable of becoming agricultural-
ists." Members were forbidden to pursue commercial activities and
had to pledge themselves to aid in the founding of other colonies. If
such groups were organized, they then had to be governed by the
same principles. A total of thirty-two young men constituted the
group, which settled on 165 acres near Crimeux, South Dakota, in
1882. Known as the Sons of Freedom, they refused outside help from
American Jewish philanthropies and tried to maintain their Russian
way of life by gathering in the evenings for entertainment and discussions. They even published a Russian-language paper. But the
crops that they planted failed to yield, and they would not rely on

outside resources. Many grew discouraged and left for New York City. The colony was liquidated in 1885.[37]

Those colonies that exhibited some degree of collectivity in addition to Bethlehem Yehuda were Painted Woods, near Bismarck, North Dakota, and New Odessa at Cow Creek, Oregon. Many of the members of Am Olam had secured work in New York City on their arrival, and between fifty and sixty of them maintained a communal household on Pell Street that was known as the Commune.[38] Household tasks were divided and earnings pooled. They maintained their zeal for collective agriculture and kept in contact with Michael Heilprin, who had organized the Montefiore Agricultural Aid Society to help settle refugees and who worked with the Alliance Israélite Universelle to place groups in southern New Jersey. Scouting parties had been sent out to look for land for the Commune group in the Midwest, Texas, Washington State, and Oregon. A member of the team looking at Oregon was none other than Vladimir Konstantinovich Geins, renamed William Frey.

The team found land in Douglass County and purchased 750 acres, 150 of which were available for immediate settlement. Heilprin had raised $2,000 from a few New York Jews, and, by July 1882, a group of twenty-five was ready to leave. The group had come to know Frey (a non-Jew and still an ardent Positivist) and asked him to lead the group. His austere and demanding manner had not changed since Kansas, and he warned the colonists that he was liable to be a "living reproach to their consciences." Presumably, the Am Olam people wanted an experienced guide, although the young people (who called themselves Friends of New Odessa) had gained some farming skills by working on farms near Hartford, Connecticut. They had done this in order to familiarize themselves with the latest farming techniques in America. On arrival in Oregon, they constructed a large building and began to follow a rigid work schedule, probably set up by Frey. He tried to indoctrinate the settlers with Comtean ideals at every turn, and held classes on philosophy for them. Mutual criticism was introduced and a session held every Sunday evening. A Festival of Humanity was celebrated on 1 January 1884, and Frey must have thought that he had found his communal home at last. The constitution that he had drawn up for New Odessa stressed the principles of altruism, self-perfection, common property, and moral cooperation.[39]

As time passed, Frey's proselytizing became a problem for an increasing number of the settlers. One visitor to the colony wrote,

"Frey's idea of happiness is to eat two meals a day of crackers and raw fruit, to touch no kind of stimulant, to do all work between meals, so as to be free often to study moral and social exhortations, in which all should join."[40] Family life was respected within the commune, yet cramped quarters made it difficult for couples to have any privacy. One group complained that there were members who confused communism with eating off the same plate and sleeping in the same room. The high point of colony life came in 1884, when there were forty members and the group's economic future seemed solid. That year they had been able to secure a labor contract from a railroad and were thereby sure of some income beyond their farming.

After 1884, dissatisfaction set in because members resented Frey's leadership, their constant hard labor, the lack of privacy, and any social amenities. Frey left the colony in that year. By 1887, it had disintegrated (hastened by a fire that had destroyed many buildings), with many of the original group returning to New York City, where they opened a cooperative laundry that lasted for a year or two. For Frey, it was his last communal crusade. He left Odessa and migrated to England, where he spent the balance of his life as a publicist for Positivism and the Ethical Culture Society. Supposedly, four Russian Jews had been converted to Positivism and followed him to London.[41] There they were reported to have lived with him in a cooperative household. In 1886, he returned to Russia, corresponded with Tolstoy, and probably served as the prototype of the character Simonson in *The Resurrection*.[42]

Frey's trip was like his earlier ventures into communal life— full of high purpose and hopes. He hoped to spread the gospel of Positivism to Russia, and, when he arrived, among the first books that fell into his hands were Tolstoy's *Confession* and *What I Believe*, then being circulated in manuscript. Frey drafted a sixty-page response to what he had read and sent it off to Tolstoy. He was invited to Yasnay Polyana, where he stayed for five days as Tolstoy's guest. Frey made a positive impression on Tolstoy, who later wrote, "I am greatly indebted to him and I always remember this saintly man with emotion." Subsequently Frey visited Tolstoy at Moscow, where he heard sections of *What Then Must We Do?* Although there were fundamental differences between Frey's Positivism and Tolstoy's primitive Christianity, the two men genuinely liked one another. Frey returned to London in April 1886. He died there in November 1888, and in a memorial statement Tolstoy described him as "a person, who, for his moral qualities, was one of the most remarkable men of our own, and not only our own, age."[43]

Frey's career, like Longley's, was a remarkable one, full of surprises, wandering, childlike faith, self-deception, and enormous variety. His life was an archetypal utopian one: eccentric, dedicated to ideas, and always looking for the ideal state. That dedication was admirable, and many people saw that quality in him. The Russian Am Olam group recognized it while they were in New York, and Tolstoy saw it at Yasnay Polyana. American offered Frey a perfect arena to test and retest his ideas. Police spies never shadowed him, no one denied him the right to print his manifestos or proselytize for his varied communal religions. Tolstoy said of him, "What is particularly interesting about him is that he is redolent of American life, of that fresh, powerful, immense world."[44]

That freshness that Tolstoy saw in Frey's life and its representation of the opportunities of American life was what the English reformer Thomas Hughes saw in the New World. Hughes was best known for his *Tom Brown's Schooldays,* and he had learned his active championing of the principles of Thomas Arnold's athletic and moral philosophy while a student at Rugby. His career in the service of cooperation began when he participated in the First International Cooperation Congress in 1869. Before that, he had helped organize the Workingmen's College in London in 1854 (later becoming its principal) and was elected to the House of Commons in 1865, supporting liberal causes while he sat. Hughes had long considered establishing a colony for the young gentry of England in either Canada or New Zealand, and a trip to the United States in 1870 convinced him that America would be the best place for "the swarming manhood of the English gentry and the middle class." He had been the London correspondent for the *New York Tribune* in 1866 and had long been in close contact with American literary and reform currents, but the driving influence on his career had been Arnold and Rugby: "You may well believe what a power Rugby has been in my life. . . . I passed all those years under the spell of this place and Arnold, who for half a century have never ceased to thank God for it."[45] Arnold's educational concerns were threefold: religion and morality, intellect pursuits, and proper gentlemanly conduct. These three concerns, plus cooperation, provided Hughes with the basis for his philosophy and the formation of the Rugby Colony.[46]

The education and training of young men concerned Hughes deeply. He believed that many of the English gentry were held in bondage by a system of primogeniture that denied them land (the land being left to the oldest son) and that left only three professions open to the younger sons of a landed family: medicine, law, and the church. If none of these three interested a young man, then he had no respectable outlet for his abilities. Manual labor and agriculture were not socially acceptable options, and Hughes hoped to provide one in a cooperative setting. In an address before the London Cooperative Congress in July 1869, he said: "Too much attention had been given to the production of wealth without sufficient cultivation of friendly and helpful relations among the workmen."[47] Although Rugby was to be directed at the middle and upper classes, Hughes saw cooperation as a vehicle for social reform for the whole society.

He came to the United States in 1870 to meet James Russell Lowell, whose *Bigelow Papers* he had edited. During his stay, he was welcomed by both senators from Massachusetts, the secretaries of state and the treasury, and such literary figures as Emerson, Longfellow, and Howells. While on this first visit, he met several prominent businessmen and tried to interest them in his colony ideas. It was not until 1878 that he purchased land for a colonization project. In that year, Franklin W. Smith, a Boston capitalist and author of *The Hard Times*, traveled throughout the East looking for a colony site for his employees hurt by the depression of 1877.[48] He secured options on 350,000 acres and settled six families on a site in northern Tennessee. Interest in the project waned, and Smith—knowing of Hughes's interest—contacted him about purchasing the land. Hughes then contacted Henry Kember, a British railway magnate, and John Boyle, a London barrister, about arranging funds and asked their advice about how to proceed. By 1880, the Board of Aid to Land Ownership, with Thomas Hughes as president, had control of seventy-five thousand acres of Smith's land: "The object of this organization is to promote associate migration to fertile, unoccupied lands; to aid their development into agricultural townships and homesteads; by means of contributing to a redistribution of labor— its diversion from trade and manufacture, where a surplus to tillage of the earth—the basis of all industries, and the primary source of all wealth."[49]

Because Hughes was such a prominent figure, the venture gained considerable attention, and Hughes published his social views in *Rugby, Tennessee* in 1881, directing his message at "young men of good education and small capitol, the class which of all others, is the most overcrowded today in England." At Rugby, young Englishmen could find their manhood and proper inheritance in good honest labor, working at some handicraft ("a country cannot be in a thoroughly healthy state in which handicrafts are looked down upon"). England was simply not the place for such an experiment: "You must begin, then, across the sea somewhere—the sooner the better. What you have to do is discover some place on the broad face of this earth where you may set to work on the best conditions; where the old blunders have the smallest chance of repeating themselves. . . . You want to get your chance, in short, in a place where we have been calling the English public school spirit—the spirit of hardiness, of reticence, of scrupulousness in all matters, or cordial fellowship . . . so that in your new house you may feel you are able to live up to your ideal."[50]

This "new home" was dedicated on 5 October 1880, with Hughes in attendance. Prior to his arrival, a hotel (called the Tabard Inn from the *Canterbury Tales*), a church (the bishop of Tennessee had written to Hughes saying, "Let me beg you to have the church organized at Rugby from the first"), and tennis courts ready to play on were under construction.[51] In his speech that day Hughes, stressed the moral nature of the community, its elevating character, and his high hope that the colonists would be ladies and gentlemen of "such strain and culture that they will be able to meet princes in the gate, without embarrassment and without self-assertion."[52]

It was a benevolent community founded by Victorian gentlemen in the hope of making men and women out of an effete class. Cooperation was begun on a modest scale—within the operation of the commissary—and Hughes hoped to see it extended to every phase of production, including herds and farming. The first settlers appeared to have been young gentlemen and ladies from England intent on roughing it in the American wilderness. A rather substantial library had been established, in part by Hughes's American publisher Estes and Lauriat, and a healthy social life centered on a literary and dramatic society, an agricultural and horticultural group, and the tennis team. By 1884, there were four hundred residents (only about 40 percent were English, the rest American), and English visitors to the United States made it a point to stay at the elegant Tabard Inn. Immigrants to the colony were told that they would find a welcome in New York at the home of Theodore Roosevelt.

Hughes's grandmother joined the colony in May 1881, and stories about this English fairyland appeared in both British and American newspapers. A typhoid epidemic struck the colony during the summer of 1881, however, crippling it. News began to spread that Rugby was an unhealthy place even though the colonists were able to pinpoint the source of the typhoid (the water at the Tabard Inn) and make improvements. A new well was drilled, the inn completely disinfected and then refurbished, and a typhoid-free manager brought in fresh from the Palmer House in Chicago.

Information about what the colonists did is surprisingly scant. All the reports emphasize the social rounds, the esprit de corps among the young Englishmen and women, but little emerges about the work they engaged in. The colony's greatest asset was its vast timber holdings, and it was from that source that the colony buildings were built. Presumably, the colonists ran a lumbering business. A fire destroyed the renovated Tabard Inn in 1884, and it took three years to rebuild it. During that period, the inn lost its clientele and reputation as a health resort. Hughes lost over $250,000 on the venture—and also his mother, who died there in 1887. He made his last visit to the colony after her death, and, on his return to England, he was forced to give up his home to pay debts incurred by the Rugby project.

It was a grand experiment that was well financed, well publicized, and, like most utopian ventures, well intentioned. It led to the construction of some impressive buildings and focused attention on the condition of the young gentry. What resulted was simply a parody of Victorian life on the American frontier, a sort of stage set for young people to play out a portion of their youth. Some of its residents went on to distinguish themselves in English life, yet the experiment has to be considered a failure. Hughes was, of course, the inspiration behind the scheme and its guiding force; however, he was rarely in residence. The colonists appear to have struggled little against the environment and hence to have continued to live as members of a favored class. Beyond that, the colony suffered from simple bad luck from the start.

Prior to the publication of *Looking Backward*, there were few dramatic turning points in the history of post-Civil War utopian thought. There were numerous efforts at collective living, but they seemed hidden away from the dominant events of the period. Of course, the Panic of 1873 made workingmen increasingly conscious of their precarious position and their need to think about alternative strategies for economic survival. A few colonies, like Oneida, had links to national influence and power, yet their peculiar social arrangements forced them to play down their connection with cousin Rutherford B. Hayes. John H. Noyes wrote to the *New York Tribune* in 1877 that they had not, as rumored, been the first to suggest him for the presidency, and, in fact, the elder Noyes noted that he "did not take part in the late election, either by pen or vote."[53]

It was usually by pen that utopian thinkers presented their schemes, though they were not shy about using the ballot box to defend vital interests once they established themselves. In some cases, these utopians were primarily engaged in self-promotion, and it was difficult to distinguish the prophet from the publicist, the charismatic leader from the crazed egomaniac. Albert Kimsey Owen, for example, was certainly not crazed but did have a career as a railroad entrepreneur and utopian colonizer. Both strands of his career were never far apart as he blended acquisitive and idealistic impulses. Those impulses came together most dramatically in his planned colony Pacific City at Topolobampo Bay on the west coast of Mexico. It was, like *Looking Backward*, dramatic and meaningful for the age. The colony's formal history extends from 1886 to 1894, but one has to turn to the 1860s to understand it fully.

Owen was born into a substantial Quaker family. Both parents were respected members of their Chester, Pennsylvania, community. Young Owen attended Jefferson College to study civil engineering and after graduation in 1867 worked briefly as Chester's city manager before beginning a career as a railroad engineer and promoter. In 1871, he went to Colorado to work for General William J. Palmer, another Quaker, who was then developing the Clear Creek Railroad and the growing town of Colorado Springs.

Palmer had completed the Denver and Rio Grande Railroad in 1869, and his work served as a model for Owen's future activities. Palmer was both an aggressive entrepreneur and an engineer. More important, however, were Palmer's definite ideas about how new towns should be developed and how their moral and cooperative features could be highlighted. He wanted to extend the Denver and Rio Grande Railroad into Mexico and, in 1872, sent Owen to Mexico City to survey land for the potential line. Owen's work took him to the west coast of Mexico, where he and another engineer explored the partially hidden Topolobampo Bay. That side trip was the highlight of Owen's eleven-month stay, and it transformed his life. While in Mexico, he also met individuals who would later be influential in helping him gain entry into powerful circles in Mexico, among them the future president Manuel Gonzalez.

The harbor at Topolobampo had always excited visitors. The American consul at La Paz had written in 1869 that it was "easy of access, a safe and secure harbor, and can be entered by vessels drawing twenty feet of water, and in my opinion, its location, good harbor and other advantages indicate the right place for the most important city on the west coast of Mexico." In addition to meeting political figures, Owen learned that, although it would be difficult, it would not be impossible to build a railroad route through the mountains. Later, he would write, "Topolobampo is the best, the most picturesque and most desirable harbor on the Pacific and Gulf Coast of northwestern Mexico. . . . I will get a railroad at Topolobampo within less than one year. . . . It will control the winter traffic, passenger and freight between the United States and China."[54]

The dream that had lured Columbus to the New World, the passage to the Orient, was rekindled in Owen's eyes; he spent the next three decades laying out a plan for both speculators and utopian settlers. Owen began promoting his ideas at the Governors Conference of the Southern States in May 1873, at which he urged consideration of the "Great Southern Railroad" to run from Norfolk, Virginia, to Topolobampo, providing a short route to the Pacific Coast. He then organized a Southern Settlement Society with the idea of placing towns along the route under the motto "Cooperation and Subsidized Colonization." In his search for financing the road, he interested Duff Green and Jesse Grant, the president's son, in a scheme that called for the issuance of special purpose greenbacks guaranteed by both the United States and the Mexican governments. Owen had organized the first Greenback Club in Pennsylvania, and throughout his career he promoted greenback financing schemes for his various projects. Between 1872 and 1876, he tried unsuccessfully to get federal support for both the survey and the greenback financing plan; however, the Redemption Act of 1876 put an end to the greenback scheme. Individual investors showed little interest, and Owen was forced to turn his attention toward the only other possible source of funding—Mexico.

Interest in the plan quickened after 1879 when Owen met with Mexican president Porfirio Diaz, who expressed interest in the planned railroad. Diaz had an even greater interest in another project—the draining of the Valley of Mexico, and Owen put together the Mexican Drainage Commission to serve those plans. That scheme never got beyond the drawing board since Diaz's financial advisers objected to the greenback method of financing. Another turn in the Mexican negotiations resulted in a concession to construct the Texas, Topolobampo, and Pacific Railroad from the Texas border with track line north to Piedra Negras and south to Mazatlan. Manuel Gonzalez had taken office in December 1881, and former president Ulysses S. Grant had now taken an active interest in the railroad.

Concessions were one thing and financing another since land and the rights-of-way had to be secured. Beginning in January 1881, Owen forged alliances, had numerous surveys made, and tried to proceed with the road, yet it went slowly. Held back by title disputes over the land and a lack of funds, he persisted with his vision while still facing the harsh engineering realities of constructing a road twelve hundred miles through the Sierra Madre mountains. As Ray Reynolds put it, "Eight times since 1872 Albert Owen had tried to climb the Sierra Madre with a railroad. Even while the eighth attempt was failing, he prepared for the ninth. Utopia was his last resort."[55]

In 1883, Mexican president Gonzalez offered free land to companies that would survey and colonize underdeveloped land. As an added incentive, he gave mineral rights for the first time in Mexican history. Owen's response to this action was to propose a planned city, Pacific City, based on the principles of "integral cooperation" and outlined in an 1885 volume by that name. In 1885, Owens put together the Credit Foncier Company for the purpose of establishing colonies all along the route, but particularly at the line's terminal point, Topolobampo Bay. The company—in contrast to the discredited Credit Mobilier project that had issued watered stock to its shareholders—was based on the "home" (foncier) credit system wherein subscribers had a permanent place in the future development site. One was not joining just another railway colony similar to the Colorado and Kansas towns of an earlier decade but participating in "the Messiah which comes to lift us out of our present chaos of irresponsibility, misery and crime to a foundation of responsibility and into a community where the home becomes the palladium of our existence."[56]

The individual home—built by the company and leased to the colonists—was to be the cornerstone of the Pacific City settlement. Owen had written earlier that "no life is worth living which is not home life," and he was going to complement that home life with a community life that had certain distinguishing features: a credit exchange economy based on labor and production units; community parks, newspapers, a library, and restaurants; a residential hotel based on Godin's Familisterie at Guise, France; a ban on lawyers, advertising, prostitution, taverns, and taxes; and cooperative enterprise as an aid to individual initiative.[57]

In addition to his utopian interests and entrepreneurial abilities, Owen was also a publicist and promoter. His hope in publishing *Integral Cooperation* was to attract investors, and he tended to paint the potential city in fanciful terms. That he oversold the site and its potential as a commercial center is without doubt, and it is best to read sections of *Integral Cooperation* as a utopian romance. The colony motto was "Duty, Interdependence and Equity." Several conditions were necessary for success in "association," and Owen assured his audience that they would be in place at Topolobampo. The first was land "within the reach of people as proprietors," the second diversified industries that "render exchanges easy and rapid," and the third a full volume of money (greenbacks) "happily termed the instrument of association." The colonists would be partners in a business that made it possible to exchange goods and services. Such a partnership would be based on new principles of cooperation rather than on exploitation and commercial aggrandizement. Community life would be based on "home life kept inviolate and public properties controlled in the interests of the citizens."[58]

His plan was drawn from such diverse sources as San Marino, Italy; Salt Lake City, Utah; Zoar, Ohio; St. Pierre, the Isle of Guernsey; and Pullman, Illinois. According to Owen, cities had never been fit places to live because they were started by chance and left to "speculators to extend and irresponsible politicians to manage." Contrary to such a hodgepodge and corrupt pattern, Pacific City had developed a comprehensive plan that integrated capital, labor, and innovative design: "Permanent and diversified occupations, wide streets, bicycles used, single homes, artesian water, river or bay for public use, sewerage recycled, wiring, pipes underground."[59] Integrated into that design was a social philosophy that stressed individual responsibility toward the community, public trust in the management, and equality between the sexes. Ideally, one would become a colonist from an inward conviction that, although society had failed to create better men and women, Topolobampo could change that condition because its environmental presumptions would be different and it was nurtured by the ethos of cooperative labor.

Among Owen's supporters was Marie Howland, whose reform career spanned a forty-year period. According to her second husband, Edward Howland, the early death of her father forced her to care for her younger sister and dictated that she work at a cotton mill in Lowell. In the early 1850s, she moved to New York City, where she taught school, completed her education at New York Normal College, and married a radical lawyer, Lyman Case. During the late 1850s, she lived at Stephen Pearl Andrews's cooperative boarding house, Unitary House, and counted among her friends Jane Mc-Elheny (the actress Ada Claire) and the publicist Edward Howland, who became her second husband in 1864. The Howlands lived in Europe during the Civil War and at Godin's Familisterie during 1864. In 1866, they returned to the United States, with Edward Howland working as a free-lance journalist and Marie as a secretary, using the phonography method that she had learned while at the Lowell mills.[60] During 1868, the coupled moved to Hammonton, New Jersey, and had among their visitors Albert Brisbane. In 1874, Marie Howland published *Papa's Own Girl*, a utopian romance that may have served as the prototype for Edward Bellamy's *Looking Backward*.[61]

The source for Howland's novel was the life and work of Jean Baptiste Godin, a French industrialist who manufactured stoves and other heating devices. During the 1840s, Godin read St. Simon, Cabet, and Owen, only to find that Fourier captured his imagination. In 1848, he underwrote a third of the cost of the Icarian expedition to Texas, and, in 1856, he began thinking about constructing a central house for his workers, a structure call the Familisterie, which was completed in 1859. Marie Howland based the novel on her impressions derived from her 1864 stay and Godin's own *Social Solutions*, which she translated for an American publisher in 1873.[62] Godin had been elected to the National Assembly in 1871, only to leave it and devote his life to his iron works and cooperative activities. Within the Familisterie, there were five elements, each complementing one with another, forming an integral community promoting collective well-being while safeguarding individuality and privacy. The five elements were a collection of united buildings called the Social Palace; a group of cooperative shops that sold bread, fuel, and food; an educational service that provided nursery care and elementary education up to age fourteen; a system of profit sharing for the workers based on the guild system; and a system of mutual insurance for the workers through old age.

At the height of its activity there were some fifteen to seventeen hundred employees, 350 of whom lived in apartments in the Social Palace. A good view of the community was given by Edward Owen Greening, the English cooperator, who visited Guise in the 1880s and wrote about it for the *Cooperative News*: "The French Society we have come to visit not only includes a cooperative store, with departments for grocery, bakery, confectionery, drapery, boots and shoes, butcher and every other article of prime necessity, but it furnishes its members with employment in a gigantic iron works, houses them in palatial buildings, nurses their babies so far as the mother desires its help in that most important department, educates their children, provides library, news-room, billiard room, refreshment saloon, theatre, music master, doctor and dispensary; assists them by machinery to wash and dry their clothes; insures them against the needs of old age, the accidents and ailments of life, and the loss by death of the wage earner; furnishes them with a newspaper devoted to their principles, including a glorious cooperative garden filled with fruits and flowers." [63]

Greening was impressed with every aspect of the Familisterie—particularly, however, the nursery and educational system run on the Froebel method. The Howlands' stay at Guise must have had a profound effect on them since many of the elements of Owen's Pacific City scheme were clearly taken from Guise. In 1874, Owen visited the Howlands at Hammonton, and after that visit their home became the center of publicity for his railroad and colony ventures. The Howlands edited a variety of publications for Owen, most notably the *Credit Foncier of Sinaloa*, which ran from June to October 1885, promoting the colony idea. Articles by Felix Adler ("On Cooperation"), about the Separatists of Zoar, and about anarchists and socialists were mixed in with lavish descriptions of the proposed colony. For Owen, the initial response to his plan was gratifying. Socialists like Peter Good, who had organized a colony in Seattle in 1885 based on the ideas of Godin and Fourier, wrote that Gronlund's *Cooperative Commonwealth* and "your book are the great texts on this great subject." Another colony enthusiast, Isaac Rumford, who had started a vegetarian colony, Joyful, at Bakersfield in 1886, wrote, "I am now fifty-two and was an old man nearly used up when forty-eight, but learning the Edenic Diet [raw food] I am now a new man and a better one than the old chap was at twenty-five. . . . I like your colonization work better every day." [64]

Letters came in from Greeley, from the leaders at the Puget Sound Colony, from parties eager to participate in utopia. By May 1886, there were 2,546 stockholders. Marie Howland emphasized the women's question in her columns and received encouraging words from dissatisfied women in faraway Laramie, Wyoming. A former member of the North American Phalanx wrote that everyone supported women's suffrage in Laramie and she was praying for the success of the colony. Another "Veteran Associationist" wrote about his interest and *very* long career with the utopian movement: "Competition has been repugnant to me from early manhood; cooperation attractive. Forty years ago I started to join the Sylvania Association, in Pike County, Pennsylvania, met Greeley in New York, who assured me that no more members could be taken. Next I went to LeRaysville [sic] in northern Pennsylvania, hoping to join the Swedenborgian colony started there by Drs. Belling and Solyman Brown, but found the enterprise in the throes of dissolution. I then went to Northampton, Mass. to visit a movement set up by G. W. Benson. Fell in with A. L. Smith of Rhode Island, at Springfield who had the same object in view. We found noble men and women there, but no room for more members. We mutually concluded to wait for the North American Phalanx in which friend Smith took stock and went with the pioneers. Sometime after I joined him there, but found him dissatisfied, through the influence of another. I then broke for Brook Farm, friend Smith leaving the colony for the purpose of keeping the Graham House, in New Hampshire. I was admitted as a member of the Brook Farm Phalanx, which has been aptly called a 'Child of Heaven.' But the destruction by fire of a well-nigh completed edifice dissolved the noble band."

One would have thought that such an adventuring lust for the communal life would exhaust the seeker, but Stephen Young continued his journey. "Next I used every endeavor to engage in the French attempt to establish a Fourierist association in northern Texas. Since then I have attempted to assist in several movements to be partially cooperative, as the Kansas Vegetarian Colony, Dr. Thrall's 'Hygenia' near Chillicothe, Ohio etc. Am I not discouraged. Not at all. I am sure that it was down on the Eternal program that a social order in which truth, equity and liberty shall be universal, is to be established. And I have implicit faith in Albert K. Owen as the man to establish it. And my foremost desire now is to witness, and if possible assist in, the laying of its foundations on the shore of Topolobampo."[65]

Stephen Young joined Topolobampo from Memphis, Missouri, and died while in the colony. Obviously, he was a dedicated utopian whose sense of the possible sustained him through several failed and missed opportunities. Most of the members who came to the colony were first-time communists battered by bad times or buoyed by the promise of an ideal life on the sunny west coast of Mexico. Of the 1,423 adults in the colony by August 1886, the greatest number were "housewives" (250), followed by farmers (196), carpenters (95), laborers (41), clerks (35), teachers (29), stock raisers (29), and printers (31). There was one brewer, one author, one elocutionist, but not a single clergyman. The occupations seemed diversified, and the colonists had the necessary skills to establish a colony in the isolated section of Mexico that their dream had taken them to.[66]

In September 1886, the board of directors of the Credit Foncier Company met and named Owen president. Out of the ten directors, the name of John W. Lovell stands out. He had printed Owen's *Integral Cooperation* as no. 665 in "Lovell's Library," was an innovator in the publishing business, and an ardent experimenter with reform schemes. In 1885, he embraced Owen's Pacific City plan and eventually spent a considerable portion of his fortune to support it and the railroad. Other members made a considerable commitment to the colony, stockholders subscribing for $102,000 in securities and pledging over a half million in cash or real estate for loan purposes. In July 1886, Porfirio Diaz granted a concession to build the Texas, Topolobampo, Pacific Railroad with the understanding that five hundred families would be settled on the land within two years and that a railroad would be built using greenbacks as the medium of exchange. The railroad also agreed to transport the colonists to the site free of charge, to give them free education, and to sell each family one hundred acres of land. Diaz wanted a railroad built; Owen wanted to create a planned community. Although these interests seemed to complement one another, they would prove, in the long run, to pull the colony in two directions.

Integral Cooperation and the Howlands' promotional work in the *Credit Foncier of Sinaloa* interested and excited potential colonists so much that, while Owen was in the final stages of negotiations with the Mexican government over the concession, a group of two hundred colonists journeyed from Denver to Mexico. On arrival, they found hard tropical conditions, a harbor difficult to navigate because of a shifting sandbar, smallpox, and an inadequate water supply. The workers were organized into labor groups, told to elect their own foremen, and paid at the same rate regardless of task. They were also encouraged to rotate their jobs. These egalitarian and Fourierist notions were not, however, what the paternalistic Owen had in mind. According to Ray Reynolds, the "theory, roundly democratic, ill-fated Integral Cooperation's fatherly approach to workers." The Denver contingent had organized themselves into groups, and, despite the abysmal physical conditions and the fact that they were considered the "dregs" by some, the *New York Sun* reported glowingly about the experiment. In 1893, Julius Wayland, the editor of the *Appeal to Reason* and founder of Ruskin, wrote that the "literature of your colony has done wonderful work. I meet it from every section."[67]

During 1886, other colonists continued to migrate south even though conditions at the bay remained hard and living arrangements primitive. A group of thirty New Englanders had sold all their possessions and were making their way to a warmer land while newspapers began to run articles with headlines that screamed "A Wicked Scheme; Taking Men Out to Sinaloa and Leaving Them to Starve" and "Horrors of Topolobampo: Small Pox, Poisonous Reptiles and Intensive Heat the Year Round." Between November 1886 and March 1887, 293 adults and 117 children had come. Out of that group, 114 were married, 165 single men, and 13 unmarried women. Seven died, and eighty four left. A rough community was in the making at four settlements on the bay. Homes were built, a headquarters had been erected, and a wagon road fifteen feet wide and thirty-five miles long had been hacked out of the jungle. Alvin Wilber, who had been at the Union Colony in Greeley, later wrote that it was all familiar to him: "Many things that happened here made me think of 1870 in Greeley. The hard fare, the hard work, the lack of tools and suitable materials, even the grumbler and the sorehead, the shirk and the man who wants to steal the colony is also here."[68]

Those who left were seen as weak and irresolute, while the ones who toughed out the first years looked back on them as a time of testing and a display of courage. Some who left commented on how impractical it had been from the start since the colonists had come from every section of the country, from an enormous range of backgrounds, and had "gathered together to put into practical operation principles of which (however beautiful they may write to you) they have only a crude understanding." Anna Norris, a Unitarian minister, later wrote to Marie Howland, reminding her that "often in such experiments there come moments when longer persistence indicates not so much loyalty to principle as blind enthusiasm and folly."[69]

Throughout 1887, conditions deteriorated as factions developed, lawsuits were threatened, and disputes between colonists wound up in the Mexican courts. Despite the problems, Christian B. Hoffman, a Kansas radical and millionaire, breathed new life and funds into the dying project.[70] Hoffman, even though he was a banker and successful mill owner in central Kansas, had joined the National Anti-Monopoly League in 1881, edited the *Anti-Monopolist*, and supported several cooperative projects prior to this. Topolobampo caught his attention in 1886, and Hoffman was deeply involved in its affairs for the next seven years. He organized the Kansas-Sinaloa Company to purchase land for the Credit Foncier colonization project and led a contingent of settlers from Kansas to Pacific City in 1891. During his brief stays at Topolobampo, he carried on an affair with Marie Howland before open conflict drove him away from the project. Later, Hoffman was to associate with Frank Parsons, Edward Bemis, and Thomas Will to radicalize the Kansas Agricultural College, of which Hoffman was a trustee. He ended his reform career as editor of the *Chicago Socialist* just a year prior to his death in 1914.

What attracted Hoffman to the scheme was Owen's idealism and his own desire to find some meaningful solution to pressing social problems. He was, he wrote, "tired, very tired, of the even recurring, never ending conflict between man and man which brutalizes and demoralizes us in savagery. I fear that capitalism and monopoly had engulfed all the treasures of Mother Earth and that mankind were orphans."[71] Unlike Edward Bellamy's *Looking Backward*, Owen's plan showed a clear path to utopia via the American and Pacific Railroad, which was scheduled to terminate at a "mystical city most true," in Owen's words.

Initially, Hoffman was going to put together a syndicate of Kansas entrepreneurs to purchase large tracts of land and support the newly formed Kansas City and Pacific City Railroad Company that was to run a line from the midwest to Mexico. One of Owen's great strengths over the years was his ability to shift the focus of his energies from one scheme to another just as it appeared that the old one was losing ground and the new one offered a better return on the dollar. He was always on the verge of both bankruptcy and enormous wealth.

In 1890, Owen traveled to London to seek additional funding for the Sinaloa project. By late 1889, it was evident that times was running out, and the London trip was designed to replenish his diminishing capital. He needed to begin the rail line, and the Mexican government was looking for some tangible proof that their concession was going to reap a reward. He even invited Edward Bellamy to invest in his Sinaloa Guarantee Trust Company, but it was a group of London investors who saved the day by agreeing to support the project if he could gain some additional concessions from Diaz. As part of the plan, Owen would become chief engineer of the railroad, and thousands of Scots would be encouraged to move to Pacific City.

In 1890, Owen published *Integral Cooperation at Work*, tracing the colony's history and restating his commitment to homes for workers. He added, however, certain features intended to interest wealthy supporters: "Persons with homes secured, beautified and endeared, are contented and hence conservative. Strikes, boycotts and antagonisms, which threaten liberty, life and property cannot occur in a community where all heads of families are the owners of their homes, free from tax, rent and mortgages." The tone of the second volume is strikingly more conservative and reflects the tensions brought about by the violent transformations that swept American labor between 1885 and 1890. The events at Pullman, the great railroad strikes, and the sudden rise in revolutionary activity made cooperators (and entrepreneurs) like Owen conscious of how cooperation might serve as a means to blunt class antagonisms: "To strike means to hit. Strikes are mobilized antagonisms against legalized and systematized combinations of business men. They are wrong in principle, because they are revolutionary in spirit because they excite the worst passions of all concerned; and, in policy, because each strike unites the incorporated classes into a closer and more powerful and more tyrannical compact, hence it makes it more difficult to start correct and well matured plans for righting the wrongs of our people."[72]

Revolution meant national chaos and the emergence of demagogic leaders who would enslave people worse than the trusts. Trusts were, in fact, steps toward "assured socialism." Cooperation was a "good" trust, and cooperators were the only ones capable of fending off the menacing and untrustworthy capitalists. Owen needed both capitalist and cooperator, and Christian Hoffman was an ideal amalgam of the two. Yet Hoffman's relationship with Marie Howland proved an embarrassment and a test for Owen's defense of the "home" as a key element in his scheme. Many of the colonists were outraged by the Howland/Hoffman romance, and charges of free love against the colony were circulated by a group of religious spiritualists. A split between Hoffman and Owen over Marie Howland did not materialize, though a great schism took place in 1892, when Owen's followers (believers in cooperation) fell into arguing with the contingent from Kansas (Hoffman's supporters) about the virtues and defects of cooperation. In May 1893, the situation came to a head, and Hoffman withdrew from Topolobampo. The specific issue that forced the crisis was reorganization. Hoffman wanted to grant the colonists considerable freedom over their affairs, and Owen opposed such a move, saying that the Credit Foncier was in "no wise a political association. Members, no matter how numerous or powerful, are powerless to alter the essential conditions of our association."[73] Throughout all this period, construction on a ditch to bring water to colony lands in Mochis Valley moved slowly, and, when, in July 1892, water moved onto the lands, it came at a time when the weather was bad and the prospects for any success even worse. Owen's supporters in the colony felt that the Hoffman faction had arrived late on the scene and was trying to run the colony that they had planted and suffered for. In a letter to Owen, they expressed their grievances: "Finally Mr. Owen, we came here for peace, reform and colonization, we have willingly endured the hardships of several years residence in the wilderness, in a struggle to settle a new country and the labor of development, but now we find a mere handful of people avowing their intentions to run the colony, offering for sale lands bought and paid for years ago."[74]

Owen left the colony in May 1893, never to return. During 1894, colonists began to leave in great numbers, and, over the next several years, Owen tried to sell his interests in the project, even approaching Thomas Lake Harris of Fountain Grove. However, the Harris colony was itself in the process of disintegration, and Owen still owed Harris $41,000 from an earlier loan.

Topolobampo's history is a tortured welter of thwarted aspirations, financial juggling and scheming, and incredible bungling. On balance, what stands out are the financial rather than the utopian aspects of the plan. The idea that Owen outlined at the 1873 Southern Governors Convention—that Topolobampo was to be an outlet to the Orient, a dream of traders for centuries—was still a potent one in 1893, though in a somewhat altered form. Writing for a special supplement to the *New City,* Owen waxed as eloquent as had Thomas Hart Benton forty years earlier. Topolobampo was to be in touch with the wealth of the Indies but was to remain untouched by the commercial aspects of that trade. His city would be self-sufficient and self-contained and reap the rewards of its location. Owen's message was both expansionist and insular, both radical and conservative. It was radical in its form, conservative in its appeal. He promised that the "New City" would put an end to municipal corruption, put an end to waste and inefficiency, and create a seaside utopia: "The best appointed, the most beautiful city."

> I love to dream of a city which will stand in the direct and best route between Europe and Asia—in the path of that commerce which has made civilization and dominion wherever it has broken bulk in the day, or has rested for a night—of that exchange and travel which has built

up Nineveh, Babylon, Thebes, Alexandria, Melbourne, New York and San Francisco.

I love to dream of a city where eclecticism will be practiced; where the best ideas, the most approved plans, will, *at once* be adopted; where the "dark tangled schemes of sad civilization" will not be preached, and where the cunning plots of deceitful "business" men will not be found to be profitable.

I love to dream of an ideal community—of an ideal folk who will be forever struggling for the ideal life, the ideal religion, the ideal home; the ideal sentiment; the ideal in industries and the ideal in perfection.

I love to dream of a city of idealists—of men and women who are to unite to work, continually and incessantly, for the best in everything; of an organized society which is not afraid to practice it convictions and which is determined to offer no compromise for the vices of cities and for the speculations of designing men.

I love to dream of a city so well regulated, by its attractions and disciplines, orderly, correct and peaceful wellbeing, that the citizens will live devout, practical, upright, cultivated lives, in their everyday interchanges and greetings, one with the other; and will show the faith that is within them and that they believe in the doctrine of doing good, but each citizen laboring every day to serve all the others and by giving his or her first thought and best skill to make Pacific City great and remarkable, by means of home industries diversified and perfected through a ways and means of payments—by the opportunity of our service by another.[75]

While Owen was writing these lines from the Hotel Iturbide, in Mexico City, another ideal city was being thrown up on the shores of Lake Michigan—the "White City" of the Columbian Exposition. Resplendent in white, organized by a corps of experts who agreed on certain aesthetic features, this city dazzled America. Like Owen's city, it was mostly facade, and it had a certain impermanence about it. Owen's vision had faltered, and he was never able to make the dream a reality. His idealized community had—by 1893—become a means to an end, and that end was the simple continuance of his scheme. Originally connected with ideas about social progress and justice, it became a series of plots hatched in New York and London that dazzled only speculators.

Despite its setbacks and the halting efforts at construction, the

Pacific City scheme did succeed in calling attention to itself and the implied dream of a cooperative city. Accounts about the project regularly appeared in papers throughout the country. Other colonies founded in this decade had greater success, but none had as large a vision. John Lovell, in an address before the Manhattan Liberal Club in November 1886, asked the question that many utopians of the era were asking and that Owen presumed to try and answer: "A cooperative city—the dream of St. Thomas More, the hope of Socialists, the Ultima Thule of those who look forward to a higher and better civilization—is the time yet ripe for its foundation."[76]

While utopias by the sea were being established at Topolobampo and Fort Myers, the older groups like the Harmonists and the Shakers were trying to make adjustments in their declining years. They still represented, and were often cited, as justifications for the cooperative life. The most eloquent statement about them and the possibilities of community life had come from Henry Demarest Lloyd when he addressed the residents of the Ruskin Community: "Only within these communities have there been seen in the wide borders of the United States a social life where hunger and cold, prostitution, intemperance, poverty, crime, premature old age and unnecessary mortality, panic and industrial terror have been abolished. If they had done this for a year, they would have deserved to be called the only successful 'society' on this continent, and some of them are generations old. They are little oases of people in our desert of persons. All this has not been done by saints in heaven, but on earth by average men and women."[77]

As Rush Welter has pointed out, figures like Lloyd were caught between two worlds. Enterprise was the basic social philosophy of the day; there was a growing acceptance of amoral social conditions arising, in part, because so many significant social problems had not been solved. The genteel tradition still held sway, and the churches seemed powerless to act. According to Welter, it was only the Social Gospel leaders who attempted to forge an appropriate new tradition. They had their counterparts in the secular world, and those who boosted cooperation sought an alternative to the amoral enterprise system and the old morality. On the whole, however, the individuals who sought this path were not just "average," as Lloyd suggests, but unique reformers willing to try something new in an age that was crushing labor and individualism.

During the 1890s, there were repeated efforts on the part of political pragmatists to establish the legitimacy of the cooperative life. The publication of Bellamy's *Looking Backward* in 1888, the great depression of 1893, and growing labor strength suggested the need for practical solutions here and now.[78] Cyrus Willard, a founder of the Boston chapter of the Nationalist Club, a friend of William Q. Judge and Annie Besant, and a labor reporter, saw the need for socialist communities: "I still regarded Socialism the instrument for bringing about Universal Brotherhood on the material plane, I was enthusiastic and no movement is successful without enthusiasm. The idea was to colonize the state of Washington, and elect the Senators and Congressman. I believed in the feasibility of the plan because by having a place somewhere where socialists and agitators could be fed, they would not be starved into silence as so many had been."[79]

Willard's career (and later disenchantment with the communal life) is an instructive one since it mirrors the many forces that went into the creation of colonies founded in accord with political and social ideas. Born at Lynn, Massachusetts, in 1858, he attended Bigelow Grammar School in Boston and, as a labor reporter for the *Boston Globe*, gained intimate knowledge of the period's economic and political currents. In 1886, he acted as a delegate from District 30 of the Knights of Labor at Richmond,Virginia (he also represented the *Globe*), and was an outspoken advocate of both socialism and trade unionism. In his travels, he got to know a wide range of labor and socialist leaders, including Samuel Gompers and Charles Sotheran, the writer, who introduced him to William Q. Judge, the secretary of the American Section of the Theosophical Society. While secretary of the Boston Central Labor Union, Willard lobbied legislators to have Labor Day declared a public holiday, and he attended meetings of the German-speaking section of the Socialist Labor party. This labor reporter, trade unionist, socialists, and member of the Knights and of the Theosophical Society read Bellamy's *Looking Backward* and was so taken by it that he wrote to Bellamy asking "how he would like to have me form an organization that would spread the ideas he had expressed in the book."[80]

Bellamy's answer was, "Go to it." Additionally, Bellamy sent along the names of individuals who were part of a reading club, and, with other names volunteered by Henry Willard Austin, he issued an invitation for a meeting. At this first meeting (held at the Merchants Exchange Building), a retired Army officer, Captain Bowers, was made president and Willard secretary. According to Willard, he later made a motion that a Nationalist Club be formed: "Rev. Edward Everett Hale, with whom I had served on the board of the Anti-Tenement House League, arose and said in his peculiar voice that sounded as tho' his mouth was full of hot mush, that he hoped to once belong to some organization before he died, that had no constitution or by-laws to quibble over. Howells, seated on the wood box, thumped his heels on it bringing forth a hollow sound that made us all laugh. Thomas Wentworth Higginson, the celebrated anti-slavery orator, also spoke." Later, Hamlin Garland and Willard's second cousin, Frances Willard, the temperance reformer, joined, and the club started its own magazine, with Willard assuming the editorship at one point.[81]

During this period he grew disenchanted with the politics of the labor movement ("the rottenness"), though he continued on as labor editor of the *Globe* until 1895. His attention now shifted to the Boston Branch of the Theosophical Society, which he had joined in 1889. In July 1889, Madame Blavatsky had written favorably about the Nationalist Clubs in her London based magazine, *Lucifer*, and Theosophists flocked to the clubs. Willard's own interest in Nationalism had preceded the Blavatsky imprimatur, and his interest in socialism remained steady during the 1890s. In 1897, he became involved with the Social Democracy party and served as secretary to the colonization committee that sought land for a settlement in the West. After playing a major role in the 1898 convention in Chicago at which the socialists split over the colonization question, he joined the Burley Colony and stayed for two years. By 1900, however, he had become disenchanted with communalism and dedicated the balance of his life to the cause of Theosophy.[82]

Willard's career moved from east to west, from hope to disillusionment, from material solutions to spiritual ones, from cooperative utopianism to individualism. From 1886 onward, he worked on behalf of labor, participated in movements that seemed to contradict one another, and yet always saw the possibility that people could come together for some common good. His criticism of the German-speaking section of the Socialist Labor party was rooted in his belief that they had to become more American in their orientation and that they could not cut themselves off from mainstream discussions. His own participation in a communal settlement was a natural outgrowth of his belief that socialism—practical American cooperation—could be realized within the framework of American life. It affirmed those values rather than denying them, as he believed the Germans did with their separate language sections. Socialists like Willard tried throughout the 1880s and 1890s to discover practical solutions to pressing problems.

Writing in 1896, Norman W. Lermond summed up the pragmatic/political position in "How to Build Here and Now A Cooperative Commonwealth." He argued that, with unemployment at over 3.5 million and with businesses failing at the rate of over three hundred a week, how long would it take to wipe out the middle class and reduce "the people to the condition of paupers and slaves. A remedy might be found and applied, or our last hopes of remaining a free and independent people are gone." The ballot box had failed them (this written after McKinley's election), and socialism was a principle to be practiced as well as preached. In an age of vast combinations, Lermond argued that there was little that the individual could do but unite with others into a "people's trust." If 100,000 cooperators each gave $100, a pool of $10,000,000 could serve as a counterweight to the oligarchic trusts of the day. With a modest $10,000, a colony of workers could build a factory and cultivate some land. "Colony No. 1 would now be in a condition to give employment to possibly 5,000 workers and thus the work would proceed—colony after colony being sent out from the parent association; new recruits constantly joining the Association to swell the funds and numbers; more and more industrial plants erected with an opportunity to work be given to all seeking employment and all the necessities and luxuries could be produced and by means of the labor check exchanged between the various colonies, thus dispensing with the use of either gold or silver money." [83]

To achieve all this, industries had to be organized on a large scale, and socialists had to concentrate in one section of the country. Socialists had to own and operate everything they used and then go on to establish "cooperative schools and colleges." Lermond believed that any state west of the Mississippi or south of Ohio contained the necessary resources to support this kind of venture. Farmers who were ground down by the system might offer their lands for colony sites, and workers from industrial centers should be willing to migrate with their families to such sites. In fact, the Hiawatha Colony founded by Thomas Mills in 1893 in Michigan operated on just that arrangement. According to Lermond, if it were only possible to "bring land and labor together, adopt an equitable system for the distribution of wealth created, and the problem of problems is solved." He believed that the best sites for such ventures would be in moderately sized rural towns, where a concentration of forces of socialists would benefit by the "society of each other." [84] Here he was quoting William Muller whose little pamphlet "One Way to the Co-Operative Commonwealth" had presented a detailed plan in 1893.

Man had been too long divorced from the land, argued Lermond, and he had to reclaim his birthright and share in nature's bounty. One sees in Lermond's appeal a mixture of industrial and agrarian idealism and a plan that had elements that one would see in the garden city plans of Ebenezer Howard. He ended his call for membership in the Brotherhood of the Co-Operative with a poem that symbolized the efforts of mankind to establish such a place where "justice, truth and love shall reign forevermore":

> How bright, how sweet, this world would be
> If men could live for others.
> How sweet, how bright, how full of light,
> This life, if justice, truth and right
> Were once enthroned; if men were free;
> If men would all be brothers!
>
> And is this nothing but a dream
> Must wrong go on forever?
> Must poverty forever be?
> And selfish greed and tyranny?
> Must hate and strife be still supreme,
> And love and peace come never?
>
> No, I will not believe it. No.
> God still reigns somewhere, brother;
> Somewhere, sometime the race will climb
> Above its selfishness and crime;
> Will gentler, nobler, happier grow
> And men will love each other.
>
> The morn is rising soft and bright,
> The way grows light before us.
> Cheer, brothers, cheer! through doubts, through fear,
> The world grows brighter year by year;
> And fast and bright a day of light
> Will spread its white wings o'er us.[85]

These ideas were sponsored by Henry D. Lloyd, Frank Parsons, Eugene V. Debs, Henry R. Legate, C. F. Taylor, Hiram Vrooman, Stephen Maybell, Thadeus Wakeman, James G. Clark, Charlotte Perkins Stetson, F. M. Sprague, William H. Muller, and W. D. P. Bliss.

The Brotherhood of the Cooperative Commonwealth did go ahead and organize a colony in 1898 after its strategy had been rejected by the Social Democracy party. Its sentiments—particularly its expansive optimism—mirrored the feelings of those socialists who were impatient with the rate of change and the setbacks that they had suffered at the ballot box. For these socialists, the colony idea was the only practical one, and its rewards were immediate. For many who participated in such colonies, the disappointments were as immediate—such was the case with Cyrus Willard. But the colony idea did suggest a practical alternative to the gradualism of the Knights, the erratic militancy of the trade unionists, the violence of the force anarchists, and the blandishments of corporate capitalism. There was no single model for these practical socialists, although many took inspiration from Gronlund and Bellamy. They were varied in their strategies, varied in their appeal, but all united on the proposition that the cooperative way was the way that grew "bright before us."

Typical of the colonies started in the 1890s was the Hiawatha Colony, organized in 1893 at Manistique, Michigan, by Abraham Byers.[86] Prior to homesteading a large tract of land with nine relatives in the Upper Peninsula in 1882, Byers had been an itinerant preacher in southern Michigan. He read Walter Thomas Mills's The Product Sharing Village and wrote to Mills, offering to deed his farm to the cause if some neighbors would do likewise. Mills, a famous temperance lecturer and millionaire who had amassed a fortune in Illinois real estate, came to Manistique and lectured.[87] Under Mills's tutelage, the Hiawatha Colony came into existence. Six other farms were deeded to the association, and Mills's father and five other members of his family came to the colony. The aims of the association were set out in their paper, The Industrial Christian, published in 1895. The colonists hoped to "inaugurate a system that will make it more honorable for the jockey to trade off his ideas for better ones, instead of trading off his old horses for better ones. Let every man, woman and child use his or her strongest energy in defending, in spreading and in perpetuating the ideas and workings of the product-sharing village already begun here. No boy will then have to become a rascal in order to support a widowed mother or sister. A never failing provision will be made for a child as soon as it is born. No unfortunate human being and no aged person on account of decrepitude will be taken from friends and home and put in an almshouse where they are looked down on as objects of pity, and depend upon the so called charity for what little they eat and wear. Product sharing for all."[88]

To become a member, $100 in cash, land, or personal property had to be paid in, but none except those who gave their land had a stake. Their assets eventually included 1,080 acres, 125 head of cattle, and twenty-five horses. They used a time-credit labor system. Members who joined later were housed with families until their own homes were constructed. They came from Iowa and Texas and had heard about the project through Mills or reform periodicals. In addition to farming, the members operated a sawmill and a printing shop, and they could join whatever "department" they wished. Mills procured for the colony a contract for canthooks, peavey stalks, and broom handles. One resident remembered the village as a happy place, but the economic difficulties that the colonists faced resulted in its dissolution in 1896. They had difficulties finding markets for their goods, and there was some dissension. Two members objected to living in the communal village and were forcibly moved from their homes at the outskirt of the village to make way for additional farmland to be cultivated. These dissidents sought legal advice, and the other colonists were forced to resettle them back on their old site.

During the winter of 1895–96, about fifteen families were still in residence, with most of the men working in nearby logging camps. Mills's family withdrew at this time, and the colony slowly disintegrated.[89] It had lasted for a little over two years, had 225 members at its height, and had grown to some twenty structures. The property was divided, some of the original settlers getting back only about half their investment. At Hiawatha there was a mixture of Christian idealism, practical socialism, and self-interest. Mills's idea had taken hold in an isolated Michigan town, and there were enough earnest believers to test the proposition that the Sermon on the Mount had meaning for the industrial age.

Another altruistic community located in Michigan was called, simply enough, the Altruist Community. It was the brainchild of a wealthy Detroit philanthropist, C. W. Gibson, who organized (with his brothers) a stock company, the Gibsonville Altruist Community. Located on 450 acres in Genesee County, it consisted of fifty of the poorest Detroit families (selected by the poor commissioners), who were settled on a cooperative and communistic farm. Gibson outfitted them with the necessary tools and clothes and spent $50,000 setting up the colony. The families were expected to live together in a hotel then under construction, with the entire proceeds of their labor going into a communal treasury.

Following this initial settlement phase, Gibsonville was opened to anyone with $100. All members were required to devote all their energies to the community, and they received, in return, all that they required. In January 1895, the colony consisted of 160 members living in forty houses. There was a basket industry, and members were building a broom factory. Plans were under way to construct a laundry and a creamery. It proposed "to be one of the largest and most prospering altruist communities in the country before many years."[90] It failed within the year.

The best known of all the Altruist colonies was Edward Biron Payne's Altruria, located near Thomas Lake Harris's settlement at Fountain Grove, California. Payne's career was a wide-ranging one. A graduate of Oberlin, he came to Berkeley in 1875 after having worked with Dwight Moody in Chicago and then leading a small congregation in Ohio. Dissatisfaction with Congregationalism in the 1880s led him into Unitarianism and pastorships in Massachusetts and New Hampshire. Ill health forced him back to Berkeley in 1893, where he became the city's first Unitarian minister. The Social Gospel aspects of church work had attracted him while working with Moody, and his conversion to that vigorous gospel was completed when he heard George Herron and Laurence Gronlund speak about the social evils of the day.

Early in 1894, a group centered in his church drafted a constitution for a cooperative colony "based on democratic suffrage, complete equality of community goods, but individual ownership of all possessions purchased with colony labor checks."[91] A 185-acre site was found at Fountain Grove, near the Harris colony. In October 1894, the Altrurian colony began, with three families and seven single men the first pioneers. Payne never maintained a full-time residence at the colony but continued to direct his Unitarian congregation in Berkeley, visiting the settlement on weekends. The colony published a newspaper, the *Altrurian*, that covered a range of reform topics, including progress reports about Fairhope and Topolobampo. Substantial support for the venture came from other Altrurian councils in California. For example, the San Francisco club sent a cow as a Christmas present, and the Los Angeles local supplied chess and checker sets for the colonists.

By the summer of 1895 no amount of goodwill, Social Gospel fervor, or enthusiasm could alter the fact that the colony was in financial trouble after only seven months. The membership fees had been set too low (at $50), and too many members had kept their outside interests separate from the colony. In order to forestall a closure, the colony divided into three groups, with sixteen going to a cooperative farm near Cloverdale, another group moving to Santa Rosa, and fourteen staying at Altruria. By June 1895, the colony had ended, and Ambrose Bierce's prediction in the *San Francisco Examiner* that these "amicable asses" would fail had come true. He called it a "flower of reform, gorgeous, exuberant, ephemeral."

More than forty years after the failure of Altruria, Payne's wife,

Ninetta Eames Payne, said that the colony was a "prolonged picnic under the stimulus of exalted association."[92] Considerably more practically minded and operating under a limited objective, the Colorado Cooperative Company organized in 1894 to build a ditch to irrigate cooperatively purchased land near Pinon, Colorado. All land was owned by a company, whose sole function was to improve that land. Improvement meant irrigation, and, after ten years of hard work, water was flowing onto land settled by between two hundred and three hundred individuals. The company was run like a corporation, but it did publish a paper, the *Altrurian*, that emphasized the possibilities of cooperation in the aid of individual enterprise. Its original purposes were to operate manufactures, "insure members against want, provide recreational, educational facilities, provide social harmony based on principles of cooperation"; in fact, all it did was to organize work around the irrigation ditch project.[93] By 1906, there were four hundred stockholders, the original settlers had laid out a town (Nucla) along single-tax lines, and this limited cooperative enterprise—in contrast to Altruria—had made a success of itself.[94]

For others, it was "Everybody's Opportunity, or Quick Socialism" the title of J. Herbert Rowell's 1901 pamphlet issued by the Chicago-based Free Socialist Union. The wealthy had no need for cooperation, and the poor had become "so machine like that they are helpless as soon as they are separated from the main shaft." According to E. Stanton Osborn, people could improve their condition by experimenting with schemes like the single tax one proposed by Rowell. Whereas the state socialists wanted "to colonize a state," the free socialists like Rowell thought it possible for single taxers to come together into a colony venture. His group had an option on some land in Minnesota and was planning to start a cooperative store in Chicago in 1901. His sentiments were as lofty and poetic as Lermond's about the necessity for a possibility of a better age: "I want to live, and help them tear down the old, decayed, rotten and vile smelling structure of this civilization (so called) and help build the new pearly palace, lofty, grand and majestic. I want to usher in the new life in which humanity will live in comfort and peace, in happiness and joy. . . . I am in favor of immediate action because opportunities are present."[95]

Under Rowell's plan, some five hundred "free socialists" could start a "colony school" or "working model or sample group or colony, whatever you please to call it," on free government land, with each member claiming 160 acres. Colonists could live in a town center and farm the surrounding area. Initially, individuals were to be housed in three-story buildings forty feet wide with broad halls and a central heating system using hall heating as a key element. Later, members would build houses to suit their tastes. There was to be a variety of trades and occupations represented in the colony, a variety of industries, and various grades of membership, depending on financial ability and participation. Rowell's blueprint was quite elaborate, and every conceivable question raised by a skeptical outsider was answered in a calm and reassuring manner. In an imaginary dialogue between a "state socialist" and a "free socialist," some key distinctions were set forth about the proposed colony:

> State socialist, question 27: "Oh, I see you will then have what is commonly called communistic colonies, but have turned out to be failures."
>
> Free socialist, answer 27: "You do not understand us; our colonies will not be communistic, no more so than a partnership is communistic today under the capitalistic system. Each member in a colony will have his own separate dwelling if so desired, but we will operate a company kitchen and dining room, so that those members who do not wish to keep house can get their meals at a restaurant, as it were. We will also operate a laundry and bakery. This will do away with the drudgery of the housewives. . . . Our colonies will be communistic in production, but in regard to consumption we will be individualists. . . . This is necessary in order to give each individual the fullest liberty which is possible; liberty is one of the main foundation stones of our entire plan. . . . Our company buildings, machinery and everything will require these things as a matter of necessity, and all other things which come under the head of luxuries and individual wants will not be operated by the company. Do you get the idea?"[96]

If Rowell's imaginary dialogue had been read in the 1850s, it would have been obvious to every reformer that what he was proposing was a Fourierist joint-stock colony. There is, however, no mention of the French sage or even of Godin, the French experimenter at Guise. Rowell's colony was to be open to all, regardless of race, color, or sex, and would be a "happy medium between the two extremes of the lonely farm house and the great overgrown city."[97] His colony—which appears never to have got off the ground—was based on two simple principles: equal liberty and voluntary and reciprocal cooperation.

Although Rowell's scheme never got beyond the imaginary dialogue stage, it did represent one part of the pragmatic political spectrum. If there was any politics in his scheme, it was the politics of Henry George. The famous Georgeist colony at Fairhope, Alabama, was started in this period, and Rowell's inspiration may have been drawn from the Alabama venture since it received considerable publicity in the press. It was a singular characteristic of these secular groups that ideology took second place to the more important concern of actually planting a colony that would work, that would serve immediate needs rather than ideological ones. The notion that such colonies would be "patent office models" (to borrow Arthur Bestor's phrase) was, of course, in their thinking; fundamentally, however, the appeal was to an immediate and concrete desire to alleviate poverty, social distress, and a sense of powerlessness felt by workingmen and women in the face of government indifference and monopolies. Support continued throughout this period for piecemeal reforms like the cooperative store, and, as late as 1904, commentators were urging laborers to support "anything that improves the present condition of the wage workers. . . . We can do it NOW! And these cooperative enterprises, of whatever nature, will help not hinder, the coming of the New Time."[98]

This coming of the "New Time" had interested labor reformers as early as the 1820s, and the cooperative commonwealth was an important part of that New Time. As a recent study has shown, laborers joined the Fourierist phalanxes in equal numbers with middle-class Whigs, and the "labor question" was on the agenda at most utopian settlements, including the religious ones. Between 1880 and 1900, there was a renewed interest in cooperation, particularly among labor organizations. Interest in cooperation appeared at three levels, according to Charles LeWarne: "Among workers who hoped that the communal experience could provide needs in uncertain times, among secondary or local labor leaders associated with labor who were responding to immediate situations, and among a few national figures who considered communitarianism as policy."[99]

A key feature in the appeal that communal colonies had was that they promised that aged, incapacitated, and sick members, as well as widows and orphans, would be taken care of. Labor leaders hoped that such colonies could serve an important educational function by instructing both laborers and the larger public about important economic issues. Cooperation was not an idea apart from the labor movement; rather it was part of a larger moral strategy that hoped to set workers free from the evil effects of the competitive system. Not surprisingly, cooperation had it strongest supporters among the Knights of Labor. In 1880, Grand Master workman Terence V. Powderly advised the General Assembly to pursue cooperation as a means to colonization. In 1882, a five-man Cooperative Board was established with the authority to support local assemblies in cooperative projects. One cooperative board chairman, Henry E. Sharpe, would have extended cooperative efforts to include planned colonies. He had founded the York Society of Integral Cooperators in 1880, and its prospectus had urged "that if a sufficient number of people, of sufficient variety of skill, go apart to sufficiently friendly locality, with sufficient funds for the first operations, they can from their own lands, by their own industry, obtain and fashion all those things according to their own ideas of equity."[100] Twelve English families acquired a thousand acres in Taney County, Missouri, in 1882, and by 1883 they had fifty members and a Knights assembly organized for sixteen.

Sharpe traveled about the country lecturing on integral cooperation and was elected chairman of the Cooperative Board. But disputes within the community soon made their way into Knights' journals, and Powderly feared that any connection between Sharpe and the Knights could be damaging. Members at Eglinton had accused Sharpe of both high-handed methods and "kidnapping," and he was suspended from his Cooperative Board position, pending an inquiry. That inquiry subsequently found that the evidence against him was insufficient, but by that time the colony was on its last legs. The Eglinton controversy led the Knights' executive Board to recommend against colonization as a policy because the Missouri colony had at its command too few resources to carry out a successful plan. Sharp continued to speak out in favor of cooperation and interested such figures as E. V. Neale, the English cooperator, and William Hinton, the English-born journalist, who later become a key figure in the Debs-supported Social democracy colonization plan of 1897.

Sharpe avoided using the word *colony* and, in fact, called such places *retreats* where the aged and infirm could raise their own food in a communal atmosphere. To his proposal, he attached the notion of a compulsory assessment on all Knights, and, when that failed to gain a hearing, his practical plans had no real basis of financial support. For Sharpe, there were three areas where communal settlements had something to offer the laboring class: insurance, education, and profit sharing. Although later expelled from the Knights, he did lay some important groundwork in the early 1880s for the idea that cooperative colonies and labor had something to offer one another. In 1889, he joined an experiment in Brazil.

Sharpe's work was followed by John Samuel, Jr., a Welsh glass-blower from St. Louis, who served on the Cooperative Board of the Knights for a three-year period. He wrote "How to Organize a Cooperative Society" and therein proposed that would-be colonists begin with a Rochdale store and expand outward to a self-supporting colony. Whereas Sharpe had emphasized integral colonies as a beginning point, Samuel saw them as the final link in the cooperative chain. Another colony supporter within the Knights was Peter McGaughey, who helped form the Pioneer Association, a cooperative agricultural association formed in 1883 by Minneapolis coopers and printers. In 1885, twelve families from the Minnesota Knights moved onto five hundred acres in the Mille Lacs region.[101]

Clearly, the influence of British cooperators made a mark on these early supporters of colonies within the Knights. As early as 1868, Richard Hinton had advanced cooperation. John Orvis (who had joined Brook Farm in 1844) had visited England in 1862 and after his return promoted association within the Sovereigns of Industry. He was elected Sovereigns president in 1873. Thomas Hughes and A. J. Mundella visited the United States in 1870, advocating cooperation and arbitration procedures for labor. George Jacob Holyoake's 1879 visit gave public notice to cooperative principles and led directly to the creation of the Cooperative Colony Association.[102]

Holyoake's visit to the United States (chronicled in *Among the Americans*) was a whirlwind one that lasted for four months and brought him in contact with leading American public officials and cooperators. His visit had several goals: to facilitate immigration from Britain to the United States, to survey American conditions, and to promote the work of the Guild of Cooperators. One of the first persons he met was P. T. Barnum's nephew, E. E. Barnum, who had directed Henry Sharpe's Cooperative Colony Aid Association in Kansas and who was secretary to the Colony Aid Association. Holyoake was in America to promote cooperation and steered wide of communal settlements, believing that "it was my duty to take care that cooperation should be seen as a distinct thing. The communist may be a cooperator, but the cooperator may not be a communist." Oneida was particularly odious to him, and "no entreaty induced me to go near." Its "immoral" features repelled him, yet the Thompson Colony in Kansas with its temperance and moral features drew his earnest endorsement.[103]

146

Yearley sums up the situation neatly: "By the mid-eighties obviously, cooperation was the panacea of the farmer rather than the wage-earner; the transition of the idea from city to countryside was to all effects complete. Some cooperators were claiming by that time in fact that 'stores on the Rochdale Plan are not adapted to large cities.'" It would not be until 1889—in New York City—that there was any effort to establish an urban base for a communal society with the dominant trend being one of concentrating energies in rural areas and attempting to combine farm and city in any new settlement.[104]

Holyoake's interest in arbitration and cooperation was directed at ameliorating the class struggle, but the sources of colony formation were varied. It was, for example, through anarchism that J. J. Martin founded a community. After working as a labor arbitrator on behalf of San Francisco seamen, he started, with Burnette Haskell, the Kaweah colony. Admitted to the California bar in 1879, Haskell had, for a time, edited the journal *Truth*; he then became involved with the labor movement to such an extent that he founded the Marxist International Workingmen's Association. Some characterized him as "brilliant," while others thought him "dishonest" and "unscrupulous." He was among the group that formed the Federated Trades of San Francisco, a mixed assembly of Knights composed of workers from different occupations. At a meeting of the assembly in 1885, Haskell presented a tentative plan for the formation of a series of industrial settlements to be established along the Pacific coast from Mexico to Canada. These colonies were to be situated as near as possible to a port to facilitate exchange between the settlements. In addition, each colony was to serve as a base for regional economic development. A temporary organization was formed and money subscribed. A stock company was incorporated for the manufacture of brick and hollow tile at Fish Rock, north of San Francisco, where there was a bed of clay. Land was purchased and machinery brought in, but in a short time it was decided that the site was inappropriate for a colony.

Shortly thereafter, C. F. Keller, a native of Tulare County, suggested Kaweah Canyon in that county, and a committee to investigate such a site was assembled. The committee report was a "glowing one" since there were substantial timber lands that could be exploited for a market in the San Joaquin Valley, fifty miles away. However, a twenty-mile road would have to be built to connect the timber land and the railhead. Halfway between the forest and the valley, there was a desirable location for a manufacturing town. The stage was set for the establishment of the socialist colony. Individual members of the colony association filed claims at the Tulare County Land Office on 5 October 1885. Fifty-three men of the Cooperative Land Association made the trip from San Francisco to claim the land under the Timberland Act of 1878 and the Homestead Act of 1862. Fear of fraud on the part of the filers caused the land office in Washington to withdraw the land from further entry a month later. The colony members had agreed (verbally) to turn over the land to the association in return for a certificate of membership in the colony worth $500.

Next, they incorporated the Grant Forest and Tulare Valley Railroad, with Haskell as president, Martin as secretary, and Keller as general superintendent. Their offices were at Fifth and Market Street in San Francisco, and they began, at once, to receive surveys of the proposed road and to purchase rights-of-way. The construction of a wagon road was begun. As stated in the prospectus, the prime reason for the colony was not to build a road or fell trees but "to insure its members against want or the fear of want by providing comfortable homes, ample sustenance, educational and recreational facilities, and to promote and maintain harmonious relations among its members and with the world." Membership cost $500, with $100 in cash at once or "approved value in material." No shares or stock was issued, and wages (based on a time-check system) were paid to all on an equal basis. In addition to the twelve square miles of timber land, a townsite of 240 acres was procured. The colony was administered by a board of five trustees and each branch of industry (collection, extraction, growing, handicraft, transportation, storage, finance, administration, education, public service, and domestic) placed under a superintendent appointed by the trustees. Haskell headed education and Martin administration. Meetings were held on the first Saturday of every month, and the superintendents gave reports to the assembled workers. These monthly meetings became the place where they argued, disputed policy, and, in general, fell upon each other.[105]

There was a large body of colony supporters of a nonresident class who paid membership fees but lived outside of Kaweah. There were clubs in San Francisco, Los Angeles, Denver, and New York. The Eastern Group of the Kaweah Colony was led by Alice H. Rhine, the author of *Niagara* and contributor of a sixty-page essay on "Women in Industry" to the volume *Women's Work in America*. Rhine lived in Manhattan and was one of six women who belonged to a group numbering twenty-two. Interviewed in New York, Rhine said, "To find out that there is more romance in the world than is dreamed of, one has only to visit the co-operative colony of Kaweah founded by practical men of business, whose vision is to make the ideal republic, that has haunted the minds of men from Plato downward, a reality. While others are discontentedly grumbling in the cities and talking revolution, the Kaweah colonists have left the centers of the population behind and settled down to practical work and example."[106]

Two members of the New York group, Ralph Pope and Douglas McCallum, visited California and came away full of enthusiasm for the project: "The morale of Kaweah is high. Think of it a town without a saloon, no profanity. . . . Marriage among them is decidedly successful. The family relation is held most dear and sacred.[107] Such supportive remarks were sometimes supplemented by gifts from the local clubs. Alice Rhine, for example, had hoped to join the colony, but it disintegrated before she had her chance. Most who did join were skilled laborers from the trade unions and recruits from the Bellamy movement. Members originally lived in a tent town; however, by 1890 a settlement at Kaweah had taken shape. There was a permanent common hall for dining, a colony store, a printing shop, a blacksmith's shop, and a barn. Social life was varied, with literature and science classes on Mondays and orchestra practice on Tuesdays and Fridays. The standard of intellectual interests as indicated by the articles in the colony newspaper, the *Commonwealth*, was high. Essays by Ingersoll, articles about the Fourierist colony at Guise, reports of Nationalist Club activities, all kept the colonists in close contact with the outside world while they were creating a community and building a road. It was the building of the road that symbolized the colonists' dedication.

As Robert Hine has noted, the road stood in the colony literature as the "symbol of future glory." Begun in October 1886, it was finished in June 1890. Dug out by hand and dynamite, this eighteen-mile turnpike was the "best built mountain road in that part of the country if not the whole Sierra range." Constructed especially to bring down heavy loads of lumber to the townsite at Kaweah, the settlers considered it a "great demonstration of the possibilities of industrial cooperation." The sacrifices they made in building the road were nothing when "compared with the prospect of well-being and comfort that presented itself with the completion of the road.[108] It was not to yield the hoped-for prosperity since the government ("a snake in the grass") worked to stop the colonists from harvesting the timber. In September 1890, Congress established the Sequoia National Park and set aside adjacent lands as a national forest. According to the government, the colonists had been squatting on the land, and, when they sought some reimbursement for the improvements that they had made on it, the government denied the claims.

The congressional action of 1890 effectively signaled the end of Kaweah, though there was continued litigation and government prosecution of the trustees for illegally cutting down a mere five trees on land that they had tended with considerable care. A second criminal case was brought against them in 1892 for illegal use of the mail to defraud; it was dismissed for insufficient evidence. The Land Claims Office had left the colonists hanging fire for five years while they built their road and tried to establish a community for two hundred people. All had not been sanguine within the colony since Haskell was difficult—"argumentative and undependable"—and the organization of business affairs cumbersome because they had long and frequent discussions about policy that made it difficult to get prompt decisions about financial matters.[109] Reports of the colony's decline were wildly reported in the press, one paper asserting that honest members were being starved out by the "rascals" and that some members were under arrest for "stealing sweet potatoes to keep themselves alive."[110] In November 1891, half the resident members had abolished the time-check system and had taken possession of the land and machinery. In the process, they repudiated the debts of the old workers. In short, the colony had turned on itself. Until the end, however, there was little negative publicity about the colony in socialist papers.[111]

In the nonsocialist press, Kaweah generated a great deal of hostility, and the colonists believed unto the last that the government had set out to harass them at every turn. That was surely the case in the two suits brought after the congressional action, but there is inadequate evidence to suggest any concerted action to deny them their land just because they were socialists. They had settled, unfortunately, on land that was at the center of a shifting government policy (and a progressive one at that), and they were its first victims. What the members retained of Kaweah were memories of an heroic attempt to claim a piece of the earth for a higher purpose and build the new commonwealth in California. One former member, Will Purdy, wrote an epic poem, "Kaweah: A Saga of the Old Colony," that caught some of the hope that motivated these San Francisco laborers to build their road to utopia:

Whilom in this titanic foretold
A group of men, by faith impelled,
Here met in solemn conclave to work out
A scheme of life dread poverty to rout. . . .

There was Martin, son of Albion's fruitful isle
A man of genial presence, kindly smile. . . .
Haskell was a man of different mold . . .
A man you'd make a poet or a dreamer
Who embittered, might become the crafty schemer

And so, in eighty-five, it came to pass
They filled their lawful timber claims en masse
The sylvan wealth that Nature here had sowed
Could ne'er be reaped without a wagon road. . . .
The toilers work was valued at the rate
Of thirty cents an hour; and they devised
A monetary system; twas compound
Of time checks based on each man's honest labor.

These earnest people with their new ideal
Were Persecuted with fanatic zeal. . . .
It robbed them of their lands—they might expect
No mercy at the hands of Uncle Sam

Yet shall their beacon, shining from afar
Be to pilgrim man a guiding star;
Brave martyrs to a cause we may not shun
This be the mead of love they, losing, won.[112]

It was after Kaweah had sunk into the western sun that a leading reformer of the day, Henry Demarest Lloyd, gave up his lifelong
commitment to Emersonian individualism to embrace communitarianism. Under the philosophical tutelage of T. H. Green, Kant, Hegel,
and Comte plus the ethics of Emerson, Carlyle, and Ruskin, Lloyd
began to believe that co-operation was the higher law and that "society must develop a cooperative cure for child labor and unemployment caused by monopoly and technological change, or submit to
catastrophe and decay."[113] His thinking about cooperation and social change had crystallized after a weekend visit to the Shaker community at Mt. Lebanon 1893.

Before Lloyd's arrival at Mt. Lebanon, the Shakers had read his
pamphlet "The New Conscience," and in the course of his visit there
developed some mutual admiration between Lloyd and Eldress
Anna White. The New Lebanon visit had a profound effect on him
as he saw in the Shaker way of life a higher form of association:
"Thus in the religious communitarianism of Mt. Lebanon, a type he

had hitherto scorned, Lloyd found a practical validation of the altruist, equalitarian, ethical and cooperative conceptions that were fundamental to his welfare philosophy. Had he not been predisposed by
preceding events to a favorable view he might have detected evidence of decay in that six-thousand acre community, where competition by commercial producers with its furniture was already felt
and young recruits were insufficient to displace the tenant farmers."[114]

Lloyd either did not see or did not want to see the weakness at
Mt. Lebanon; instead, he chose to view it as a prototype of the future.
He accepted the stone factory, well-kept farms, and huge barns as
evidence of impregnable prosperity and proof of the practicality of
the "Cooperative Commonwealth." Thereafter, he valued communal
colonies as having experimental and symbolic meaning. Later, he
visited cooperators in England and Ireland, finding that they, too,
had an interest in Ruskin. At the Delft Conference in 1896, he reported on it for the assembled international cooperators. At Ruskin,
he later told an assembled audience, "The communes are its [polit-
ical economy] new pioneers. They are the monasteries in which the
light of the new faith is kept burning on the mountain tops until the
dark age is over. These little societies must be generalized into a
society which will, like them extinguish the degrading dependence
of the many on the few for a chance to work and for a share of the
product."[115]

Between the onslaught of the 1893 depression and the outbreak
of the Spanish-American war, the number of colonies and the interest in colony settlement leaped. The pages of the *Coming Nation*
were filled with statements of intent, with inquiries, with invitations
to join, and with travel plans. In February 1896, the Ohio Colonization Society, based at Dayton, announced that it was "organized on
the George system of mutual cooperative colonization, and is looking for land in Tennessee and other Southern states. A certificate of
membership costs $100 payable in 50 cents weekly installments." In
March, the society's two representative, I. S. Bradley and Dr. Samuel
F. George, were looking at land in Georgia, and in June all sixty members of the association "with bag and baggage" left for the Equality
Colony in Washington.[116]

Nearly every Midwestern and Southern state had its cooperators. The Ridgeville Cooperators in Illinois had land and $2,000 in
cash and were looking for members. The South Missouri Christian
Colony had purchased four thousand acres, had a $150 entrance fee,
and was establishing (as of 1 March 1898) a "Christian colony where

Christ's law shall reign supreme, where God's word shall be a text-book." Some groups copied from others like the colony at Greenwood, Arkansas, which had, in 1894, adopted the bylaws of the Ruskin Association and were organizing. There were town developers such as J. S. Mann of York, Florida, who had "land, timber and climate second to none in the world to produce and manufacture our raw material, saw, shingle and grist mill now on the ground and doing a good business. Will start a town as soon as 100 cooperators will come and subscribe to our by-laws." Another cooperative colony was begun at Montecello, Jefferson County, Florida, in February 1898, only to have failed by September because of "poor land."[117]

Charles H. Bliss of Pensacola was typical of the cooperators who believed that the only answer to the current economic crisis was cooperation. His long life story printed in the *Coming Nation* is, I think, an emblematic one for the 1890s:

> I was one of the enthusiasts that helped to organize the Populist Party having the honor of coining the name and publishing the first paper with that title, published the *Populist Compendium* and works on silver that reached an immense circulation, and spent much time and money in that cause, but like many others my fondest hopes were not realized. I did not expect all that was claimed, but I did expect that a respectable number of the oppressed would act in their own defense.
>
> I have not given up the work of reform, but I have turned my efforts from those of political endeavor to a line of cooperation. This country offers exceptional advantages to colonies. Land is cheap and abundant and productive. The country is less developed than in the "wild west." Winters are extremely short and very mild, permitting gardens to be grown in the winter months. . . . Aside from this one must not overlook the facts that this is the most healthful part of the United States, good water exists everywhere, fruits and flowers may be produced in profusion. . . . I have secured a large tract of fine land upon which I shall establish a cooperative colony. A portion of it is upon the immediate sea shore, where the scenery is grand and the fishing and oystering superb. On account of the surpassing beauty of the surroundings the future town will be called "Dreamland City."[118]

For a membership fee of $100, Bliss was offering workmen the security of a home where land could not be sold out from under them or where they could not be thrown out of their houses to pay their debts. Land tenure was but one form of security offered as part of the many appeals to workers to organize into colonies. In 1894, workers interested in a Colorado colony were urged to write to Seibert, Colorado, or Ashtabula, Ohio, workers interested in southern California had a chance to settle in Paso Robles, and those in Texas had only to contact R. S. Price in Waco to start a "Lone Star Association."[119] The labor-exchange movement started by G. B. DeBernardi with his *Trials and Triumph of Labor* (1893) had created—contrary to DeBernardi's wishes—one cooperative colony, the Freedom Colony, at Olathe, Kansas, in March 1897. By 1900, that group still had only thirteen members, among them the eccentric reformer Carl Browne, who had served as "Chief Marshall" in the Commonwealth Army of Jacob Coxey in 1894. By 1905, the colony had ceased to exist. Its original members had moved away, but it had served its modest purpose in those years by sheltering a few families from the uncertainties of American economic life.[120]

The Grander Age cooperative at Co-opolis, Mississippi, was, like Freedom and all the others, born of enthusiasm and died at the hands of individualism. Begun by E. A. Cowell, publisher of the *Cooperative Age* at St. Paul, Minnesota, and S. W. Rose, of Handsboro, Mississippi, it started with high hopes in January 1894, only to announce its end in Rose's *The True Story of a Cooperative Village*, published in 1898: "Co-opolis no longer desires to be advertised as a co-operative village. It will take its place along with other villages of the Gulf Coast and while it will welcome the coming of good, intelligent people who do not subsist off the efforts of others, it earnestly hopes that those who are looking for the seventh heaven of delight, and will be mad if they don't find it, will not come to us, for we wish no more disappointed ones, who will claim that we have deceived them. We are not angels by any means. We are only common, every-day people who WORK for a living the same as they do at Biloxi, or Gulfport, or Handsboro, or any other Gulf Coast town."[121] Such candor was rare when colonies, socialistic or religious, were wound up.

Although Kaweah was the first of the workers colonies to attract national attention, it was not until 1894 that the greatest test of practical socialism was made. It was formed largely through the efforts of Julius A. Wayland, the Indiana-born editor and reformer, who made a fortune in Colorado real estate before being converted to socialism by the English radical William Bradfield. Wayland started his paper the *Coming Nation* at Greensburg, Indiana, in 1893 and with aggressive journalism made it into the largest-circulation radical newspaper in the country. The *Coming Nation* was read from New York to California, and Wayland (who had not read Marx before starting the colony) used the paper to promote the colony.

During the latter half of 1893, Wayland ran an announcement in the paper urging the formation of a cooperative village on the following terms: "I am not only willing to give up all that [profits] and more to founding a village on economic equality that I may live and labor with my neighbors, but would love to do so. . . . If you will increase the circulation of *The Coming Nation* to 100,000 . . . This money will buy 3,000 or 4,000 acres of land and pay for it. Those who send in 200 subscribers or more or contribute as much, will be charter members who will proceed to organize the colony on such a basis of equality as in their judgement will produce justice. . . . Now go to work for subscribers, and show by your zeal that you are worthy a fellowship in such a community. You Can Do It."[122]

Following this crass commercial appeal to boost circulation, Wayland gave his justification for the establishment of the village: "The masses are ripe for something which promises relief from the unequal contest with corporate capital. Look about you start some cooperative industry." Wayland was combining both Sharpe's integral cooperation with Samuel's gradualist approach in an effort to get some social movement started in the midst of the 1893 depression. For Wayland, "cooperation was the way out."[123] Clearly, it was not *just* a scheme for boosting circulation, or *just* a plan for implementing practical socialism, but an effort (and here it was unique among the political societies) to implement an experiment in aesthetics as well.

Wayland had been profoundly influenced by the writings of John Ruskin, the English art critic and aesthetician. Ruskin had been the inspiration behind the earlier failed St. George's Guild in England, which had been the practical application of ideas that he had expressed in *Fors Clavigera*, a monthly series of letters addressed to the workers and laborers of Britain first published in 1871: "We will try to make some small piece of English ground, beautiful, peaceful and fruitful. We will have no steam engines upon it, and no railroads; we will have no untended or unthought of creatures on it; none wretched, but the sick; none idle, but the dead."[124] This Guild of St. George was slow to come into existence, and in 1874 Ruskin made his first concrete proposal to buy some land for "young couples of the higher class," then settle them on the land in a self-supporting community that needed a minimum of modern machinery. There were to be three classes: the "companion servant," who spent the day in guild work (artisans); the "companion militant," who worked the land; and the "companion counselor," who remained in his own profession yet supported the guild by tithing.

All these would be under the direction of a "Master of the Guild," Ruskin himself. With the help of Sir Thomas Acland and William Cowper-Temple, Ruskin established a St. George's Fund, then accepted seven acres of woodland in Worcestershire from a merchant, George Baker. Still, progress was slow since funds failed to come in, and there were difficulties establishing a legal trust, though he was able to accept more land from another benefactor, Mrs. Fanny Talbot. A public appeal for funds was launched in 1882 through the publication of a pamphlet that outlined the four major activities of the guild: agricultural labor, historical investigation and illustration, completion of a mineralogical collection, and the purchase of manuscripts for the St. George's Museum. Some tenant farmers were settled on guild lands, but it was the museum at Sheffield that took up most of his funds and efforts.

This mixture of lofty sentiment and contemporary concern caught Wayland's eye, and he patterned his appeals to readers of the Coming Nation on the Fors Clavigera letters. As the subscription list of his paper neared 100,000, Wayland set out to purchase some land.[125] An agent purchased a one-thousand-acre tract at Tennessee City, Tennessee; however, the site proved so unproductive that the colonists moved four miles north to an eight-hundred acre tract. On this new town site, Ruskin, Wayland located the Coming Nation. There were 175 acres of arable land, two large caves that provided temporary shelter, and a base for colony activities.

Colonists were asked to contribute $500 per family, refundable if they left. Most were garment workers or mill workers from New England thrown out of work by the depression and eager to get out of the economic cold. The colony's stated purpose was to "own and operate manufactories, to acquire land, to build homes for its members, to insure the members against want or the fear of want, to provide educational facilities of the highest order, and to promote and maintain harmonious social relations on the basis of cooperation." Membership qualifications were broad. Individuals had to be of a "good moral character, be well informed in the principles of cooperation and socialism and be able to pass an examination in these principles." Twenty-one was the minimum age for admittance, and membership was granted by a majority vote of the members. There were separate departments ranging from Public Works to Printing and Publishing. A day's labor could be no longer than ten hours, and all workers were paid at the same rate even when they were sick and unable to work. Although the general rules emphasized the rights and benefits of association, there was considerable precision about some obligations that membership entailed. Article 9 of the bylaws tried to depoliticize this political settlement by barring members from voting for themselves or asking others to vote for them. Another article stated that no member would be allowed to have children "grow up in ignorance," which presumed compulsory schooling. Although it was not spelled out in the colony literature, women had an equal vote in colony matters.[126]

As in all such enterprises, the first members to arrive (though initially discouraged by the first site selected) were imbued with enthusiasm and a zeal for the place that only time would test. Theodore McDill later wrote about the "Happiest Days of My Life": "The Great Cave was the center of Ruskin. The main room was about thirty-five feet high and perhaps two hundred feet back to the lake. . . . Sometimes the young folks played ball in the big cave." McDill worked in the chewing gum factory and found Ruskin a happy place, a place where socialism was being practiced and where there was hope. He had arrived at a forlorn railroad stop, Tennessee City, in the middle of the night, and what he could see of the colony suggested that he might want to take the next train out: "The colony proper was about four miles away. I followed a foot path up hill and down dale through the unbroken forest. The hotel was another barn built of rough boards with a rough board roof. Every time it rained more water came inside than ran off the roof. There were a dozen or so rough tables with benches for some fifty people. Visitors stayed at the hotel. . . . The wives and daughters of the members kept the hotel in order. The rooms had no ceilings. Conversations floated over the partitions. There were a dozen or so rough houses where the various families lived. The colony store was a room built in front of the dugout, in the hillside. The solitary goat spent most of the time browsing off the roof."[127] What made McDill stay is unclear. Stay he did, however, and married a Ruskin colony member (as did his two brothers).

The center of activity at Ruskin was the Great Cave, which acted as a storage area, a garden, and, at times, a baseball field. Initially, the only industry was the newspaper, but the colonists soon expanded into the manufacture of stump pullers, hay presses, and other machines. In numerous ways, Ruskin was an un-Ruskin-like colony. Unfortunately, these businesses were failures, and all the colonists had for their efforts was the time-check script printed on the community press. At first, they lived in the Ruskin Cave; however, it was soon recognized that they needed some focal point, and a three-story Commonwealth House were erected to serve as a hotel, dining room, nursery, theater, and printing shop. It contained a theater with two hundred seats where the colonists put on performances and art shows. Creative work was encouraged, one of Ruskin's principles. A painting of *The Master of The Guild* done by a colonist was on display. They had a band that went on tour, and the Ruskin Dramatic Troupe gave performances in nearby villages. Piano recitals took place occasionally and included some original compositions such as "Salut de Ruskin" and the "Village Where Labor Is King."

The economic base for all these activities was equally varied. Wheat, corn, and tomatoes were grown for home consumption, but they had to go to local markets for much of their foodstuffs. A rhubarb crop was grown in the cave yet never marketed because the colony was too far from commercial centers. For a time, the colonists published some reform literature, and, when the project lost money, they abandoned publication. One observer noted that there was not always enough work to keep the members profitably employed, yet outside labor was used to chop wood and logs. Other lumber-based industries were begun with mixed success: "Bath cabinets were manufactured on which the profit was large but the demand for them was very small, and they sold not more than one per week. Chewing gum was manufactured but there was scarcely any demand for it. The tailoring shop made a small profit on its outside trade."[128] There was a sawmill, a steam laundry (most of the workers were women), and other small businesses (cereal, coffee, and leather suspenders). None was successful enough to carry the colony.

By 1895, Ruskin was, in effect, a small town of two hundred people. When Issac Broome first visited the colony in March 1896, he found thirty-one new homes, the hotel, and a variety of industries. He was not impressed by the quality of the people who came and noted that the presence of "coarse" individuals came as a blow to those colonists who believed that utopia would contain only persons of quality and bearing—particularly a colony named after Ruskin: "Imagine the shock to this idyllic when expectation is wrecked by finding within the magic circle characters so deficient in moral principles as to be outlaws. Character so besotted in ignorance as to be beyond hope."[129]

There were several communal features that bear special mentioning. The colony laundry required fifty women to work five hours a day to take care of seventy families. The colonists believed that it was a great labor-saving device, and, along with the common dining room, it was seen as the most efficient colony operation. There were four cooks and thirty-five waiters, plus helpers and a manager serving what many considered excellent fare. Like the laundry, food preparation was in the hands of women whose children were taken care of in the Commonwealth Nursery. In a two-part series published in August 1895, Ella Jennison, M.D., wrote about the "Women of the Ruskin Colony" for the colony paper. She found that, despite the fact that they had not been consulted during the site selection process, they were keenly interested in the home sites and colony life.[130]

The colonists had, in spite of the hardships, been able to create proper homes for themselves. One woman's garden showed "evidence of thrift and industry"; another's living room reminded Jennison of the saloon of a sailing vessel and had rugs and "evidence of culture and refinement." A former resident of Topolobampo, Mrs. Isabel Herring, was involved in educational affairs, and she described the principal occupation of most women in summary fashion: "Housekeeping would cover it." She was willing to bear with this labor until the cooperative industries were in place: "We are content with our seemingly hard lot, isolated from civilization, because we hope to establish a precedent or live out a principle which we hope to see followed by others with less hardships because of our sacrifice and the example of our combined efforts. In our new cooperative kitchen the people can be fed at the cost of eighty cents to one dollar a week, a great saving upon the individualistic plan of single homes."[131] Most of the women believed in the suffrage, although they had not organized in any formal fashion to press that claim at Ruskin.

One member, Mrs. Eschmann, had been born in Zurich and had acted as a midwife in the first colony birth. She had come to America to improve her material situation and believed that the colony would show the "possibilities of socialism." Although intended as a piece of propaganda for the colony, the Jennison article did indicate that Ruskin, socialism, and the suffrage were all of a piece in the women's minds. Willingness to shoulder their hard domestic tasks was both a necessity and a first step toward true socialism and cooperative equality.[132]

The colony had a distinctive educational cast to it, and the establishment of the Ruskin College of the New Economy symbolized the members' desire to build for the future of the race: "An institution is necessary where students activated by the new social motive may be equipped for intellectual battle with the emissaries of capitalism, an institution where the new economy, setting Man above Money, Worth above Wealth, Progress above Party, and Growth above Greed, may be taught, and those who teach it will be free of time serving."[133] Seven trustees were to be chosen to represent different geographic areas of the country, and the laying of the cornerstone of the college was a gala event. The college, however, remained an idea despite the elaborate plans.

Although there were years when the colony tried to put some solid ground under itself in terms of land, buildings, and resources, it was the human resources at Ruskin that were counted on to sustain the colony in difficult times. Between August 1894 and June 1899, it admitted 171 members (222 if one includes nonvoting wives and minors), and, of that group, eighty-six remained until the end. An average of 19 percent of the resident population left every year; Julius Wayland, the founder, left after only eleven months. Only seven of the original fifty-nine who came in 1894–95 remained until the end. In 1896, less than 15 percent withdrew, and, in 1898, there was a jump in new members to bring the core group of men to seventy. Ruskin's collapse was a quick one and precipitated by the demands of one group to divide the assets. In 1899, the property (worth, they believed $100,000) was sold for $10,000 to satisfy claims.[134]

Theodore McDill recounted the last days at Ruskin. The hostility that local residents had shown when the colonists came had now passed, and their neighbors were sorry to see them leave. At their last Fourth of July celebration, fifteen hundred neighbors came and purchased anything they could to help out the debt-ridden colony. In the end, they even passed the hat for their socialist neighbors. Whatever uncertainty McDill had had on entry was now all gone, and he saw in Ruskin—this failed experiment—hope for the future: "In Ruskin Colony we found the answer to the problem of the unemployed. The problem which threatens to destroy our entire civilization. And I want to tell the world. Let every county establish a colony for the superannuated and unfortunate. Where the unemployed can be self-supporting in slack times and from which skilled labor can be drawn when needed. With no taint of charity and no donations for upkeep. . . . Self supporting, self respecting all around good citizens."[135] As he wrote those words in 1932, the Roosevelt administration was considering a plan for subsistence homesteads.

In the throes of this profound and often bitter struggle to determine the course of American radicalism, an organization emerged

that over the next few years tried to act as a clearing house and catalyst for cooperators. The American Cooperative Union emerged
from the 1896 National Cooperative Congress in St. Louis, which
was held at the same time as the tumultuous Populist party convention.[136] Henry D. Lloyd had been in correspondence with Wayland
and George Howard Gibson about cooperatives and colonies, and,
when asked by Lorenzo Wardell, a Topeka socialist, to participate in
such a congress, he agreed. He had been stimulated by the World
Congress of Cooperatives held during the World's Fair, by news
about the success of Knights of Labor cooperatives, and by his visit
to the Shakers at New Lebanon.

The Brotherhood of the Cooperative Commonwealth was
founded by a Maine reformer, Norman Wallace Lermond, to educate
Americans about socialism. It had, according to Howard Quint,
three objectives: to unite all cooperators into a fraternal organization, to colonize a western state with individuals eager to live in
socialistic colonies, and then to capture control of state governments. Lermond had convinced Lloyd to head the brotherhood at
the St. Louis convention (to which both Lermond and Imogene Fales
were delegates) because it seemed an appropriate place to promote
the cooperative cause. Yet populism occupied everyone's attention
at St. Louis, including Lermond's—so much so that Alcander Longley reported that, when the congress did meet (there were less than
one hundred in attendance), the sessions were all taken up with
speeches.[137] The congress accomplished one thing—the formation
of the American Cooperative Union headed by Wardell and Imogene
Fales.

In her opening address to the congress, Fales said that their one
definite aim was the "overthrow of the competitive system" and that
there would be a department "devoted to the formation and development of colonies, located near each other, or near some central
point, for the purpose of exchanging surplus products, and buying
and selling by a system of checks receivable in all the colonies." It
was, according to her, the "manifest destiny" of the United States to
"lead and reconstruct the world." But it was the evolutionary rather
than the revolutionary principle that she stressed, with cooperation
the top rung on the social ladder that man was climbing: "cooperative colonies, the natural expression of the illimitable west will
be prosecuted by those to whom community is the Alpha and
Omega of all reforms; who see it as a remedy for existing ills, and an
opportunity *to put in practice the principles* that ere long will be
politically and otherwise expressed throughout the nation. The col-

ony movement is distinctively American. The broad lands of the West and South call for cooperative communities with their colleges and communities and the new education for the new civilization on which the world is entering."[138]

Just prior to the organization of the congress, the *Coming Nation* agreed to keep the cooperative flag afloat by printing reports and news from Wardell and his associates.[139] The call to the convention had been signed by a national coalition that included figures like Lloyd, Gibson, Ralph Albertson, Frank Parsons, Morrison Swift, Eugene Debs, Myron Reed, and Alice Hyneman Sotheran. It was McKinley's victory in 1896, rather than brilliant organization or the clarion call of socialist worthies, that caused workers to join the brotherhood. By June 1897, it had 125 branches and a membership of two thousand. Eugene Debs was, for a short period, the national organizer, but his interests eventually turned toward socialist politics. For the moment, however, he, like other socialists, saw the cooperative-colony scheme as a way to give shelter to the unemployed and blacklisted union men.

During the 1897 meeting of the American Railway Union, Debs (with the help of Victor Berger) steered the railwaymen toward the creation of another organization, the Social Democracy of America. The colonization issue was a central part of their constitution, adopted in June 1897, but only part of a broader program. Within a broad spectrum of issues that concerned them, cooperation was seen as a strategy that could lead toward the takeover of a single state for socialism. A Colonization Department was established with the objective of finding suitable sites for a colony.[140]

Debs, in fact, sent a letter to John D. Rockefeller asking for financial support for the colonization idea. The railway people had taken over colonization and made the notion subservient to their own ends. Colonization and the Social Democracy party were not the same thing, as many members came into the party from the Socialist Labor party because they had failed to follow the strict De-Leon line. The colonization idea did have an appeal, and, as Debs toured the country, he found that outside the urban centers in the South and Midwest "men and women came up to him after his lectures to inquire of the progress of the three man social Democracy colonization committee which had been appointed early in August."[141] The committee consisted of Richard Hinton, William Borland, and Cyrus Willard. From the start, they were hampered by a lack of funds and their decision to look at states other than those in the trans-Mississippi West for the colony. They investigated a site near Crossville, Cumberland County, Tennessee, just twenty-five miles from where Rugby had stood, but decided against it. Colorado next seemed a possible site, and, as the 1898 convention of the Social Democracy party drew near, the commission made an offer on some land in Colorado. Hinton tried to enlist the support of figures like Charles Sotheran who had signed the original call for the National Cooperative Congress only to find out that he had changed his mind:

> My dear Richard, when I tell you that I do not believe in the colony project and will not go into it, I'm still more sorry for myself, for the blighted hopes your letter conjures up of the American people in which I could once more become an ardent useful worker. . . . But my objection to joining your colony is not so much the idea of failure as a strong conviction that socialistic work must be done in places where workers live; the socialist agitator must live in cities, in mill towns, mining districts, to teach the exploited a knowledge of the wrongs they are up against and show them how to break from slavery into freedom, how through the intelligent use of the ballot they will gain the right to live life's highest best.[142]

Willard wrote to Edward Bellamy seeking his approval for the project and an article from him for the *Social Democrat* on "Building a State." Willard saw it as an extension of the idealism of Nationalism and the culmination of the ideas put forward in *Looking Backward*: "Even in the most enthusiastic days of the National movement, there was nothing like the present move of the Social Democracy. You would be astounded at the offers of money and contributions of all sorts, land, etc., which the commission is receiving. The organization of the Social Democracy is going on at lightning speed, and huge masses of men are being enrolled by competent and skillful officers, and it appears to be in fact the mustering of that industrial room you portray. . . . I want you and all the rest of the old boys in the Nationalist Movement to realize that this is only the continuation and realization of that movement."[143] Bellamy did not respond.

The supporters of colonization, however, found themselves in conflict with those elements of the Social Democracy party inclined toward political solutions. All this came to a head in June 1898, at the convention. On one side stood Berger and his allies and on the other Willard and his friends. Debs was, as usual, of two minds. After a heated and faction-ridden convention, a majority (fifty-two to thirty-seven) came out in support of colonization over political action. The political group then bolted the convention, and Debs sent them a letter of support. The colonists had won, but at a terrible cost. The Brotherhood/Social Democracy group soldiered on in the form of the Cooperative Brotherhood movement and issued a call, in the fall of 1898, for a colony.[144]

What did all this maneuvering, all this political infighting, mean to the average socialist? The disputes between Berger and DeLeon, the intrigues of Debs and Willard, shaped the organizational pattern, but colonization was still a potent idea to the maverick socialist willing to chance something on a new journey. George W. Quimby, a civil engineer from Verdigee, Nebraska, was such a socialist. Writing in December 1897 to a socialist "brother" in Washington, he said that he was an "enthusiast" on the colony question. Possessed of several mechanical skills, he saw himself as an asset to any colony, but he admitted that he did bring some liabilities to the venture: "I would like to inquire what effect your climate has on cases of catarrah." Quimby knew of other interested families in his town (he had recently started a paper in Verdigee) who were thinking "favorably on the question" but who were unwilling to risk the chance that it might be unsuited for them and "then they would be just that much money out."[145]

Some did chance it, and, in August 1897, Willard and J. S. Ingals purchased land near Henderson Bay in Washington at Equality. Those who came were, like Harry Ault said, "interested neither in the gold rush, the impending war, nor the rivalries of competing real estate agents—we were part of a vanguard of the army that was to cover the thinly-populated State of Washington with a network of cooperative settlements and quietly and peaceably—and quite legally—transform it into a cooperative commonwealth." He believed that the purpose of the settlement was to "prove the soundness of their principles by practical example." The Brotherhood of the Cooperative Commonwealth had commissioned Ed Pelton, a Maine lumberjack, to find a proper site. After looking at land near the Mississippi River ("but the number of Negroes and the attitude of white residents toward them caused him to search further"), Pelton went West and picked a site in Skagit County, Washington.[146] He convinced a local socialist, Carey Lewis, to deed his twenty-five acre farm; then he purchased an additional 280 acres of cutover land while taking an option on an additional 160 acres.

On 1 November 1897, fifteen people gathered at the Lewis home to start a colony. They called it Equality and after Edward Bellamy's latest novel. Settlers came from all over the United States, including a contingent of sixty socialists from Dayton who stayed but briefly. By the summer of 1898, there were three hundred people in residence living in rude houses and struggling to establish a cooperative life. Most lived in two-apartment houses, with families occupying two rooms, while all the bachelors lived in the attic. A farm, a mill, a school, and a communal dining hall all came into existence quickly, and the members organized themselves politically. Their printing plant published a paper, *Industrial Freedom*, that ran news notes and articles by leading socialists and cooperators. By 1901, their weekly had become a monthly, and, in 1902, it ceased publication at all. As early as 1898, there were signs of trouble within the group, as Ed Pelton demanded that the brotherhood move its offices from Maine to Washington, give the colony more funds, and halt its plans to open a second colony at Edison until the first one was secure. The brotherhood and Equality did become one; however, the flow of new members ceased, and it struggled ahead until 1904. Pelton's death in 1901 stripped it of a tireless leader, and the character of the settlement was altered in 1905 with the arrival of Alexander Horr, a New York anarchist. With his arrival, the constitution was changed, and Equality became Freeland, after the utopian novel of Theodore Hertza. In February 1906, it went into receivership; at that point, the membership was less than forty. During its heyday, the colony could boast of an active social life, fishing boats, an eighteen-ton sloop, *Progress*, and its commitment to practical socialism. Harry Ault reported that on "winter evenings the big living room would be the scene of wonderful debates on aspects of the radical movement that would leave the listeners all at sea and the debaters physically exhausted. These debates took the place of similar discussions in various churches . . . which finally resulted in the disruptions of many congregations." It was "on little matters of difference" that the entire colony experiment was wrecked. Those differences were argued about in the General Assembly, and such issues as the appointment of a new postmaster almost "resulted in bloodshed."[147]

The work of the colony was carried out by departments (transportation, construction, printing, exchange, horticulture, mill, and timber) under a superintendent appointed by the General Assembly. The assembly ruled all and "debated everything from the question of whether Comrade Stiebritz was using too much charcoal gas with the bees, to how to nail boards on the new printing press or whether the timbers in the new barn were big enough."[148] One of the major sources of difficulty was the conflict over the General Headquarters, first located in Maine and then at Edison, Washington. Monies paid in by new members ($160 admission fee) plus membership dues from the brotherhood (ten cents a month) were administered by salaried officers of the brotherhood who had better accommodations than the colonists. Workers were paid in greenbacks based on a time/labor scheme, but, during the 1898 controversy, the organization and the newspaper were moved from Edison to Equality. An analysis of the application forms for Equality indicates that most applicants had read Bellamy. In response to the question, "What books on socialism have you read?" several answered by saying, "Nearly everything." The names of Bebel, Marx, Wilshire, and Gronlund appeared regularly. When he entered, Alexander Horr offered to donate 160 copies of *Freeland.*

Whereas Equality progressed from socialism to anarchy and changed its name to signify that shift, another Washington-based colony, Home, was always loudly and unabashedly anarchist. It was the most volatile of the Pacific Northwest colonies and had its origins in the desire of three anarchists from another group, Glennis, near Tacoma, to live in a freer community. Home, "neither socialistic nor communistic," was really an anarchist town whose residents leased their two-acre plots from the association. Whereas the single-tax philosophy distinguished Fairhope from its neighbors in Alabama, it was a belief in high individualism that set the colonists at Home apart from their neighbors. From 1898 to 1901, this small group (sixty members) lived in relative peace and quiet, publishing their newspaper, *Discontent,* and tending their gardens. It was in 1901, when the Pierce County Superior Court judged the Home printer guilty of distributing an obscene article and McKinley was assassinated by an anarchist, that problems developed.

From that point on, the Tacoma newspapers launched tirades against the colony that led to the formation of a crusade against them by a Loyal League of North America. The colony tried to defend itself by inviting members of the public to visit; however, the attacks continued, and, in September 1901, three members were arrested for mailing obscene literature. Thus, the stage was set for a show trial between the "free lovers" and the respectable citizens of Tacoma. The judge ruled in the colonists' defense, but it was a short-lived victory as a jury—in another case—found colonists guilty on a similar charge. The colony post office was closed in March, and that ended efforts to promote the cause of anarchism. *Discontent* folded and was replaced by the *Demonstrator,* but the thrust of the community had been blunted. It still welcomed distinguished visitors in its Liberty Hall and did become embroiled in various controversies in subsequent years, with Jay Fox taking the lead in such episodes. Its impact was less enduring than that of Fairhope, and it provided— for a short period—a haven for anarchists trying to form a community based on liberty and personal freedom.[149]

The driving force behind Home was liberty, that behind Equality was economic socialism, and that behind another late 1890s invention, the Christian Commonwealth, was a redefinition of the gospel that included social programs. Populism, like anarchism, had many faces, and one of them was the Social Gospel, an effort to put sociology in the service of Christ and to make Christianity a working religious ethic. The movement's name was taken from a periodical issued from the Christian Commonwealth in Georgia, the end result of several efforts at collective living in other parts of the United States. Two individuals figured prominently in its formation, Ralph Albertson and George Howard Gibson. Albertson's career will be examined in relation to his Massachusetts colony of a later date. Gibson's career was at the center of both populist and Social Gospel agitation in the 1890s.[150]

Gibson began his reform career in Omaha in the 1880s as owner/editor of a temperance paper, the *Rising Tide*, then moved to Lincoln in the 1890s, where he worked for the Farmer's Alliance and the People's Independent party, becoming editor of the *Alliance-Independent* in 1893. His populism was Christian, and he announced that belief to his reader: "I believe, religiously, morally and very definitely in the fatherhood of God and the brotherhood of man. . . . God's priceless abundant gifts must not be used for purposes of oppression and robbery. Society owes as much help to one individual as to another. Monopolists are in a word all these, kings, despots, robbers, slaveowners and they must with such be classed. In the degree that I love liberty I hate monopoly." The *Alliance-Independent* was run as a cooperative, and Gibson used the paper to advance populist causes and condemn individualism. Gibson's intellectual and social mentor was George Herron, whose applied Christianity complemented the work of Walter Rausenbusch in the Social Gospel movement. Under the influence of Herron, Gibson became, in late 1894, interested in cooperatives and, after attending the 1894 populist meeting in St. Louis, became even more radical in his views. Late in 1894, he turned away from politics to work for a "farming, stock raising, fruit-growing, manufacturing and love educating paradise."[151]

In April 1895, the Christian Corporation was chartered, claiming ninety-nine members, assets of $30,000, and 1,360 acres of land, including a 480-acre site near Lincoln. Gibson characterized it as a "democratic industrial equality [sic] communal organization and an association of Christian communes to equalize conditions and allows none to lack." Soon afterward, he sold his paper, the *Wealth Makers*, and led a group to Georgia to found the Christian Commonwealth Colony. Gibson was one of those socialists who believed that populism failed to encourage the generous cooperative spirit and had allowed individualism and profit taking to predominate within its ranks.[152] During 1895, a debate had occurred in a small socialist magazine, the *Kingdom*, over the merits of cooperative colonies. It had been set off by a letter from John Chipman urging those who "love Christ" to come "together and put all we have, little or much, into a common fund, buy a tract of cheap land and go to live there and work all good works in Christs name."[153] Ralph Albertson, recently forced from his Springfield, Ohio, pastorate and living at the Willard Cooperative Colony in Andrews, North Carolina, joined in the debate and urged readers to participate in a "Christ-filled" society by abandoning private property. Gibson wrote in January 1896 that the churches themselves were the greatest obstacle to Christian socialism.[154]

As the result of these exchanges, Gibson's Christian Corporation and the Willard Co-operative Colony merged to create the Christian Commonwealth Community.[155] In November 1896, Chipman made a down payment on a 931-acre cotton plantation thirteen miles east of Columbus, Georgia, after Albertson had visited several sites. The Willard group arrived first and was joined by the Nebraska contingent in two waves from December 1896 to August 1897. In February 1898, the first issue of the *Social Gospel* appeared, edited by Gibson. Members, both resident and nonresident, were asked to sign a covenant pledging themselves to follow "Christs law," to dispose of private property, to "withdraw myself from the selfish competitive strife and devote myself to the co-operative life and labor of a local Christian Commonwealth."[156] Although primarily an agricultural colony, the community did attempt (unsuccessfully) to establish a mercantile base with the manufacture of Turkish towels, but their quality was so inferior that few were sold. Another practical experiment involved the teaching of industrial subjects in the colony's normal school, yet the project never got very far, and the colonists had to content themselves with a primary school and an adult education program. The colony's principal financial success was its printing service, which constituted the main basis of financial support in the first two years.

The *Social Gospel* had a circulation of two thousand and considerable influence—So much so that, when Charles Hopkins came to characterize liberal Christian thought in the period, he took the magazine's name. Despite the brave beginnings and its distinguished name, life at the colony was hard and members' efforts unrewarded. Housing was always a problem, food was poor, and they were constantly begging for funds through the *Social Gospel*. Donations did come sometimes in the form of a press from the Vrooman brothers and looms for the Turkish towel venture, but there was never enough. When in May 1899 a group within the colony asked that a receiver be appointed, the dream began to disintegrate. Complaints then surfaced about the open-admissions policy, about inept management, and about favoritism. The court rejected the petition, but the damage was done. Shortly thereafter, a typhoid epidemic swept the colony and administered the final death blow. During this period, Albertson left, leaving Gibson to struggle with the mortgage and a demand from the Right Relationship League that their $2,000 loan be repaid. Gibson blamed the collapse on economics, others cited the lax admissions policy that admitted the lazy and shiftless, and others saw it as just a typical failed colony.

In the 1890s, political pragmatists had begun to turn away from the limitations imposed on them by the shifting currents of American radical politics and place themselves on what they thought was firmer ground. That firmer ground was the colony idea—an idea that proved both alluring and elusive. But for one group it proved to be secure as they took the principles of Henry George's single tax and put them into practice in a small Alabama town. "Fairhope was the creation of a dozen Iowa Populists," Paul Gaston has written, "made skeptical of electoral politics by their poor showing in the 1892 and 1893 Iowa elections." [157] Its leader was E. B. Gaston, who had studied Bellamy and Gronlund, joined the Populist party, and edited the *Farmers Tribune* in Iowa before turning toward the single tax philosophy.

"Cooperative individualism" was just one of a series of alternatives available to midwestern populists. As early as 1890, Gaston had drawn up a proposed constitution for a colony scheme and was in readiness when the Lasallean alternative—the ballot box—failed in Iowa. He had studied the histories of Kaweah and Topolobampo and believed that a greater emphasis on individual freedom than those groups had allowed would give a colony a chance at success.

It was at one of the meetings of the Des Moines Single Tax Club that Gaston put forward his plan for a colony run on Georgeist principles.

Four years after its founding, the colony outlined, in the pages of the *Fairhope Courier*, its views on cooperation: "Those who organized the Fairhope Association believed, and yet believe, that all of those who had previously attempted 'working models' of correctly organized communities had failed to recognize both the fundamental principles of human rights and the dominant forces of human nature, and that to their failure to recognize these and build their models upon them was due to their discouraging round of unbroken failure."[158]

The men who organized Fairhope were political pragmatists in the sense that their commitment to utopianism was muted by a conservative political philosophy operating within the radical tradition. They were distrustful of grand schemes, though it has to be said that, while Henry George's scheme was grand in theory, it was simple in operation. Eleven members of the Des Moines Single Tax Club met in late November and early December 1893 to discuss the colony idea. Their December meeting was held in the home of General J. B. Weaver, a leading populist and their candidate for the presidency in 1894. The *Fairhope Courier* carried a quote from Weaver on its masthead; presumably, the single taxers hoped that his imprimatur would attract other populists: "That which Nature provides is the Common Property of all God's children that which the individual creates belongs to the individual; that which the Community creates belongs to the Community."[159]

A committee was formed to seek out a site, and, after visiting seven states, it settled on 135 acres in Baldwin County, Alabama, on the eastern shore of Mobile Bay. Only twenty individuals (including eight children) made the trip from Des Moines to Fairhope. By early 1895, there were thirty-three members (not including wives of members), and interest had spread beyond Des Moines. The early members were drawn from populist supporters and single tax circles. In addition to E. B. Gaston and his wife, there were his niece and her husband and Mrs. Gaston's brother and his family. There were also former officials from single tax associations in Vancouver, British Columbia, and Indiana and trade unionists from the Hoosier state. The groups formal statement of intent and incorporation had that ring of high purpose and legalese so common to such documents: "Believing that the economic conditions under which we now live and labor are unnatural and unjust, in violation of natural rights, and at war with the nobler impulses of mankind . . . and believing that it is possible by intelligent association, under existing laws to free ourselves . . . to establish and conduct a model community, or colony, free from all forms of private monopoly. . . ."[160] Authority was vested in the membership, with rights of initiative and referendum guaranteed. After a brief rebellion by some newcomers, and after some hard economic times, the colony settled down to its modest Georgeist function: to ensure individual liberty and to collect land rent under Gaston's leadership.

There was considerable interest in the project in the socialist world, and the colony newspaper, the *Fairhope Courier*, tried to encourage membership by publishing letters to the editor, newsy notes about visitors, and an occasional social commentary. There was, of course, a steady stream of information about the single tax. A typical letter to the editor came from a cold Northern reformer interested in some southern sunshine and relief: "I have been living in Detroit for over sixteen years, having left England in 1881. Ever since I was old enough to vote and express my views I have been associated with reform movements; and like you and your friends, I have got disgusted with the populace who vote blindly against their own interests. I have worked and toiled for my bread. . . . I am getting older, and with it comes the dread of old age and nothing provided for it. I am good for twenty or thirty years more work; and being a single-taxer direct legislator and a Populist. . . . I am sick of these northern extremes, that are worse than Englands weather. . . . I feel I must change my climate. I suffer with the cold, and have a cough during the winter which I would not have in Fairhope."[161]

The site on Mobile Bay was warm and beautiful but on marginal agricultural land, and the colony's holdings were too small to dominate economically or politically the surrounding area. Colonists were expected to build their own homes, clear and fence their own land, and find their own employment. There were socialists among the early settlers who wanted community of property and possession to go beyond the limitations of a single tax, so there was constant debate about political questions. The community site, despite its limitations, continued to attract settlers, and by 1900 there were one hundred and by 1920, 849.[162] There was a continuing need to establish industries that could use the raw materials from the hinterland. Most of the colonists farmed their limited acreage, and some started small businesses or engaged in trades. All the while, Fairhope remained a vigorous and intellectual center. In 1904, it was incorporated under Alabama law as the Fairhope Single Tax Corporation, a landlord administering the single tax colony by collecting rent from the lessees. By 1908, the town of Fairhope was incorporated, and the village government served both colonist and noncolonist. Among the most interesting settlers in Fairhope was Marie Howland, the longtime reformer and author of *Papa's Own Girl*, who had come to the colony during the disintegration of the Topolobampo Colony. She worked on the *Fairhope Courier* and was responsible for starting the town library from her own book collection. She lived at Fairhope until her death in 1921.

After ten years, Fairhope was no longer a colony but a municipal center with a unique history, a unique population, and a unique system of taxation. Another unique element was added in 1907 with the establishment of the School of Organic Education led by Marietta Johnson. One of the first progressive schools in America, it emphasized a child-centered education based on the growth of the "whole person." By 1913, Johnson was able to open a second school at Greenwich, Connecticut. She was encouraged by the single taxers and the socialists in her efforts since they saw the organic school as a natural extension of their own colony idea. There were two complementary principles at work in the development of Fairhope as a unique town. First, there was a belief that community was possible without coercion if men and women could overcome the inequitable capitalist system based on land use. Second, there was a spirit of individualism that recognized the need for creative and fluid social arrangements. The existence of the organic school did much to enhance the flavor and quality of life and give to this small Southern town a distinct liberal atmosphere. Its liberality, however, did not extend to race relations, and the colony was never open to blacks, though in 1903 there was talk of organizing a separate black colony.[163]

Even though there was, by 1900, considerable evidence to suggest that cooperation, in the form of either stores or colonies, had not been a success in America, there were still those who urged its use. The organization of the Cooperative Association of America represented another effort by political pragmatists to hoist the banner of cooperation over the nation. The major figures behind this surge were Hiram Vrooman and Bradford Peck. The Vrooman family had been involved in varied phases of reform activity since before the Civil War and was particularly active in labor and cooperative circles in the 1880s. According to the family biographer, Ross Paulson, there were two things that the Vrooman brothers agreed on, "that social problems arise from selfishness in man and selfishness is caused by an unfavorable environment."[164] During the 1890s, they had signed the call to the St. Louis populist convention and had worked with Frank Parsons to implement his People's University. In 1902, Hiram Vrooman announced that the association was going to open two centers, one in Boston, the other in Lewiston, Maine, to promote cooperation. The Boston center would house the Co-Workers Fraternity or Workingmen's College. The Worker's Cooperative Association, also in Boston, was dedicated toward finding work for the unemployed. The Lewiston association was headed by Bradford Peck, whose novel, *The World a Department Store*, had caught the imagination of some socialists in the same way that Bellamy's works had. With Peck, however, they had a successful businessman who had over several years run a successful business enterprise along cooperative lines and who was now dedicated to spreading that idea.[165]

The Cooperative Association of America was essentially a "good" trust, as opposed to the prevalent inefficient and inhuman variety used by the Morgans and Rockefellers. One major aspect of the association was its plan to purchase large tracts of land and then sell the land in small-acreage farms and city lots to cooperators who would develop the area and benefit, as a group, from increased land values. The title to all land would be held by the association, but every worker would be given perpetual use of a home lot to build his house. At the center, there would be a townsite and, on that site, a workingmen's college. In an interview in *Arena*, George Washburn, owner of the Washburn Department Store and a reformer, said that the association was a "substitute for the chaotic struggle in the competitive shambles" and was at the same time "progressive yet conservative, venturesome yet substantial, radical yet rational, the brotherly yet business system of Cooperative Combination."[166] The supporters of the association were people like Henry D. Lloyd, Frank Parsons, N. O. Nelson, B. O. Flower, Charles Caryl, and Ralph Albertson.[167]

In 1906, the association tried to establish a cooperative colony in Oregon based on these principles after purchasing land in Florida and Massachusetts to settle individuals on. The colony never materialized. The Vroomans had been impressed in the 1890s by Topolobampo and its efforts to direct a large-scale resettlement project that guaranteed homes. By the time they started their association, Topolobampo had vanished, but that cloudy image had been supplanted by the fresher one set forth in Peck's *World a Department Store*. Following Bellamy, Peck had his narrator, Percy Brantford, fall asleep, awaking in twenty-five years to a world transformed. The transforming agency had been the Cooperative Association of America—a "Peoples Trust." The world is now a department store where all needs are met from a central source and where coupon books are used instead of money. At birth each child receives an income that steadily advances, and, by the time he is ready to marry, he has enough to have a family. In this new world, people labor for six hours a day and are part of a universal trust where they are the owners. The association, like the novel, promised that "men will live with a sense of security, each one doing his or her task with cheerfulness and joy. All will receive enough to enjoy the beautiful world in which God has placed them." [168]

Among the supporters of the association was Ralph Albertson, who had co-founded the Christian Commonwealth and who was, in 1906, the president and publisher of the *Twentieth Century Magazine*. Influenced by George, Bellamy, and Gladden, Albertson was educated at Oberlin and held pastorates in Ohio before resigning from a Springfield church because his Christian nonresistance principles made it impossible for him to support the workers. In 1895, he was a member of the Willard Colony; he then joined the Christian Commonwealth, where he edited the *Social Gospel*. After its failure, he worked at publishing in Boston and established an almost communal atmosphere at his home just outside Cambridge. [169]

The servant problem, the labor problem, the land problem, the money problem, the urban problem, the industrial problem—all these problems that reformers struggled with in the 1890s were addressed by the political pragmatists of the day. Willard, Nevins, Sharpe, Haskell, Lloyd, Albertson, Gaston, and Sinclair all believed that you could erect "good trusts" in opposition to the oliogarchies, that cooperation could engender a full political life based on obligation and mutual respect, that labor could regain its rightful place as a producer of wealth rather than face continuous exploitation, and that community was possible in a competitive world.

Their vision was surprisingly bright given the conditions of American life and the forces aligned against them. Those forces did not actively seek to crush them in the marketplace or deny them their day on collective farms and factories. They were allowed to pursue their destiny within a system that allowed new patterns to develop, new ideas to be tested in small commonwealths, and energy to find its own future. By and large, these colony efforts failed because they were unable to surmount the internal disputes that have plagued such efforts since Robert Owen, and they failed to offer a better material life for laborers.

4 "New Movements": Missions or Retreats?

> The colonies of Free Comrades are to be regarded as nuclei of
> the New Life. They are to be free, peaceful, self-sufficient little
> worlds, to illustrate what the whole world will be when free. As
> they increase in number and contiguity they need not be so self-
> sufficient, but can specialize function and exchange products to
> increase economy. Aside from their agreement in the great prin-
> ciples, the different groups may have exceedingly different
> ideals, a common sympathy with which will unite the majority
> of the members, tho individual variation be never denied—thus
> one Colony will be artistic, another scientific, another religious;
> one varietist, another monogamic, another celibate. It does not
> matter, if all are free and kind."
>
> *Free Comrade* 2, no. 1 (March 1901)

The thirteenth-century Hohenstaufen emperor Frederick II reportedly asked the court astrologer, Michael the Scot, a simple
question, but one that was fraught with meaning for the medie-
val mind. Frederick wanted to know, "Where was Paradise?"
Was it in Africa, in Asia, or in some remote island still to be
explored? Would it be like the original Eden or be filled with
new wonders and delights as yet untasted? Melvin Lasky, in
Utopia and Revolution, notes that a "historical observer may
be tempted to think that the European mind was here on the
great borderline between old nostalgia and new hope, between
a golden restoration and a revolution of the new."[1] Utopian
communities—as practical manifestations of the utopian
wish—often sit on that borderline between restoration and revolution and waver between the pull of the past, the lure of the
peaceful garden, and the promises of change and revolution.

Some have a mission to the world since they see it as a
place flawed by men or events, and they seek to change it by
action or example. Some communities organize themselves
around a core set of beliefs and begin to recruit a body of believers. The political pragmatists, for example, rallied to the
cry of "socialism"—usually write large—and constructed an
oppositional ideology to capitalism. For the cooperative colo-

nizers, the call centered on the issue of "moral cooperation" and the necessity for concerted action to cope with a destructive and rapidly shifting social order. Charismatic and perfectionist groups heard a trumpet ring out the tune of "Redemption Now!" and they gathered to purify themselves and the world.

These small communities all represented strategies for reform that would lead to a more general reformation of the society. John L. Thomas quotes H. D. Lloyd on this point: "Cooperation can be made to succeed . . . only by uniting small groups of men engaged in something that brings them together into personal daily contact, so that they know each other and each knows what the other is doing."[2] These organic communities could, by example and action, act as a weight against a world that grew less personal with each passing decade. Yet there was an essential question that they all faced in common. Should they engaged with the world and present an aggressive program for action and emulation, or should they retreat and form a perfected enclave of believers who would ensure the survival of those values for a future generation?

In order to start such communities, men and women had to journey (both literally and symbolically), propose an agenda that could rally supporters, and provide both more freedom and more security than the world offered. A core issue for many groups in this period was the "family," its current status and prospects. Certain groups, like the Shakers and Oneida, had offered radical solutions; others, like the North American Phalanx, had adopted policies that tried to modify it and limit its destructive tendencies. The issue of whether to abolish the family or to acknowledge its role within a community always sparked a debate in the formation of any group. In addition, such debates focused discussion on the allied issues of women and children. One group discussed earlier, the Women's Commonwealth of Belton, Texas, and later Washington, D.C., faced some of these questions; however, its primary concerns were spiritual rather than social.

Another major issue centered on the contemporary spiritual character of American life and the emergence of new religious traditions and practices. Spiritualism had, since the 1850s, been a growing force in American life. Thomas Lake Harris, for one, operated within the tradition for a time until he was able to construct his own religion based on a redefined social, sexual, and spiritual family. In another colony, Shalam, the issues of family and spirituality came together in an unique experiment. In the free-love colony of Spirit Fruit, one sees many of these late nineteenth-century social issues emerge, and, in the Straight Edge Society, we see the problems facing the family, religion, and the new industrial order given a Progressive solution.

A third major issue throughout the late nineteenth century, and one that cooperative leaders from Albert Brisbane to Albert Kimsey Owen focused on, was the evils generated by an urban society. The twin evils of industrialization and urbanization were realities that few reformers could ignore. As the century wore on, they were increasingly cited as the source of man's misery, his selfish individualism, and his unhappiness. For most communal and utopian reformers, the antidote to that sickly condition was in pastoral retreat rather than confrontation, removal to a safe place rather than engagement with the devil. Many hoped to create industrial villages where a community of workers could share in the wealth of their productive labor and participate in a varied and active social life. It was possible to flee from the grog shops, from the poverty and despair, and create within the new colony a cleaner and more humane industrial order that had within it the culture, the excitement, and the variety of town life. By the end of the century, however, a few communal and cooperative groups squarely confronted the urban and industrial future and became urban missionaries. They had, of course, the settlement house ideal, the Social Gospel, and the growing Progressive spirit to spur them on to action. The Straight Edge Society and the Francisco Ferrer movement were both (in their initial phases) urban oriented but later sought retreat in the countryside for their members.

During the 1870s, labor had not responded to the communal call. It was an alternative that simply could not and did not compete with the promises and potential of either individual effort or collective power in the form of unionism. Although labor failed to indicate any interest in communes, there was a steady interest in a kind of anarchospiritualism that emphasized individualism and, sometimes, free love. Fourierism had always appealed to such individuals, though its "scientific" character often failed to spark an interest among deeply spiritual seekers. One community founded in the mid-1870s and the careers of two communards indicate this persistent interest in communal living that enhanced high individualism and spiritualism. The community was Dawn Valcour located on an island in Lake Champlain. It was the brainchild of John Wilcox, of Chicago who advertised in *Woodhull and Claflin's Weekly* and other journals seeking members for his "Head Center of Advanced Spiritualism and Free Love."

Wilcox's request was responded to by Orrin Shippman of Colchester, Vermont, who offered him eight hundred acres on Dawn Valcour Island plus a nursery on the Vermont side of the lake in return
for payment of his debts (some $9,000) and $26,000 for land reportedly worth $100,000. In August 1874, twelve individuals came to
the island. A few left immediately, and the remaining core group not
only faced the future with diminished numbers but was surrounded
by a hostile local population. The "Head Center" members decided
to call a meeting to explain their philosophy and recruit new members, if possible. In speeches by Wilcox and Hannah White, the colony's free-love intentions were made clear: "We have come among
you to demonstrate the fact that any evil that afflicts humanity today
is the result of false and underlying conditions, mainly attributable
to the unjust distribution of wealth, and the cruelties perpetuated
under the hell-begotten phase of the present marriage system."[3]

In a series of letters to the Plattsburgh *Republic,* Hannah White
elaborated on those views. She said that families should have rooms
in a common house, be served their meals restaurant style, have a
child-care center at their disposal, and work only three days a week
with the same wage rate for all employment, skilled or unskilled.
All community decisions would be made by vote, with everyone
over the age of fifteen having a vote. The Fourierist ideal was obviously at work, as was free love. Social freedom, according to
White, was the "right of each to regulate their own sexual regulations as they please."[4]

The community was never able to establish a real foothold, in
part because Shippman had deceived the emigrants about the extent
of his indebtedness and the fact that the land did not have a clear
title. In their first "Letter of Appeal," the community had said that it
was erecting a "*Commodious House*" for forty or fifty members and,
in their second appeal, revealed that five hundred "faithful liberal-
ists" had written to them. In November 1875, the remaining colonists left for New York City "in hopes of starting all over again."[5] It
must have been a bitter experience, particularly since they had announced so boldly in January 1875 that they were fleeing the city:
"We have virtually fled from Sodom." To Sodom they returned after
nine months in the North Country. What makes the Dawn Valcour
group noteworthy is not their failure but the continuance of the
Fourierist dream well after what historians believe to be the "Fourierist period." What one finds in many of these communities is an
intense desire to mix individualism with another social program,
whether it be free love, associative labor, or diversified industries, as

with Dawn Valcour. The Fourierist ideal of attractive labor, of the boarding-house community, of the promise of an independent life, was still a powerful draw for those interested in community.

Spiritualism, social reform, and a concern for the plight of urban children all came together in a community in the West. It was the result of a combination of the charismatic and perfectionist traditions, plus a quarter of a million dollars. The 1884 colony, Shalam, under the leadership of John B. Newbrough and with the financial support of Andrew Howland, was both mission and retreat. The community grew out of the social concerns of some spiritualists and Newbrough's mystical qualities. A dentist, Newbrough had a varied career that included authorship of a travel romance, *The Lady of the West, or the Gold Seekers.* In it, he wrote about his travels to California and attacked suffragettes and abolitionists.[6] Later, he published *A Catechism of Human Teeth* (1869) and *Nitrous Oxide Gas* (n.d.), the second a defense of his own use of nitrous oxide that had resulted in the death of a patient.[7] During the early 1860s, he was on the board of the New York Spiritualist Society and, for a short time, was a member of the Domain, a spiritualist community at Jamestown, New York.[8] In 1882, he published, with Elizabeth Rowell Thompson's help, the *Oashpe,* written "automatically" under spirit influences and in a language of its own, "Paneric." The *Oashpe* traces the history of man on earth through twenty-four cycles and seventy-three-thousand years of history.[9]

His mystical writings found a group of readers, and two communal societies were based on his vision and the care of orphaned children. The idea of a "Cooperative Orphanage" had been set forth by Dr. Rutherford, who wrote of the need to provide a home for the orphans of cooperators. It would enable the cooperators to put their principles into action, serve as an altruistic model for the nation, and provide a means to understand the ways of training youths. Rutherford outlined a plan of education for the orphans up to age fourteen and noted that "on leaving the orphanage at that age [the children] would have a better preliminary scientific training than nine-tenths of the foremen in our largest manufactures receive." This elite corps ("a phalanx of brave spirits led by capacity, integrity and intelligence") would go into industry, where they would "sweeten the relations between labor and capitol."[10]

This grandiose vision was coupled with another practical suggestion for educating poor children set forth by Elizabeth Thompson in her 1873 book *Kindergarten Homes:* "The present public schools are of no advantage to the class that ultimately fills the prisons and poor houses. These people have no avenue open to them to rise in virtue and industry. Everything is against them. And since we cannot reform the grown up people let us begin with the little ones."[11] Thompson's support for the Chicago-Colorado and the Thompson Colony in Kansas came out her lifelong belief that the cities of the United States were breeding places for crime and social corruption. Concerned about the problem of drink, she was motivated to support projects in Kansas, a state that enforced prohibition.

Her kindergarten homes were intended to be places where children would flourish under the benevolent rule of house parents. Such homes would have verandas that let in fresh air and ample space for children to play within because "children should not be put in straight-jackets or made to stay in little shut up corners, like the present asylums." Children would be taught practical skills such as housekeeping and cooking and then progress to gain other skills like carpentry, blacksmithing, weaving, and spinning. These skills encouraged self-sufficiency and industry: "It is probable that a man could build up a Kindergarten home, with hundreds of children, which he could make [sic] it a very profitable institution, after the children were ten to fifteen years of age."[12]

Her correspondence with Loring Moody, director of the Institute of Heredity, was published in 1882 under the title *Heredity*. She wrote, "If people eat, drink and breathe sin, disease and damnation they must propagate and spread disease and damnation over the face of the earth."[13] She believed that, if experiments were made with children instead of adults, the results would be better. Orphan and castaway children could be "molded into the nucleus for a higher mode of life. In the cities they are tempted by whiskey, tobacco, extravagance, profanity, crime, idleness and 'uncertain associates.'" She drew little comfort from the previous experiments by famous communal groups: "Their [Shakers, Rappites, Fourierists, etc.] experience has proved them entirely incompetent to reach the masses. While they get one convert to join them, there are born into the world hundreds of little ones with no more opening, but crime and poverty before them."[14] It was her association with a dentist turned spiritualist, John Newbrough, that made her theories the basis for a remarkable "Children's Colony" in New Mexico.

John Ballou Newbrough was born on the Ohio frontier at Mohicanville, near Wooster, in 1827 to a farm couple recently moved into the Miami Valley from Virginia. When he was seventeen, he left his father's farm for Cleveland, where he apprenticed to a dentist and at the same time pursued a medical career at Cleveland Medical College. His first job after graduation was at the Ohio State Insane Asylum, where he practiced his newly learned arts. Whether he worked as a doctor or a dentist is unknown, but the asylum did not hold him for long. In 1849, he journeyed overland to California in search of gold. The gold fields failing him, he then traveled to Australia with a gold party and struck a claim worth $25,000.

After making his fortune, Newbrough circled the globe before settling first in Cincinnati and then in Dayton in 1855 to practice dentistry. From 1853 until 1855, he worked on a romantic novel growing out of his California experience. *The Lady of the West, or the Gold Seekers* was published in 1855 "for the purpose of social reform" and attacked nativism and discrimination against Chinese laborers while at the same time taking a dim view of certain reformers, particularly suffragettes and abolitionists. Newbrough championed the creation of a true democracy based on free and open mingling of the world's races. There is no hint of support of spiritualism or cooperation in the novel, though Newbrough must have been influenced by the spirit rallies in the Miami Valley in the early 1850s.

Cincinnati was an active spiritualist center, with reports of spirit manifestations as early as 1845. The Fox sisters had made a triumphant visit there in 1851. Emma Hardinage, in her *Modern American Spiritualism*, commented that "spiritualism is a fixed fact in Cincinnati and warm hearts and willing hands are there, just as zealous in its belief as ever."[15] Nahum Koons's feats of automatic writing in 1853 in Athens, Ohio, received wide attention, and it seems reasonable to conjecture that Newbrough's first contact with spiritualism may have come during his stay in Dayton and Cincinnati, 1853–57.

From 1857 until 1881, Newbrough's career took a number of detours before he sat down at a Scholes typewriter and produced an "automatically" written bible for the new age, the *Oashpe*. The first detour took him to Scotland, where he married Rachel Turnbull, the sister of a gold-field partner. After his marriage in 1857, he started a mercantile firm in Philadelphia, only to return to dentistry in New York, where he lived from 1859 until the move West in 1884. During the 1860s, he was active in the spiritualist movement in New York, serving on the board of the New York Spiritualist Society and at one point becoming a member of the Domain, a spiritualist community in Jamestown, New York.

Spiritualism was torn apart in the 1860s by disputes between two factions. The philosophical spiritualists saw the movement as part of a larger pattern of ethical and moral development that encompassed humanitarian and reformist measures. Andrew Jackson Davis, the "Poughkeepsie Seer" and driving force behind American spiritualism in the 1850s and 1860s, led some spiritualists in their attempts to prevent the "phenomena" spiritualists from dominating the scene. The phenomena spiritualists emphasized séances, mediumship, and psychic manifestations. They were less concerned with moral or social reform and tended to attract the extravagant members of this volatile movement.[16]

Davis saw spiritualism as a positive force moving society in progressive ways and served as the spokesman for such views at reform conventions. In 1863, he founded the Children's Progressive Lyceum and the Moral Police Fraternity as vehicles for spiritualist reform. The lyceum spoke to the needs of spiritualists to educate their own children outside Sunday Schools that stressed conventional Christian precepts. The Children's Progressive Lyceum would not only develop sound minds and sound bodies but aid in the "progressive unfolding of the social and divine affections by harmonious methods."[17] The Moral Police Fraternity was a social service agency made up of spiritualists who wanted to aid the destitute of New York. Davis hoped that the fraternity could secure a home near New York City for indigent mothers and their children; however, the plan never materialized, and the fraternity lapsed. What both organizations did suggest was that spiritualists were actively concerned about the plight of children and that they were actively working toward creating a harmonious and poverty-free society.

In founding Shalam, Newbrough brought together both branches of the spiritualist movement. First, he emphasized the community as a special place for children, and second, the community grew out of the ultimate in phenomenal practice, automatic writing. Newbrough first attracted attention and a small corps of disciples with the publication of the *Oashpe* in 1882. It took him some fifty weeks to put the book together, though he played no active part in its composition. All the illustrations and text came through Newbrough, as medium, from some higher power. According to Newbrough, "One morning the light struck both hands on the back and they went for the typewriter, for fifteen minutes, very vigorously. . . . One morning I looked out the window and beheld that the line of light that rested on my hands extending [sic] heavenward like a telegraph wire toward the sky."[18]

The title *Oashpe* means that the book is a record of heaven and earth. It traces the history of man on earth back some seventy-three-thousand years and through twenty-four "arcs," or cycles of history.

The first race on earth took place in "Wan's Arc," and its history—the story of Adam—has been preserved in myth, folklore, and legend. Throughout the text are elements of Hinduism, Buddhism, and Christianity that reflect the true history of the arc. For example, there was a dark age in "Arbrookus Arc" (twenty-eight-thousand years ago), which was followed by the great deluge during "Noe's Arc." Several individuals escaped this great cataclysm that had sunk the island of Pan (the Atlantis of the Pacific). These individuals were scattered throughout the earth and founded the various races. They then began a cycle of birth, growth, and decay that can be found in every subsequent arc. Because this cycle occurs in each arc, the *Oashpe* has great prophetic powers—if read correctly. To the unbeliever, the *Oashpe* is incomprehensible because it is full of neologisms (Paneric words) and has little obvious coherence, but, to Newbrough's followers, it charted the way to the good, the society based on a children's commonwealth.

Elizabeth Thompson supported the publication of *Oashpe* with a $1,000 gift. Some of her other philanthropic efforts included support for research into yellow fever and aid to the American Association for the Advancement of Science. Thompson believed sufficiently in Newbrough's message to underwrite the cost of three thousand copies. A small group of enthusiasts then decided to establish a colony in Woodside, New Jersey, in late 1882, but the project did not prosper. A convention in New York City in November 1883 provided a second catalyst for the communal venture. Delegates from eleven states to the Faithist Lodge of Oashpe met for three days at Utah Hall in New York "to commence work on a new foundation." According to the *New York Times* report of the convention, "they would not begin with adults but with children, whom they would teach to regard virtue and industry as the strongest virtues of benevolence." [19]

The genesis of the colonization scheme found in certain passages in the *Oashpe* that emphasized the unique contributions that the young would play in the future society: "The young are your angels given to you by the creator and ye are their gods. Consider ye, then, what kind of Kingdom ye raise up. Better it is to labor with a child from infancy and then to maturity to teach it aright than to strive with a score conceited adults and fail to redeem." [20] A colonization committee was formed at the convention and a gathering-in home established at Pearl River, New York. An organization called the Tae of Faithists was formed, with Newbrough as "C'Chief" and Dr. H. S. Tanner as secretary. Tanner was a practicing physician and a famous "faster" who, in 1881, fasted for twenty-nine days in order to break the record of the Brooklyn faster, Mollie Fancher. There were twenty others involved in the Pearl River community, where members followed a vegetarian regime and waited for the establishment of a permanent colony.

At this point, Andrew Howland became interested in the Faithist communal project. Howland was a member of a distinguished New England family and heir to a vast whaling fortune. A wool broker by profession, he came into contact with Newbrough in the 1870s and made his fortune available for the scheme. Newbrough brought about $25,000 to the project, but it was Howland who poured over a half million dollars into Dona Ana County, New Mexico, and Shalam from 1884 till 1901.

In early 1884, Newbrough and Howland set out to find an appropriate site for the colony while the others waited at Pearl River. They traveled to New Mexico and selected 1,490 acres in Dona Ana County within sight of the Rio Grande, choosing what they thought was a fertile tract of land because they saw abundant cottonwood trees. Unfortunately, they were ignorant of the flood plains that nourished these trees and of the arid conditions in the Mesilla Valley. It was a land of dust and flash floods rather than milk and honey. By all accounts, the first winter was hard, and it seems doubtful that they would have survived without Howland's immense wealth. He imported foodstuffs by the trainload when conditions proved too hard for the first contingent.

Newbrough set forth the principles on which Shalam functioned:

> There is no intention of forming here a community of adults. This is not a work of charity for either children or adults. This is no place for adults, however spiritual they may consider themselves, or however, "advanced" they may be, or however high their aspirations, and yet are too lazy to work.
>
> Here an attempt is being made "to found on earth a place (like which there shall be many in time to come) where will rest perpetually a system that will provide a new race, where poverty and crime and helplessness cannot enter" and to do this by means of the young and not with adults. Gathering up in the world orphan babies and castaway infants and foundlings.
>
> And they shall grow up of all nationalities and races, being raised from infancy to live communally, and to eat not fish nor flesh of any creature alive, but to nourish and

build up their corporeal and spiritual bodies upon a pure diet.[21]

How to get from such a set of principles to the creation of a viable utopian community would tax the capacities of a Solomon, yet the spiritualists headed by Newbrough believed that the impossible was possible. During the first winter, there were a few deaths; however, the communists survived and began constructing two-room adobe houses before beginning work on the forty-two-room central home, the Fraternum. A letter from Shalam in 1885 indicated that they felt sure of their mission and confident of its success: "There is plenty more land here to be bought cheap. So we feel there is plenty of room here for a community here of two or three thousand people. We design planting about fifty acres in grape vines, for the raisin grape. Also a large number of apple, peach, pear and other kinds of fruit. . . . Yes, we are strictly herbivorous, or vegetarians, and we enjoy our diet. We eat but two meals a day, and like the plan. We work in groups, and frequently change off, so that no part can be severe on any body. But you must not lose sight of the fact that ours is a community not for ourselves but for the children we are going to raise."[22]

The children were recruited in the most remarkable fashion. They were "gathered-up" from foundling homes, donated by indigent mothers, handed over by police sergeants, and left in Faithist depositories. During the 1880s, Newbrough and his wife traveled to San Francisco, Kansas City, New Orleans, and Chicago in search of children for Shalam. In an interview with the *San Francisco Chronicle*, Newbrough made no secret about his mission: "I have come to San Francisco," said he, "to gather any infants I can find, and will take them back to New Mexico with me. I do not, of course, expect parents to give up their children to me though there will doubtless be some who will go with me to grow up in our colony. Previous to coming to San Francisco I was in New Orleans, and there I gathered six young babies and took them to Shalem [sic]."[23]

The Newbroughs lived in New Orleans for a full year after founding Shalam and built a receiving home for infants; it consisted of a receiving room that contained a cradle and a perpetual light over an inviting sign: "Any Babies Welcome, No Questions Asked." In addition, there were children taken from the Lily Dale spiritualist camp and others who came with members. All in all, the Newbroughs collected about fifty children, nearly all under two years of age. On their arrival, the children were given white linen garments, placed on a nourishing vegetarian diet, and given "Oashpean" names like Havrolo, Nin'ya, Thale, Pathodices, and Dis. They were, by every standard of their age, pampered and treated with great loving care. In 1890, a separate Children's House was constructed containing twenty rooms and a special bathing area that had ten infant's tubs. Visitors to Shalam always commented favorably on the health, vitality, and interracial composition of the children's colony since there were Chinese, Caucasian, and black children in this new age community.

From the outset, the community suffered from the naïveté of its founders and the incredible harshness of the land. To be sure, there were internal disputes and the inevitable court case brought by a disgruntled member, yet the community grew, held séances, and gathered children. A number of substantial buildings were constructed utilizing Mexican labor and the Howland fortune. The Fraternum housed adults and children, and a conical building, the Temple of Tae, served as a spiritualist church. Another building, the Studio, was where Newbrough withdrew to meditate and paint his remarkable canvases. The paintings were, like the *Oashpe*, done automatically. A photograph remains of a portion of one of the paintings, *Three Worlds*, suggesting something of the artist's abilities. There were numerous other paintings similar to *Three Worlds*; however, descendants of the Newbrough family found them offensive and put them to the torch.

Newbrough's contemporaries at Shalam considered him a prophet and a mystic who was driven by a divine spark and possessed with a remarkable vision. On 22 April 1891, the colony's fortunes took a rather abrupt turn when John Ballou Newbrough died of influenza. At the time of his death, Shalam consisted of the Fraternum, the newly constructed Children's Home, and a few out buildings, including the church and the studio. Just prior to his death, Newbrough had added another chapter to the *Oashpe*, and it fell to Andrew Howland to carry out that final chapter. In 1889, Newbrough had begun writing the "Book of Gratyius," and the message that came through was clear. There was a class of individuals who fell somewhere between the people of the world and the "Kosmon" people who inhabited Shalam. These were the "Leviticans," and they should be encouraged to come to Shalam and found another type of colony "for adults, single and married, with their own children, and especially such as desired to live in isolated homes and to work and manage in their own way."[24]

The second colony, Levitica, was situated a half mile from

Shalam on 365 acres surveyed into one-acre lots. Howland constructed twenty two-room houses at a cost of $2,000 each in order to make the rural, cooperative life "open for them [young men and women] in the country, for a higher and holier development. And the cares and fears of making a living shall pass away from them. Unto all such, here are homes without money and without price. Come, O ye with Faith in Jehovih, and inherit them."[25] And they came by trainloads from Kansas City and Denver to squat at Levitica and hasten Andrew Howland into bankruptcy. After two years, Levitica ceased to be an experiment for adults as Howland sent some twenty families back north and admitted that the newcomers had been a lazy bunch.

Improvements continued at Shalam despite the Levitica failure as Howland transformed the 1,490 acres into a garden by a massive irrigation effort. Furthermore, he imported a herd of Guernseys from New York, built an elaborate chicken farm, and experimented in agronomy. As a result, the community became a showplace for scientific farming; it was too much and too soon for the Mesilla Valley, which did not see the possibilities of such schemes until the Elephant Butte Dam was constructed in 1933. In addition, Howland started a cooperative store for the large Mexican labor force that he employed when it became obvious that they were being cheated by local merchants.

All the schemes were to no avail. The numerous projects and the lack of markets for produce and cattle proved too much of a strain for even Howland's wealth. By 1900, it was evident that Shalam had overextended itself. The community had been forced by finances to send the children to local schools, and there were only a handful of Faithists still working for the community. The Howlands (he had married the former Mrs. Newbrough in 1893) petitioned the Las Cruces court to restore the property to him and agree to place the children in proper homes. There were twenty-five children, all under fourteen years of age. Arrangements were made with private homes, an orphanage in Denver, and the Buckner Home in Dallas to take the children. The Howlands remained at Shalam until 1907, when the doors were locked and never opened again. They lived in California for a short time and then made a permanent home in El Paso, Texas, where he was looked on as a "colorful" figure until his death in 1917.

Little remains of Shalam except in the minds and hearts of contemporary Kosmons, who sit and wait in California, Arkansas, Indiana, and Colorado for the true gathering-in colony to appear. Since 1901, the *Oashpe* has had a curious career on the cosmic underground and in spiritualist circles.

An obscure publication based in Santa Cruz, California, the *Buddhist Ray* ("Devoted to Buddhism in General and to the Buddhism in Swedenborg in Particular"), commented in 1890 that there were movements in the United States that failed to display that "reverence for established formulae, laws and orders" that seemed to be a "virtue, or weakness with all our citizens." Singled out for praise by the *Buddhist Ray* were "cooperation, the single tax, nationalism, the Theosophical Society, anarchism, Faithism."[26] This motley assortment of ideas, tendencies, associations of individuals, and cults all came under the heading "New Movements." By 1900, single tax, as a political force, had died with Henry George, sustaining itself only at Fairhope; Nationalism had spent itself as a movement, yet the memory of *Looking Backward* still caused Bellamy's readers to look for utopia; Faithism was still functioning at Shalam in New Mexico; and anarchism and Theosophy were still to have their day and their colonies. As for cooperation, it was still alive and surviving, not as a separate entity, not as a social movement (though efforts were still underway to make that a reality), but as an alternative solution seized by both religious and secular men and women intent on constructing their own formulae, their own laws, their own order.

Although the decade of the 1890s was dominated by political pragmatists in search of some solid ground for their socialist dreams, there was a continuing interest in groups promising another and more spiritual road to salvation. In the same year that the Burley Colony began, Point Loma was opened by the Theosophists in California. In 1899, a small group of spiritualists (some called them anarchists, others free lovers) founded a colony in Ohio based on sexual liberation and social freedom.[27] They were to be driven out of Ohio just as the Nicholses had been fifty years earlier, but they took up residence north of Chicago rather than leave the country. During the 1890s, a remarkable colony, the Holy Ghost and Us, transformed a hill in Maine into a holy spot and sought to convert the world by example and prayer. All these groups represented older traditions of association and older patterns of spirituality that attached themselves to contemporary issues and personalities.

Walt Whitman, in the *Song of Myself*, struck the note that characterized the position taken by the founder of the Spirit Fruit Society, Jacob Beilhart:

Through me forbidden voices
Voices of sexes and lusts,
Voices veiled and I remove the veil
Voices indecent, by me clarified and transfigured.

The story of Spirit Fruit is largely the story of Jacob Beilhart, whose leadership led the experiment from its origins to its conclusion. Through Beilhart's life, one can see the shifting patterns of American religious life, the nature of his charismatic leadership that brought together a millionaire and a labor leader, and the anarchism behind his religiosity.[28]

Born on 4 March 1867 on a farm in Columbiana County, Ohio, Jacob Beilhart grew up in a mixed religious environment. His father belonged to the German Lutheran church while his mother adhered to the Mennonite faith. The ten Beilhart children, however, were christened and confirmed as Lutherans.[29] Reflecting in 1903, Jacob wrote, "Religion was always a very sacred thing to me." Lacking much formal schooling during his youth ("Work was about all I received as an education"), he left the farm when he was seventeen to labor in a brother-in-law's harness shop in southern Ohio. When the relative moved to Kansas a year later, Beilhart accompanied him. Apparently not much interested in the harness trade, Beilhart became a sheepherder shortly before his twentieth birthday. The Kansas family for whom he worked were Seventh-day Adventists: "They read the Bible to me and I would see that I had not read it right before; and on many doctrinal points . . . I could see that they were right in their beliefs." He quickly embraced the new faith: "I accepted their doctrine in its entirety."[30]

Typical of religious converts, Jacob Beilhart dedicated himself to the church. In time, he abandoned the farm to serve the Adventists full time. He initially disseminated their denominational literature in western Kansas but subsequently moved to Colorado. As he later recalled, "I broke all the records of all the canvasses which they ever had selling the books—thirty orders in a day being the highest mark, while I took fifty." After a winter term at an Adventist college at Healdsburg, California, Beilhart embarked on a preaching career, first in Ohio and then in Kansas. He excelled in his new vocation, yet he terminated it. "Two years of preaching alternately with another man, meeting every evening, and then one season alone," he wrote, "brot [sic] me to the time when the 'Brethren' decided that I should go South." Jacob refused. "I had decided that I would preach no more until I could do something besides talk."[31]

A burning desire to help the sick led him to enroll in a nursing program at the Seventh-Day Adventist sanitarium in Battle Creek, Michigan. Tired of preaching, he found his new work meaningful. After completing the course of study, which emphasized natural and rational health remedies, Beilhart remained at the sanitarium; in fact, he became a staff nurse associated directly with the institution's founder, Dr. John Harvey Kellogg, one of the nation's leading health propagandists and the originator of flaked cereals.[32] While employed by the Battle Creek Sanitarium, Beilhart underwent another religious transformation, one that led him to sever his ties with the Adventists. Continual Bible study convinced him that the sick could be made better, even cured, through prayer rather than diet. In an autobiographical sketch, he related the incident that established his reputation as a faith-healer:

> One day I was called to see a sick girl who had heard me tell of my faith in healing by prayer. She had typhoid fever and was very sick. Doctors had but little hope for her. I went to see her, and she asked me to pray for her to be healed. This I did, annointing her after the instructions of James, 5:14. She was healed immediately; the temperature going from 104 1/2 to about normal in a few minutes. She got up and dressed, drank milk, and retired for the night in about an hour.[33]

Beilhart's life changed. His continued faith-healing activities and his rejection of the Adventists' strictly vegetarian diet ("My stomach would not digest the grains and vegetables") prompted sanitarium officials to ask for his resignation. Shortly before he left, Beilhart had been nursing C. W. Post, later the wealthy food manufacturer but then operator of Battle Creek's La Vita Inn, an institution for healing by the practice of mental suggestion. Beilhart claimed that it was Post who introduced him to the healing potentials of Christian Science. Yet subsequent instruction in this faith left him dissatisfied. After Christian Science, he studied Divine Science, Spiritualism, and Theosophy, but none kept his interest. "I soon settled down to this," he remembered later; "all these theories are very nice, but it is hard work to run the universe when you know as little about it as any of these folks seem to know who claim to be teachers."[34]

While groping for the true religious perspective, Jacob Beilhart remained in Battle Creek. He and his wife, Loruma, whom he married in 1893, had two children, Harry, born the next year, and Edith, who came nineteen months later. Harness making and odd jobs sustained the household.[35] By the late 1890s, Beilhart was less interested in his family and even more preoccupied with religion. Calling his faith the "Universal Life," he developed a philosophy that blended aspects of the various religions that he had encountered, particularly Christian Science. He repeatedly argued, for instance, that "jealousy, doubt, and fear of losing love, are the causes of more disease than all the healers can ever cure." Yet, unlike disciples of Mary Baker Eddy, he blasted materialism. Private property should not be held. "Oh! Do you not know the joy of willingly giving up all that self holds dear?" Rejection of possessions, according to Beilhart, became one means of achieving the "Fruit of the Universal Spirit."[36]

At a time of intense national political activism, Beilhart remained apolitical. A true religious perspective and not a particular political scheme was the secret to happiness: "You may speak of socialism; you may speak of single tax or no tax at all; you may depend on good law makers and good executors to carry out those laws; you may have all material things, the necessities of life, in common. All these thing will not give you peace."[37]

Resembling other religious zealots, who likewise had messages to share, Jacob Beilhart decided to launch an intentional colony in 1899. By "living in community" he also hoped to attract attention to his new-found positive faith. The colony "is practically our work shop, our demonstrating station."[38] Between 1899 and 1907, Beilhart and his small band wrote, printed, and distributed two periodicals, *Spirit Fruit* and *Spirit's Voice*.

Beilhart selected a colony site on the outskirts of Lisbon, Ohio, the seat of Columbiana County. As he described it in the June 1899 issue of the *Spirit Fruit*, "The Home . . . contains five acres of good ground with plenty of fruit trees, a fine spring of water, and a large fifteen room brick house, in need of repairs."[39] Why he picked this particular location is not clear. That it was in the immediate vicinity of his boyhood home is a probable explanation. Also, the Columbiana County area boasted a sizable population of spiritualists, individuals who might find his teachings appealing. The site, moreover, was inexpensive; it was accessible to both steam and electric interurban railways; and the climate was temperate.[40]

Spirit Fruit drew few to its communistic fold. The dozen or so residents came mostly from outside Ohio, particularly Chicago, a city where Beilhart regularly conducted meetings. From Chicago, he attracted an unlikely pair, Robert G. Wall, a former labor leader, and Irwin E. Rockwell, the wealthy president of Idaho Consolidated

Mines. (It was Rockwell who emerged as one of the society's "financial angels.")[41]

Officially incorporated in 1901 under the laws of Ohio as a religious organization "to teach mankind how to apply the truths taught by Jesus Christ," the internal governance procedures of Spirit Fruit are unknown. Beilhart probably made all important decisions, and most of the minor ones, too. Internal splits, that often haunted cooperative and political progmatists' communities, were absent from the Beilhart utopia.[42] While the Spirit Fruit colonists enjoyed domestic peace, their daily routine initially was likewise uneventful. Local residents seemingly knew or cared little about this tiny religious settlement in their midst; the Libson newspaper paid it scant attention. But these conditions changed.

While the exact date is unknown, two years after Jacob launched Spirit Fruit Lisbonites started to talk about the settlement about 1901. Rumors spread of "unusual proceedings" at the colony, that it had become a "free-love" nest. When a child, Evelyn Gladys Beilhart, was born out of wedlock to Beilhart's thirty-one year old sister, Mary, local moralists vainly sought to bring legal action against the group. "If the laws of the land are violated," remarked the *Lisbon Buckeye State*, "the society has been able so far to prevent outsiders from obtaining any proof that would enable them to take action against them."[43] But Evelyn Gladys, the "Love Child," continued to remind many Lisbonites that Jacob Beilhart and his Spirit Fruit Society damaged the community's image.

Coinciding with the "Love Child" incident, Chicago journalists came to cover the "abduction" of the wife of a prominent local physician. A Dr. Bailey had thought that his spouse was visiting in the East, but, when she did not return home, he hired investigators to find her. When Dr. Bailey at last received word that his missing wife had joined the Lisbon utopia, he sought immediately to retrieve her. But she refused to leave. Bailey next tried to have family members persuade his wife to return home. Failing that, he sought unsuccessfully a writ of habeas corpus. After this setback, Dr. Bailey, undaunted, hired legal counsel to prepare papers to have his wife declared to be of "unsound mind." She was soon brought before the probate court, and, when confronted with the prospect, she reluctantly agreed to return home. The Chicago press dramatically described the final episode in the alleged abduction: "As they were at the [Erie] station and about to leave the city, Beilhart made his appearance to bid the woman good-bye. When the husband assaulted him and slapped him in the face several times, Beilhart offered no resistance but rather extended the other cheek. The incident ended without further violence and the Doctor and his wife left on the train."[44]

Although Jacob Beilhart and the Spirit Fruit Society weathered the early storms, they proved harbingers of future difficulties. The turning point for the utopia came in 1904, when extensive journalistic "exposés" made life uncomfortable for the colonists as local opposition mounted. In May 1904, the Chicago press once more focused attention on them. Reporters visited the society's city branch (rented rooms on Clark Street); their accounts correctly noted that Jacob was a "tireless worker," but the thrust was the colorful and sensational. The group was labeled a "fantastic" religious sect. To underscore such a claim, journalists attempted to show that Beilhart, whom they said claimed to be the "Messiah," held unconventional ideas; for example:

> "Do you believe in divorce?" was asked.
> "We pay absolutely no heed to institutions that man has established," was the answer. "But I will say that if I were married to a woman whom I hated I should not hesitate to seek out my proper affinity. If I did otherwise, according to our belief, I should be practicing hypocrisy."[45]

The *Buckeye State* seized on the Chicago revelations. The 2 June issue carried the large headline "'SPIRIT FRUIT' SOCIETY HAS TAKEN CHICAGO BY STORM." The next edition, published a week later, contained the damaging story of Katherin "Blessed" Herbeson, one that received national attention. It paralleled the Bailey incident three years before. Once again Beilhart had attracted a Chicago woman to the colony, in this case a "beautiful, well-educated, musical and independent" eighteen-year-old. When family members learned of her new association, her lawyer father and a brother-in-law traveled to Lisbon to retrieve her. Again, Beilhart did not resist. Nevertheless, the press gave the impression that the Spirit Fruit Society either "abducted" innocent females or was at least guilty of brainwashing them. Even though the *Buckeye State* mentioned that "Mr. Beilhart seems to think that this additional episode ["Blessed" Herbeson] is only one more link in the chain that is going to give publicity to his religion and cause it to be spread to all parts of the earth," talk of a special grand jury investigation must have given him pause.[46] There also existed a more immediate concern. Two weeks after the initial local coverage, the paper reprinted "A Warning" that angry Lisbonites had circulated on printed cards: "Wanted—Fifty good women, over twenty and under fifty years of age; also fifty good honest-hearted men with families, to meet upon the Square when called upon, and go to the Spirit Fruit farm and tell them to take their departure at once or take the consequences, as tar is cheap and feathers plentiful.[47]

Beilhart reacted this time. This passive advocate of peace and love decided to leave temporarily for Chicago. During this period, he probably reassessed the future of the Lisbon colony. By November 1904, the *Buckeye State* reported that "he has about decided to sell the community home here and buy another location."[48] More unfavorable publicity came in December when Loruma Beilhart, his wife, sued for divorce. The *Youngstown, Ohio, Telegram*, for one, argued that this "proves that the peculiar brand of religion in the 'Spirit Fruit' cult is wrong, for the religion that causes domestic woe and strife has a yellow streak in it somewhere."[49] Liquidation of the Ohio utopia began in late 1904 and continued throughout most of the next year. In August 1905, Jacob, for the society, petitioned a Columbiana court to encumber the Lisbon property for $3,000. Two months later, the court agreed to this request. Yet Spirit Fruit did not dissolve; it merely relocated.[50]

The Buckeye communitarians selected Ingleside, Lake County, Illinois, as the new home for their utopia. Forty-five miles northwest of Chicago and twenty miles west of Lake Michigan, the location in Grant Township on Wooster Lake enjoyed close access to the mainline of the Chicago, Milwaukee, and St. Paul Railroad, important since Beilhart sought to continue operations of his Chicago branch. Much larger than the Lisbon holdings, the society's Ingleside acreage totaled ninety acres of the "finest land." Soon the colonists rented an adjoining farm, and, by 1908, they either owned or leased three hundred acres of "well-tilled" real estate.[51]

By summer 1906, the thirteen utopians (eight men and five women) were creating an impressive physical setting. The colony boasted fine crops and a purebred dairy herd. The main building, however, became its showplace. In June, a reporter from the nearby *Waukegan Daily Sun* described the dwelling, then under construction:

> The home of the society is planned on massive lines. Large concrete blocks have been formed in moulds and these are raised by means of an elevator run by horse power to the top of the wall. . . . To go around the building which when completed will contain forty rooms, full

seven hundred feet of wall has to be laid. As many tiers of walls and cross walls compose the entire structure, some idea of the work these quiet artisans must do to raise "Spirit Temple" from its foundation and make it a house of abode can be gained.

Practically all the work so far is of concrete. The basement floors, the fireplaces, even the ceilings crossed with massive iron beams are of arched cement. And by no means will the building be an ill one to look upon. The design is as original and unique as the society itself.[52]

Beilhart and his Spirit Fruit compatriots worked hard. While few primary records tell of the daily rounds of the Ingleside settlement, one newspaper account suggests that members voluntarily labored at the gigantic house-building task and sustained their farm. Although Beilhart apparently continued to make the decisions, he did not act in an autocratic fashion. For instance, he told a reporter, "I give a yell and then if any of the boys feel like getting up to help it is all right, but if they don't, nothing is said."[53]

Except for the rigors of farming and construction, life must have been pleasant for the colonists. Visitors sensed a strong esprit de corps. "It is clearly the intention of the people to improve the property," concluded the Cleveland Leader. "Flowers and shrubbery are being planted, and the site of the building is one of rare natural beauty, overlooking one of the most charming litte [sic] lakes in the country."[54]

Intentional experiments have sometimes proved fragile; Spirit Fruit was no exception. The fatal blow occurred in 1908. Stricken with appendicitis on 19 November, Beilhart was rushed by train the next day to Waukegan for an emergency operation. Surgery was termed "successful." Unfortunately, "the rupture of the appendix was too far gone to permit of treatment."[55] Jacob Beilhart died early on the morning of 24 November 1908 at the age of forty-one and was buried in an unmarked grave on the colony site.

While a Waukegan paper carried a front-page story with the headline "Beilhart Colony Not to be Dissipated; Members to Remain in Same Mode of Life," the community lost its vitality.[56] "After [Jacob's] death his work ceased," wrote a follower in the mid-1920s. "There was no one to take his place and not again for many centuries."[57] Yet a nephew of Jacob's remembered that the colony did not die immediately. "Miraculously, they remained together, in diminishing numbers, for 21 more years. . . . The group had diminished

. . . to eleven, and the impact of the great depression was upon us—
there was nowhere left for them to go but their separate ways."[58]

The story of the Spirit Fruit Society differed little from some
other contemporary charismatic perfectionist experiments. The colony was based on the teachings of a single individual, it never attracted a sizable following, and it was ephemeral. Also like some
other colonies, it encountered external resentment—indeed, in this
case forcing relocation. While a "failure," Jacob Beilhart's sincerity
and persistent labors at creating a utopia are admirable. One eulogy
to Beilhart came from a fellow utopian, Elbert Hubbard, founder of
the Roycroft Colony in East Aurora, New York:

> Here is what I think of Jacob: If there were enough men
> like him in mentality and disposition we would have the
> millennium right here and now.
>
> Jacob does not believe in force. He has faith—more faith
> than any man I can think of at this moment. He has faith
> in God, and God is us—God is Jacob, and Jacob is a part
> of God. God wouldn't be God without Jacob, and Jacob
> acknowledges this himself.
>
> Jacob wants nothing and has nothing, and so he is free
> to tell the truth. He deceived no one—disappoints no-
> body, excepting possibly the people who want something
> for nothing.
>
> Jacob accepts life, accepts everything, and finds it good.
> . . .
>
> Jacob works with his hands, and works hard—he does
> good work. No one can meet him without realizing his
> worth—he has nothing to hide. He does not seek to im-
> press. He is a healthy, fearless, simple, honest, intelligent,
> kindly man. Therefore, he is a great man. But being free
> from subterfuge and hypocrisy, he is, of course, eccentric.
>
> Jacob is a bearer of glad tidings—he brings a message of
> hope, good-cheer, courage and faith. He affirms again and
> again that God, which is the Everything is good—he puts
> in another "o" and spells it Good.[59]

There are several prominent themes that run through the eclectic philosophy of Jacob Beilhart, and they stand for more than the
isolated facts of his career as prophet and colony organizer. He both
saw and presented himself as a redeemer who could save men and
women from selfishness, what he called "ego-mania," which "strips
man of all but the mere pretense of caring for the welfare of his nation or race."[60] Beilhart wanted "to make men become men and to

free women." Both were shackled by convention, by an inability to let their higher natures (their true selves) find an outlet. There was a "spirit voice" within each person, and it was "Jacob" who could draw it out. His simple message was, "Be a Man, Be a Woman."[61]

The appeal was libertarian and erotic. Men and women could be as free as he was. Beilhart had known loneliness and pain and by yielding to his true nature had found pleasure and happiness. One of his followers later described the process Beilhart had gone through: "To him, severe physical pain was the caress of God, cleansing him for the clearer sight of the universal harmony and a keener appreciation of joy. Sickness was God's own surgical operation removing outgrown conditions and cleansing the inner eye to see what IS." What was inside Beilhart was a dual nature: part male, part female. When he was six, his father died, and he became "well acquainted" with his mother. "She gave me my nature and a great deal of trouble it made me." She imparted a feminine and sensitive conscience to him that would not let him be as selfish as those around him. In Beilhart's spiritual autobiography, he wrote that he "seemed to have developed the feminine side of my nature first, and only in later years did the real manhood become uncovered."[62] What real manhood consisted of is ambiguous, but there was a strong homoerotic element in it.

In fact, on reading Beilhart one is struck by the similarities between him and Edward Carpenter, the English socialist and writer. It was Carpenter who, in the 1890s, first wrote about and dared to have published essays on homosexual love in *Homogenic Love* and *Sex, Love and Its Place in a Free Society*.[63] There is in Beilhart the notion of the "Androgynous Superman," a phrase coined to describe both Carpenter and D. H. Lawrence. The Androgynous Superman is "a seer, a redeemer who has solved the contradictory male and female passions implicit in every human being and has achieved a spiritual state beyond sex. He has accepted the world and all its contradictions and gave Whitmanesque encouragement to individuals dwelling in personal darkness."[64]

Jacob Beilhart's message was a reassuring one, promising security and freedom: "You need not fear when all is dark, and you cannot see, and do not know what to do. For then you may know that I in you will know just what to do and how to do it." His appeal was to private self locked inside a body that yearned to be free, but was fearful of the consequences of such freedom. As a lover, Beilhart promised to be gentle, to accept fully and without reservation his bride: "Do not shrink when I touch you with my Love. While you are in pain or darkness, look for me. I am there. I will surely meet you if you will let me in." [65] This is, of course, a paraphrase of the closing section of *Song of Myself*.

The Whitmanesque and heroic sexual pose is repeated when Beilhart refers to himself as the "masculine nature that lives in the feminine nature that she may become free." [66] Through the seer and lover, a woman was set free and became free to explore her "spirit voice" and to bear spirit fruit. That masculine appeal of Beilhart's earned for the colony the title "free love," though he protested that it meant nothing more than the epigram that adorned one issue of Elbert Hubbard's *Philistine:* "I believe that love should be free, which is not saying that I believe in free love." [67] However, the scandals in Ohio and the sensational accounts in the Chicago newspapers lent credence to the view that free love was practiced at Spirit Fruit.

Much of Jacob Beilhart's appeal—as was Carpenter's—was directed toward women and their special needs. It was the "feminine" that Carpenter idealized. This yielding, passive, and noncompetitive ideal he placed in opposition to the harsh, corrupt, and destructive natural order that man had created. Women were kept in bondage by "jealousy, fear and doubt," yet they could be saved by the "unselfish love of Man" with a love that encouraged "absolute abandonment, absolute non-resistence [sic]." He wrote, "Let him [man] not bind her for one moment and she will become free." [68] Once free, this "spirit fruit" will blossom and find true freedom.

Edward Carpenter believed that his mission in the world was to free man from custom, to established him in freedom with "whomever he may choose." Jacob Beilhart's aim was much the same. He wanted his followers (even though he denied any desire to have disciples) to "relax and become nonresistant," to allow the natural forces within them and the world to move them, to feel comfortable with their impulses. His role was to encourage openness, and his career after 1897 was directed toward that goal. A millionaire and laborer joined hands with him in the colony, his sister had an illegitimate child, women left their families to join "Jacob" at Spirit Fruit, and for his labors he was nearly mobbed and driven from one midwestern state into another.

After his death, some of his writings were published by "Freedom Hill Henry" at Burbank, California. J. William Lloyd, the anarchist editor of the *Free Comrade* and author of the utopian romances *The Dwellers in Vale Sunrise* and *The Natural Man*, headed a group at Freedom Hill on an estate near the San Fernando Valley. [69] Lloyd had urged the adoption of rural decentralization and colonization in the 1890s and was an exponent of sexual radicalism throughout his career. He was also a contemporary of Beilhart's though there is no evidence that they knew each other. *Jacob Beilhart: Life and Teachings,* however, was published posthumously at Freedom Hill by an admirer in 1925.

William Lloyd had traveled throughout the United States in the late nineteenth century before resettling in his hometown of Westfield, New Jersey, where he farmed and wrote. Leonard Abbott, the anarchist and later member of the Stelton Colony, wrote of him in *Mother Earth* in 1908: "He is a free spirit, asking only that he be allowed to develop in his own way, and claiming the same rights for all others."[70] Lloyd's heroes were Emerson, Morris, Whitman, Markham, E. H. Crosby, Darwin, and Thoreau. His message, like Beilhart's, was both anarchist and socialist, with an emphasis on freedom for the individual through community living. Through his work with the Lloyd group at Westwood, Massachusetts, and later at Pasadena, Abbott was a potent force in the new aesthetic movement through his writings in *Ariel* and other journals that exhalted the craft tradition. In the preface to Beilhart's writings, similar heroic influences are cited for his works: "The practical teachings given by Krishna, Buddha, Jesus, Emerson, Whitman, Carpenter and Gibran."[71] (Beilhart must have had spirit communication with Gibran since his works were published after Beilhart's death.)

Jacob Beilhart and his Spirit Fruit colony tell us a good deal about free love in the Midwest. This seemingly isolated colony in Ohio and later in Illinois was part of an emerging social and sexual movement that drew its inspiration from native American, European, and Eastern sources. Emerson and Whitman inspired radicals in New Jersey and Kansas; Carpenter and Morris suggested social plans for political anarchists like Leonard Abbott and mystical entrepreneurs like Elbert Hubbard; and Eastern-oriented philosophies like Theosophy and Vedantism saw individuals and groups adopt a path laid down by adepts and seers.[72]

Beilhart was a seer for a small band. He preached that it was possible to alter one's consciousness and to live a perfected life within his aura and the boundaries of a select community. He was not alone in the late 1890s when he tried his experiment where "human nature, motives and feelings are treated [here] as a medical school treats human anatomy." When he died, the *Waukegan Daily Sun* said that "he was one of the gentlest and unassuming of men" and that after residing three years in the area had farmer friends who "would have fought in his behalf." [73]

Like the Salvationists, the Theosophists at Point Loma tried to combine both mission and retreat, with greater success. The key figure at Point Loma was Katherine Tingley, who, like Sandford, was a New Englander and, like Wilbur Copeland, had been involved with a series of reform and benevolent groups. At various times, she had organized a home for the aged, an emergency relief fund on the East Side of New York, and a children's home on the Palisades. During the 1880s, she became a Theosophist with its leader, William Q. Judge, her mentor. Just before his death in 1896, Judge designated her as his successor and "Outer Head" of the Theosophical Society. Founded by Helena Blavatsky as a spiritualist religion, under her guidance and that of Henry Steel Olcott (one-time agricultural editor of the *New York Tribune*) Theosophy had grown to embrace a hundred chapters in the United States, with California its leading center.

Theosophy was an international movement, and it attracted a remarkable set of followers, including Annie Besant, a leading English reformer and Fabian Society member, and Albert Spalding, the sporting-goods magnate. A split developed in the society in 1891 after Blavatsky's death, with the Theosophical Society of America going its own way and an Adyar branch centered in India led by Olcott and Besant. Simply put, the Theosophical creed emphasized three basic doctrines: the universal brotherhood of man, the study of Aryan and Eastern literature and religion, and the investigation of hidden secrets in nature and psychic phenomenon. As noted earlier, there was a close connection between the Theosophists and the Nationalist movement, particularly as both emphasized the brotherhood of man. As part of a World Theosophical Crusade and Katherine Tingley's ascension to the leadership of the society in 1896, Point Loma came into existence as the center of her international organization. Land was purchased in that year, and in 1898 she invited Theosophists attending the annual convention to join her in building the community. Although conceived of not as a separate community or a commune but as an expression of Theosophist ideals, it was in the words of Robert Hine "as good an example of a religious utopia that can be found in California history." [74]

Members who came (by 1903 there were three hundred) lived either in a large communal dwelling or in separate bungalows scattered over the grounds. Meals were served in a common refectory, with a separate dining room provided for the children. Parents left their children—shortly after birth—in a communal nursery and saw them regularly on Sundays. The children were taught to be self-reliant, and their education emphasized the arts, particularly music. On reaching school age, they lived in groups of ten or twelve with a resident teacher. A majority of the students were sent to Point Loma by their Theosophical parents, but there was always an interesting mixture of pupils. In 1901, a large number came from an orphan and settlement house in Buffalo, and another thirty-five came from Cuba. Katherine Tingley had—on her world tour—made converts in Sweden, so there was a small contingent of Swedish children. The school was called Raja Joga, the name taken from Sanskrit literature and meaning "holy union." [75]

In addition to musical training there was an emphasis on theater at Point Loma. The first Greek theater in California was built there (it seated twenty-five hundred), and in 1901 the colony purchased the Fisher Opera House in San Diego (renamed the Isis Theatre), where classical and Shakesperean plays were performed. According to Robert Hine, the performances were "gigantic cooperative efforts" and were well attended by local people. Although thousands attended these lavish extravaganzas, they created more goodwill than profits. Money from outside contributors was always necessary to sustain the colony, which, at the time of Tingley's death in 1929, was heavily in debt. As the acknowledged autocratic leader of the group, she had been given a free hand in developing the community, and she spent lavishly. She wrote that "there is a top rung to every ladder," and she stayed perched there till her death.

There was a certain martial air about Point Loma, with men and women wearing uniforms and Tingley directing the whole operation like a general in battle. Most of the members were middle class and well educated, and a few supporters were wealthy businessmen like Spalding and William Chase Temple, the Florida fruit grower. In many ways, the community members were like the Salvation Army, although clearly without the Salvationists emphasis on lower-class reform. Both groups were interested in the welfare of children, in brotherhood, in moral education, and in the redemptive power of music. Tingley never had to confront hostile crowds, though for a period the editor of the Los Angeles Times, Harrison Grey Otis, did lead an attack on the colony, which resulted in Tingley's bringing a libel suit. A jury awarded her $7,500 in damages. Tingley's higher spiritualism had a practical side to it, and Point Loma set out to show that brotherhood and idealism could be passed on to another generation, that Theosophy had a future, and that its future lay in the education of the young. The colony barely survived Tingley's death and the Depression, and by 1940 most of the three hundred acres had been sold. From that point on, the group (under Gottfried de Purucker) emphasized work with local lodges and a publications program to spread the Theosophical message.

For Tingley, Point Loma was to be the center of her religious crusade—a counterpoint to Adyar in India, where her opponents had their base. For Charles Sandford, his base was in a small town in Maine, but his vision radiated outward to include Jerusalem and Alexandria. All these prophets were restless and peripatetic yet still eager to provide a secure home for their followers—a gathering-in place safe from the larger world. The tradition of the gathering-in place where the elect could come together has a long history, and numerous American colonies saw themselves, in one way or another, as places for the elect. Such communities served as both missions and retreats.

Few utopian colonies were ever located within the growing metropolises of America. Stephen Pearl Andrews's cooperative boarding house, Unity House, founded in the 1850s, did attract a few followers, and Oneida had a Brooklyn commune for a time, but the overwhelming thrust of most communal groups was away from urban sites and industrial problems. Even an organization that few would describe as retreatist, the Salvation Army, used the American frontier as a setting for rehabilitative work. The Salvationists were born amid the religious turmoil of the 1880s and in the crucible of London's desperate social conditions. William Booth's crusade against poverty and neglect shocked Victorian England, and nothing shocked it more than the publication, in 1890, of *In Darkest England and the Way Out*.

Taking his title from the bestseller *In Darkest Africa*, by the explorer Henry Morton Stanley, Booth set out, with the aid of William Stead, to show that for the slum dwellers of London all the world was a slum. This brought the Salvation Army to the forefront of the reformist fight to solve industrial problems. His solution was to apply the Christian ethic, and, beyond Bible thumping and singing, he had a plan. The plan involved three elements: a farm colony idea that presumed to take London laborers to a site near the city and give them a chance to rid themselves of urban habits (drink, disease), city colonies directed at immediate problems (rescue homes, food shelters), and overseas colonies where emigrants from London could get a completely fresh start in life: "Only those whom the Salvation Army observed to be sincere in their willingness to reform and work would be allowed to emigrate." The farm colony was started at Hadleigh in 1896, and, when Frederick Booth-Tucker became commander of the Army in the United States in 1896, he proposed a colony scheme: "Place the waste labor on the waste land by means of waste capital, and thereby convert the trinity of modern waste into a trinity of production."[76]

The idea was hailed by Grover Cleveland, Theodore Roosevelt, Henry Lodge, and Mark Hanna, and, during the fall 1897, Salvation Army officials traveled from Chicago to California looking for land. Three sites were chosen, and, during 1898, colonies were established at Fort Herrick, Ohio; Romie, California; and Amity, Colorado. Of the three, the Amity Colony was the most successful and the one that had the greatest amount of cooperation. Six hundred forty acres located six miles west of Holly in eastern Colorado were purchased from the Amity Land Company. The first settlers were fourteen families from the Chicago area, and all had farming experience. There was a careful selection process, and research went into the choice of participants. Booth's plan for the overseas colonies (he envisioned them in Africa, Australia, Canada, and the United States) contained several sound features geared at promoting successful experiments. First, they had to change both a man's character and his surroundings. Second, they had to be large scale if the problem was widespread. Third, they had to be permanent and immediately practical. Fourth, they were not to hurt those they helped and should not interfere with others in society. The practical aspects of the American colonies as stressed by his son-in-law, Frederick Booth-Tucker, involved increases in food production, decreases in taxation, and security for the families involved.

During the first year, the fourteen families at Fort Amity farmed communally and lived on small farm allotments so that they would be near one another. After the first year, they were urged to be independent. By 1903, there were 450 people on the site, and they had purchased more land, bringing the total acreage to 1,830. The colony's failure was not due to inept planning, or inadequate leadership (though the loss of Colonel Thomas Holland in an accident was a blow), or malingering. Rather, Army officials had chosen a site where the alkaline deposits were so great as to make productive farming impossible. In 1909, the Salvation Army decided to relocate all those who wanted to move and would up their involvement in the plan. Amity was essentially a huge colony of independent landowners drawn from cities and given administrative and financial aid to get them started on the land. Each family was given ten acres and, according to Marie Antalek, "one horse, a small plow, one shovel plow, a pair of gas pipe harrows, two cultivators, one of five and the other of fourteen teeth, a set of harness and such spades, hoes and shovels as were deemed necessary in order to properly cultivate the land."[77] The Salvationists built an orphanage, and the colony served as a place where "Farmers Institutes" were held to spread the intelligent use of agricultural techniques in the area.

The two other Salvation Army projects, Fort Herrick, twenty miles from Cleveland, and Romie, in the Salinas Valley, California, never made a significant impact and had no cooperative features. The Ohio colony proved too expensive to run and was turned into a fresh air camp for city youths, and drought conditions ended the California colony. H. Rider Haggard, the novelist, was asked by the British government to look at such settlements, and his 1905 report, though generally favorable of the idea, criticized the poor land selection.[78] The whole thrust of the overseas colonies was to make men and women independent, free them from the social addictions of city life, and put them on the Christian road to salvation. It was a clear response to urban conditions but essentially within an individualistic framework.[79]

It is not until the establishment, in 1899, of a community in New York City that we see a direct confrontation between the communal ethic and urban life. Even here, the emphasis was on giving skills to the unemployed so that they might lead lives of true independence and freedom. One of the features of William Booth's farm colony idea was its belief that certain industrial skills had to be mastered if the destitute of London ever hoped to lead productive lives. The Straight Edge Colony drew directly, like Booth's crusades, out of the conditions of urban life, and, for a time, its members struggled to maintain themselves in New York City. Eventually, they did succumb to the advantages of rural life and removed themselves across the Hudson.

The colony's founder, Wilbur Copeland, was born in 1869 into the family of a Methodist minister; he was later educated at Ohio Wesleyan University, from which he graduated in 1889. While an undergraduate, Copeland had become a Christian socialist, falling under the influence of Bellamy, Gronlund, and Tolstoy. He worked briefly for the president of Ohio Wesleyan after his graduation but then headed east to New York City to work for I. K. Funk's temperance paper, the *Voice*.[80] During the 1890s, Copeland tried to raise money for a cooperative society but was unable to find any backers. He wanted to respond to the social distress that he saw around him and to make that response a practical as well as a religious one. His work with the Board of Education of the Methodist Church had brought both him and his future wife, Ella, into close contact with the urban poor. In May 1899, he place an advertisement in the *New York Herald:* "Wanted—Men and women who take the teachings of Jesus Christ seriously, and who want to go to work in a cooperative enterprise founded upon the Golden Rule; state age, occupation, marriage relations, school of method, etc." Over a hundred responded to the call, and, after a meeting held at One Seventh Avenue, a School of Methods for the Application of the Teachings of Jesus to Business and Society (their cumbersome corporate name) came into existence. According to William Hinds, the Oneida historian, the bylaws of the organization were the briefest ever written: "All things whatsoever ye would that men should do to you, do you even so to them." That Golden Rule was buttressed by six equally simple bylaws beginning with "Thou shalt love thy neighbor as thyself" and ending with "Whatsoever things are true, honest, just, pure, of good report, virtuous, praiseworthy, think on these things."[81]

This School of Methods had its offices near Fourteenth Street, and Copeland believed that there were particular groups of urban dwellers for whom his program was particularly appropriate. His Christian socialist message was particularly addressed to women with children and no adequate means of support, men and women who had passed the age when they can readily secure employment on their own, the disabled, and educated and cultured people who have become dependent on others. These individuals had become "unfit" under contemporary industrial standards and were in need of training. That training would teach them to be efficient, to gain skills that they could turn into jobs. What Copeland offered was a collective environment—not a communal home—where the urban disadvantaged could learn the skills necessary to survive in a productive and moral manner: "The ultimate object of the School of Methods is to embody the results of our study in a School of Cooperative Industry, in which there will be finished opportunities to learn, under favorable conditions and by practical and experimental knowledge, the highest of all arts, namely the art of social and individual cooperation."[82]

Copeland's followers did not wish to separate themselves from the world and form a "clique," to use their own words; rather, they organized themselves into three industries in the heart of New York

City with "our fellow victims."[83] There was the Straight Edge Press, a printing establishment that did job printing, the Sunnyside Industrial Company, which produced useful objects, and the School of Cooperative Industry, a training center. During the first eight years of its existence, the group relied heavily on the contributions of the reformer Ernest Howard Crosby, who had a particular interest in the training of children in the areas of human service and natural resources. As early as 1901, the colony operated from several bases, including an old twenty-six-room mansion on Staten Island. Later— in 1906—its members did relocate to New Jersey, but in this early period their dedication to serving urban needs made them stay close to Manhattan. Their fourth-floor walk-up headquarters near Fourteenth Street housed the press and the school, and it was from this location that they publicized their efforts. In their periodical, the *Straight Edge*, they sought advice and asked their readers to send them information about a range of cooperative activities, including "Ruskin, the Christian Commonwealth, Amana, the Shakers, the English cooperative companies, the French industrial colonies such as the one at Guise, the Cooperative Merchants Company at Chicago, the Right Relationship League, the Battle Creek Sanitarium and allied industries, the Roycroft Shop, the Acme Sucker Rod Works, the National Cash Register Company, the Nelson Manufacturing Company at Leclair." The range of enterprise that they were interested in was certainly wide, but within traditions that were cooperative, industrial, and social.[84]

Although the colony had, initially, a simple plan of organization and a rudimentary set of bylaws, that gave way to a formal set of articles of incorporation. (The "School" was incorporated as a religious, though nonsectarian, organization.) Workers in its industries were free to organize themselves as they saw fit and to divide the profits. Both authority and responsibility were to reside with the workers, with no stockholder having no more than five shares. Shares were assigned to workers on the basis of time spent in the association, and the company directors had limited and oversight roles within the corporation. The corporation would have no vested interest in its allied industries and would act as a legal holding company in name only. During their first year, colony members tried to stimulate interest by publishing the *Straight Edge*, by holding open house during the week, and by having a series of public lectures and discussions on topics such as "The School of Cooperative Industry—What Is the Next Step to Take toward Its Establishment," "A

Cooperative Store—How to Start One and Run It on Correct Fundamental Principles," "A Cooperative Apartment House—Is It Practicable for Several Families in New York to Be Their Own Landlord," and "Do We Need Capitalists to Furnish the Funds Necessary to Start Cooperative Enterprises." Ultimately, the Straight Edge Society had to answer yes to the last two questions, but the greatest test would come in implementing those answers.

Although information about membership in those early years is sketchy, a clear picture of the group's numbers and progress emerges by 1906. At that time, it was located at Abingdon Square, and its principal industry was a unique line of food products. The group's "center" housed a bakery, a store with a parlor floor (Neighborhood Hall) used for lectures, and a reception room for the workers. The upper three floors of the house contained living and sleeping rooms, with one large room set aside for the children of workers, where "they [the children] play and receive industrial training, under the comradeship and direction of Mrs. Copeland." In addition, there was a sewing room and a place where one worker ran a laundry. The colony saw such an activity as an "embryo industry" and as a necessary service to the other workers. What one had at Abingdon Square was a combined settlement house, cooperative home, and cottage-industry center. From their own perspective, the members thought that they "took on more the character of the Shakers in this country and the Great English Cooperative Society." Their method was a slow one, and they rejected the criticisms of those who wanted a "quick action" plan of social or religious improvement. In 1907, there were forty-five "workers" connected with them, twenty-three of whom were children in the Play-Work School. In the first seven years of their existence, they had 170 workers associated with them. Most had become self-reliant. That Emersonian axiom was at the heart of their enterprise as they labored to bring disabled workers, young mothers with children, and the destitute back into a productive relationship with society.[85]

Initially, the Copelands had rejected the idea of leaving the city, but, in 1906, they took the large step away from that ideal with the purchase of a four-acre tract on the western slope of the Palisades at Alpine, New Jersey. La Hacienda was to house industries, but its primary focus was the Play-Work School, a unique experiment in industrial democracy. It was a place where the children of workers could learn useful skills (particularly domestic ones) and relieve their mothers of "that crushing routine of household drudgery that stifles the life out of so many women and *even* drives some to prefer being childless renters." Being released from the pressures of household work by their own children would enable "the woman who knows how and wants to do other work part of the time may have a chance to follow her preference without disaster to her home."[86]

According to the Copelands, the most "hopeful" class that they worked with were mothers with children who had no help in their struggle to survive on their own. They wanted to work and—as a group—contained fewer grafters and panhandlers than did their male counterparts. When a mother became associated with the Straight Edge, colony members assisted her in the care of her children so that she might work, but the children were her responsibility at the end of the workday. The children were not in an institution but in what we have come to call day-care centers. During the day, the children attended the Play-Work School, which combined informal schooling with work of commercial value, "as happiness permits." These little industrial workers helped wrap packages of the food business that the colony maintained through two stores in New York City and seventy-three other outlets. The first day that a child worked was considered an important one, and they received dividends for any commercial work they did. Between 1899 and 1913, the Copelands worked with seventeen single mothers and their twenty-three children and with seven families containing twenty-five children. The Copelands themselves had eight children. In 1916, there were twenty-eight workers entitled to share in the Workers Fund, with three branches of industrial association: La Hacienda, Distributing Corporation, and Baking Company. The wholesale baking operation remained in New York City but was crippled in 1918 by war measures that limited its operations. The company never recovered, and, after that date, the Straight Edge industries were located only in New Jersey.

Workers in all locations were graded on their industrial efficiency and awarded points by their fellow workers after a monthly meeting at which they discussed labor practices. The qualifications used to grade a worker tell a great deal about the values that they were trying to impart and their perception of the industrial order:

1) Does necessary and useful work that adds to the efficiency of the organization, and as much as can be reasonable be [sic] expected;

2) Puts in the time and energy necessary to do his work to the best of his ability;

3) Knows how to set himself to work and to keep at work without needless supervision;

4) Carries responsibility continuously, never throwing his work upon somebody else or leaving without having it done properly;

5) Requires no waiting on, is willing to do anything there is to be done;

6) Cleans up after himself, keeps his working place in order, is clean about his work and personal habits;

7) Takes care of tools and utensils with which he works;

8) Works in harmony with others, shows respect for his fellow workers and consideration for their rights, convenience and comfort;

9) Watches the economies of the place, saves material and expense, makes and helps carry out helpful suggestions;

10) Has worked long enough to earn the proportionate share of working capital required to provide an industrial opportunity.[87]

From these requirements emerges a clear sense that workers had to be efficient, that they had to understand their role within the industrial order, and that they had to be responsible. After the loss of the wholesale food business in New York City, the enterprise seems to have drifted, with the Copelands issuing occasional newsletters filled with schemes for trust funds, building bonds, and, in 1928, the Copeland School. The Copeland School was really just an extension of the School of Method and the Work-Play School for it argued that "genuine education must be acquired by actual contact with Life and Reality."[88] They offered a series of fellowships to attract students and hoped that patrons would come forth as well. A Howells Fellowship and a Crosby Fellowship tried to suggest the glories of the past, yet the school attracted few students. In 1934, the Copelands made an application to the subsistence homestead program of the Farm Resettlement Bureau for a grant of $48,000. The application was rejected.

The careers of Wilbur and Ella Copeland span the idealism of the late nineteenth century to the practical politics of the 1930s and the faith that both generations had in cooperation. The Copelands were inspired by Tolstoy, Gronlund, Bellamy, the Shakers, and the English cooperative tradition and spurred on by their own interpretation of muscular Christianity. That interpretation stressed the need to respond to social problems, not simply to pray. Yet there were also classic Progressives who emphasized efficiency, the use of the settlement house, and education as the tools for survival. They were, like the radicals at Stelton and the Nearings, responding to urban problems; they were, however, eventually forced to retreat from the industrial complex, and it was at Sylvan Park that the community seems to have found its proper home. This combined school, residence, and day-care center was a small but innovative effort toward aiding widowed, divorced, or abandoned women who needed a hand at becoming self-reliant and sufficient in a man's world.

At just the point at which the Copelands were planning to move to New Jersey, another radical couple, Upton and Mina Sinclair, was wrestling with that unique American social problem—the servant problem. This impelled Sinclair and his wife into a cooperative arrangement: "My family had been wrestling with this problem for six years. About a year ago we concluded to kick over the traces; we concluded that it was not enough for us to sit by helplessly and dream about how happy men and women would be in cooperative homes of the future, but that we should go out and find a half dozen other persons and establish a cooperative home and be happy ourselves."[89]

Sinclair was interested in the same questions as Wilbur Copeland, but his colony was a community of intellectuals seeking to solve a personal problem, whereas Copeland was looking for answers to much more fundamental economic issues. The servant problem had long plagued nineteenth-century America. Figures like Charlotte Beecher gave practical advice on scientific housekeeping, and women like Melusina Fay Peirce tried to organize cooperative households to attack the problem. Sinclair's ideological godmother was neither Beecher nor Peirce but Charlotte Perkins Gilman, whom he misread. His reading of her *The Home, Its Work and Influence* led him to conclude that cooperative housekeeping was the solution to the servant problem. Gilman was vague about the subject in her works, yet in her *Autobiography* she took Sinclair to task for attributing to her a system that was "inherently doomed to failure."

Doomed to failure or not, Sinclair outlined his plan for a colony in the June 1906 issue of the *Independent*. In a prospectus for the colony, he said that his planned venture might be described as a "home club, or hotel which is owned by its guests and run by them for their own benefit." There would be a resident manager, and all expenses would be shared equally. The only qualifications for residence were "social compatibility and freedom from communicable diseases, and the payment of weekly bills in advance."[90] This was just the sort of club that Fourier would have joined. Like all good

211

Progressive institutions of its day, it provided for initiative and referendum plus a secret ballot in all elections. Four to five hundred persons indicated an interest, and, after a series of meetings in New York City, some sixty members were chosen. According to his own estimate, Sinclair provided 90 percent of the funds for the colony.

The colony site was a former boys school located in Englewood, New Jersey, purchased for $36,000. It was on nine and a half acres of land and included a comfortable dwelling. In the colony prospectus, several features of the central building were emphasized. The rooms were, for example, grouped around a courtyard filled with tropical plants, and there was over six thousand feet of space on the ground floor alone devoted to rooms for "social purposes." There was a pipe organ, a swimming pool, a bowling alley, a theater, and a billiard room. Rugby had had a billiard room and a substantial organ, and several groups had theaters (Oneida and Point Loma, e.g.), but Helicon Hall was certainly the first colony that could boast about its swimming pool and bowling alley. The colony was connected to the public utilities system of Englewood, and the buildings were all well ventilated and heated. The physical plant was outstanding.

Charges for the residents ranged from three to five dollars a week, which included "all services and the cleaning of rooms."[91] A colony store was organized and the theater turned into a separate dormitory for the children, who were placed in the care of mothers paid a wage by the colony. There were plans to construct separate cottage facilities on the grounds that would be kitchenless and without dining rooms since all meals could be taken at the main building. The staffing problem was a vexing one. The colony needed servants and had to address the problem as a serious social one. At first, Sinclair's idea was to have college students act as servants in the belief that they would improve the social tone of the place and they could be treated as equals by the other intellectuals. Sinclair Lewis and his roommate, the poet Allan Updergraph, joined but left after a few months because they found the work too hard. Lewis did fall in love with Sinclair's private secretary, Edith Summers, and later they were engaged. What made Helicon Hall interesting to the New York press was its varied collection of members and its impressive guest list. Among the members was Michael Williams, later founder of Commonweal, who declared that "never since the episode of the Tower of Babel, I dare say, has there existed a place as saturated in language as Helicon Hall."[92] William Pepperell Montague, later a distinguished philosopher at Columbia University, lived there with his family. His wife was a medical student, and he, likewise, was beginning a career. Edward Bjorkman, the critic and translator of Strindberg, was another prominent literary figure in residence.

The visitors were even more distinguished, with William James leading the pack and John Dewey making regular excursions out and even considering joining. Dewey and his colleagues at Columbia took an active interest in the project and came on a regular basis. During its brief history, the colony was surrounded by publicity, mostly because of Sinclair's involvement and the fact that the members and guests were such good copy. Reports about a "love nest" on the Palisades were regular fare in the press, and such reports embarrassed people like Montague in the faculty rooms at Columbia. An even greater ordeal was the servant problem that the group had banded together to resolve. Originally, the members had hoped that professional managers would run the colony, but they found that the hoteliers who wanted to work for such a motley lot were few in number. Instead, regular servants were employed under the direction of Anna Noyes, whose husband William was a professor at Columbia. Anna Noyes was a disciple of Charlotte Perkins Gilman and had a professional interest in scientific homemaking. With more time, the Noyeses might have been able to solve the problem, but the experiment was such a short-lived one that they tried to make the servants comfortable and spread the child-care labor. Just five months after they had begun, a fire broke out that swept through the main building, completely destroying the building and killing a maintenance worker.

Writing in his *Autobiography*, Sinclair stated that, when he began Helicon Hall, he had "thirty thousand dollars in hand, or on the way and it was burning holes in all his pockets."[93] He admitted that his experiment was neither unusual nor radical and was, in fact, being carried out by others during the summer months in the Adirondacks, where clubs were started by like-minded individuals. (Thomas Davidson's Summer Brook is a good example of another intellectuals' retreat started in the 1890s.) On balance, Sinclair thought that the children benefited most from the scheme and learned to be self-reliant in ways that would have eluded them in an individual home. Although claiming that the moral standards at the colony were above reproach, he was at the time engaged in an affair with Anna Noyes.[93] Later, he said of his experiences that he "had lived in the future"; it was an insufficiently powerful motive, however, to bring the colony alive again. Sinclair did visit the single tax colonies of Fairhope and Arden and maintained a strong utopian element in his work, but he never entered a community again.

With Copeland and Sinclair we have the Social Gospel and Progressive agendas exemplified. Both focused on domestic issues and saw the solution to those problems in cooperative living, in an emphasis on improving the material and spiritual environment. Both operated within the cooperative colonizing tradition and the early Owenite assumptions about the need for order and rationality. Both had a mission to the world. Newbrough, Thompson, Beilhart, and Tingley were, on the other hand, more concerned with spiritual matters and with achieving a full expression of human potential. They, in turn, represented the latter part of Robert Owen's life, the spiritualist phase. In two of the colonies, Shalam and Point Loma, their spiritualist energy was focused on the care and feeding of children so as to improve their prospects in the coming new age. The children who came to Point Loma (dubbed "Lotus Buds" by the press) were to be molded in community and their character given shape by dance, theater, and Theosophy. At Spirit Fruit, the emphasis was on the expansion of sexual roles and the quest for higher spirituality. All these groups answered Emperor Frederick's question about where paradise was by simply constructing one. They stood, as Melvin Lasky has written, on the borderline between restoration and revolution.

FIG. 1. The Children of Shalam. Museum of New Mexico

FIG. 2. Thomas Lake Harris. Harris-Oliphant Papers, Rare Book and Manuscript Library, Columbia University

FIG. 3. Japanese at Fountain Grove. Harris-Oliphant Papers, Rare Book and Manuscript Library, Columbia University

FIG. 4. Count de Boissiere (white beard) and the Silkville colonists. Kansas State Historical Society

FIG. 5. Silkville colonists. Kansas State Historical Society

FIG. 6. Cyrus Teed and Victoria Gratia with Koreshan Unity colonists. William A. Hinds Papers, Oneida Community Collection, Syracuse University Library.

FIG. 7. Koreshan Unity women. William A. Hinds Papers, Oneida Community Collection, Syracuse University Library

FIG. 8. Holy Ghost and Us Colony. Public Record Office (FO 115/1508), Kew, England

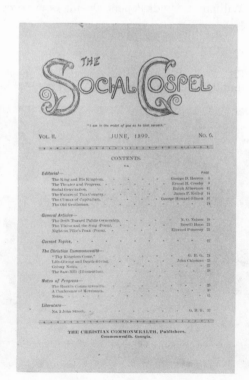

FIG. 9. The Social Gospel. William A. Hinds Papers, Oneida Community Collection, Syracuse University Library

FIG. 10. Proposed College of the New Economy, Ruskin Colony. Ruskin Cooperative Association Papers, Tennessee State Library and Archives

FIG. 11. Ruskin Colony, 1900. Ruskin Cooperative Association Papers, Tennessee State Library and Archives

FIG. 12. Ruskin workers at the Great Cave. Ruskin Cooperative Association Papers, Tennessee State Library and Archives

FIG. 13. Women of Ruskin Colony. Ruskin Cooperative Association Papers, Tennessee State Library and Archives

FIG. 14. Ruskin Band. Ruskin Cooperative Association Papers, Tennessee State Library and Archives

FIG. 15. Colonists at Brotherhood of the Cooperative Commonwealth. Ault Collection, University of Washington Library

FIG. 16. Cooperative Brotherhood Band. Ault Collection, University of Washington Library

FIG. 18. May Day celebration at New Llano. Robert Carlton Brown Collection, University of Illinois Library, Urbana-Champaign

FIG. 19. The Children of Shalam. Museum of New Mexico

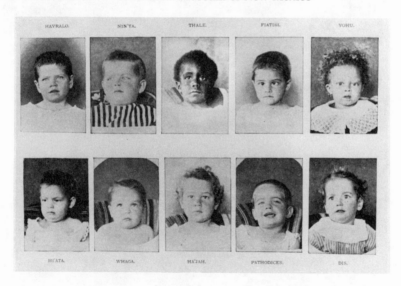

(Facing page) FIG. 17. Colonists at Brotherhood of the Cooperative Commonwealth. Ault Collection, University of Washington Library

FIG. 20. Three Worlds by John Newbrough. Museum of New Mexico

FIG. 21. Spirit Fruit—Religion the Crowning Glory of Capital and Labor.
H. Roger Grant Collection, Lisbon Historical Society

FIG. 22. Spirit Fruit colonists with Jacob Beilhart. H. Roger Grant Collection, Lisbon Historical Society

FIG. 23. Jacob Beilhart and the men of Spirit Fruit. H. Roger Grant Collection, Lisbon Historical Society

FIG. 24. Helicon Hall. Tamiment Institute Library, New York University

5 "The New Altruistic Leviathan": Conclusion

> The best thing for us to do now, and keep on doing, is to live the Golden Rule Life; for out of the midst of Golden Rule folk is to come the Mighty one, the new altruistic Leviathan, who shall lead us into the Cooperative Commonwealth. Then shall faith and justice, religion and righteousness be brought into everyday life, for all God's children be guests and kings.
>
> George Littlefield, *Ariel* 6, no. 10 (May 1902)

Communities founded between the Civil War and the First World War were self-conscious "enclaves of difference" that sought to establish religious, social, and economic institutions that supported island values and, at the same time, tried to create new patterns for emulation and hope. Often these groups were both backward and forward looking at the same time.

Foremost among the patterns one sees is an ancient one that continued to find expression in the American West and South, and even abroad. It was the idea that a perfected community molded by the dreams and visions of an inspired leader could, by the act of journeying, create utopia. It was the vision of Cyrus Teed, Martha McWhirter, and Charles Sandford. A second pattern developed in response to the labor question. Free land and labor had, of course, been a potent cry in the 1850s, and, even though there had been changes in production techniques and the growth of a labor movement, there were still those who embraced communal settlements at the same time as they adopted the new manufacturing. A third suggested that communities could be places of spiritual or sexual experimentation. Spiritualism and the acceptance, in certain circles, of Eastern-oriented belief systems became prominent with the emergence of Theosophy and, later, Christian Science, with the Vedanta movement representing that shift. Within these new mystical traditions, and in some socialist groups, there were specific concerns about the family and children.

These patterns sometimes overlapped, and, in some cases, there were groups who defied easy categorization and who remained wedded to an ideal of community that was distinctly their own. For example, Cyrus Teed's vision of the future was clearly his own, but he might find a place alongside both Thomas Lake Harris and Jacob Beilhart for typological purposes.

The career of one community organizer and seeker recapitulates many of these themes and issues. While Upton Sinclair was surveying the ashes of his short-lived experiment in community living and education and Benjamin Purnell (at the House of David) was readjusting his millennial predictions and scheming to escape the clutches of the law, an older and somewhat battle-worn socialist (in the mold of Ralph Albertson) was in the midst of a campaign to make cooperation new again.

It was 1907, and George Littlefield was promoting his Fellowship Farm. He would, like Sinclair, spend his last days in California, but, before retiring there, he had pursued a varied career that included work as a radical printer, a socialist politician, a Unitarian minister, and a colony organizer. When he did move to California, he mixed, in his own words, "spiritual truth and simple economics" and like his friend H. William Lloyd promoted the simple life, the life of an aesthete in community. Littlefield, Lloyd, H. Rowell, and W. E. Smythe all ushered in, in their different ways, the decentralist phase of communal history during which the home became a self-sufficient entity supported by a colony or community structure. These community-minded figures were closer to Ebenezer Howard's garden city movement than to Fourier. The Topolobampo experiment lay somewhere between the old Fourierist dream of a colony of individuals and the new vision that talked about individualism residing in home ownership and community existing in common landholdings necessary to support that home.

Littlefield began his career as a Boston printer employing a dozen hands in 1882, then turned his business into a profit-sharing scheme as a protest against the capitalist system. At age twenty-six, he met Edward Bellamy, joined the Nationalist Club in Boston, and was subsequently sponsored for admission to Harvard by Edward Everett Hale. In 1892, he became a Unitarian minister and actively worked to extend the Social Gospel to workers. He held pastorates at four churches, with his last one at Haverhill, Massachusetts.[1] It was at Haverhill that he made his break with the church and moved into the colony-development business. He started the Ariel Press and published several works on early New England booksellers and schools. When he was forty, he "took his ideas outdoors, into the real world and began telling the people how to get away from the old gnawing fear of losing their jobs."[2] He bought a farm at Westwood, and forty people joined him in working the Fellowship Farm. He made enough of a success of it that, in time, others interested in cooperation came to him asking for guidance in setting up similar projects. Littlefield believed that most colonies failed because of "isolation, fanaticism, pure communism, uncompromising anarchism and unfavorable time."[3]

To counteract this historical tendency toward collective colony failures, he proposed to establish colonies near large cities, combine individualism and collectivism, and use modern business methods to create a community of small landowners who would use intensive agricultural methods. Such colonies, however, would be more than mere economic arrangements; they would be spiritual and social centers where individualism would blossom. Taking his cue from J. William Lloyd's *The Dwellers in the Vale of Sunrise* (which he had printed in 1904), Littlefield advocated a return to the simple life based on intensive agriculture: "The simple Eden life, always in sight of one's home and family, ever blest with a few true friends; with up to date intensive methods of working the soil, and a determination to escape and keep clear of the enslaving commercial system of our era as much as possible—the simple producing life, on an acre of one's own, with an unquenchable passion for freedom—a passion concomitant with lofty ideals for the world's workers liberation to art, beauty, joy—that is the opportunity we open to our brothers and sisters, if they be aroused to nobleness."[4]

It was this nobleness—a combination of Emersonian self-reliance and Elbert Hubbard aestheticism—that made Littlefield combine his interest in socialism, religion, printing, and community life. For Littlefield, socialism was science and justice in government, honorable promises made and kept (contrary to most political declarations), and the brotherhood of man. Capitalism was a "vampire system that doomed every man to an early death."[5] It was to his Haverhill congregation that he made his initial plea in 1906. In that sermon he painted a society on the verge of annihilation with two contending forces in the world: socialism and capitalism. He combined images of an imminent apocalypse reminiscent of Ignatius Donnelly's *Caesar's Column* ("now it is darkening and people battle in the increasing storm and stress and cannot see clearly"); yet there was hope. There were new leaders capable of seeing the opposite shore and moving mankind toward it: "The new Columbuses and

Vespucci's and Cabots—have the vision of sagacity so that they see, westward, ho! the Co-operative Islands, and the mainland of the beautiful Co-operative Commonwealth just beyond that."[6]

Littlefield wanted to turn his Unitarian church into a "cooperative church." He had in mind more than a cooperative store attached to the church to serve local needs. He saw the church becoming the nucleus of a United Church of America that would combine all the reform interests in the city—the new thoughts cults, the ethical culturists, the cooperators, the socialists, the trade unionists, the spiritualists—into one "Grand working Fellowship."[7] They could all then draw strength from one another and turn the tide against capitalism. Workers were leaving the churches, small businesses were going under, and the new age (a "sociological" one, he thought) needed to move beyond genteel religion ("pink tea") to a church that abolished rent pews and established cooperative enterprises. Littlefield—like every good utopian—believed that Haverhill was the beginning of a movement, that hundreds of cooperatives would spring up in the country, and that the churches would become forums for social questions.

Initially, the response to his call consisted of some several hundred supportive letters; however, his congregation was not interested in that radical a transformation. He then resigned his pastorate and devoted himself to an even broader idea—the Fellowship Farm. Since his church had turned its back on him, he now turned away from it and retreated into a world based on one-acre plots and land deals. Whereas the church was presumed to be the forum for social change, now the farm-fellowship scheme became the means to the utopian end. Throughout his career, Littlefield shifted back and forth between grand visions of an apocalyptic future wherein either capitalism was destroying the world or socialism was saving it and a more personal and limited vision best exemplified by his *Ariel* essay "Farming by the Square Foot."[8]

Writing in 1911, Littlefield said that it had taken him five years to prove that he could make three cents per square foot on his acre at Westwood and that fifty workers pooling just a few dollars each month could buy a farm, equip it with tools, start a collective garden, divide the best acreage for individual holdings, and then pay a dividend. By that time, he believed that he was in a position to offer advice about fertilizers, about poultry, and about marketing. In 1911, flush with the success of running two farms in Massachusetts, he organized the Fellowship Farms Founders Association and branched out to New Jersey and Missouri. His colony in New Jersey was at Stelton, where several years later the anarchists from the Francisco Ferrer Association in New York would start their colony, but, over the years, the two groups (the Fellowship Farm still existed in the 1920s) had nothing to do with one another, although they were within a mile of each other. What Littlefield promised would take place in these new locations was again both simple and far reaching. In two short poems, he outlined his dream for the settlers on these farms:

A little land; a job at hand
A little home of your own
A sweetheart true to share with you
A king and queen on a throne

Get an acre and live on it
Get a spade and dig
Get off the backs of the workers
Get the shirkers off your backs
Get honest
Get busy

The plan for Stelton and the other sites was to group twenty to fifty residents ("as educated, progressive, refined and congenial a group as ever came together"), give them a resident adviser, and set them to work on their acre plots and on the common lot. Membership fees from $3.00 to $5.00 a month would (with dividends from the cooperatively run gardens) enable each individual to hold a perpetual lease on the land. Littlefield emphasized the steady accumulation of land and was willing to tolerate part-time involvement in the colony: "A few may merely join to help the colony and have a camping spot amidst congenial associates with a thought that in case of misfortune and need they, too, can come to their acre as a haven of life and security." There were five potential sources of income within these Fellowship Farms: gardens and poultry, dividends from the collective garden, home industries (unspecified), summer guests, and "off and on" jobs in towns and cities. Prospective members were invited out to the colonies in the making.[9]

One hundred sixty-two acres were purchased for the New Jersey colony in Middlesex County, three miles from Metuchen, for $25,000. Potential members had subscribed for $10,000, and the land was subdivided into one-acre plots, with no member allowed to hold more than three. An initial payment of $50.00 per acre was required, and a monthly installment of $5.00 expected of everyone. The central dwelling house on the property was to serve as a fellowship house, meeting hall, library, and inn. The fellowship "plan" had five elements to it and was implemented at Stelton: first, to get "landless men and manless land"; second, to make a tenth of the land (the common land) pay the whole capitalization of the property; third, to utilize a model acre in such a way that inexperienced farmers would learn from others; fourth, to organize purchasing and marketing; and, fifth, to make it easy to transfer holdings through the association's real estate bureau. As the number of Littlefield's projects grew in 1911–12, so did the problems. His involvement with a Kansas City group is a case in point.

He had been invited to Kansas City by Christian B. Hoffman, the millionaire socialist, who had been a major backer of Topolobampo and other projects. Hoffman published an article in *Ariel*, "Let the Common People Unite," reiterating several classic socialist themes about the divisions within American society and the impending crises it faced, and he then went on to urge his readers to join "Cooperation Fellowships": "They will secure to each member a home, a place of joy and rest, a place of recreation and inspiration, a fort from which to rally for the emancipation of the race." [10] Hoffman had resigned as editor of the *Chicago Daily Socialist* in September 1910 over a dispute about policy and may have been seeking another outlet for his energy when he contacted Littlefield. In October 1911, it was announced that the national headquarters of the Fellowship Farm Association would be moved to Kansas City, that Littlefield and the Ariel Press would move westward, and that a colony of forty families was to be set up near Independence, Missouri. Press reports emphasized that this group denounced no one, and it was their belief that both millionaires and paupers were victims of the oppressive system. The thirty-five-acre plot was subdivided into third-of-an-acre building lots, with a communal garden of twelve acres set aside for the very center of the colony. Hoffman and Norman Chamberlain, a railroad developer, had purchased the land for the association. Like Hoffman, Chamberlain was a socialist who felt squeezed by the capitalist system that denied employment to socialists and squeeze their life from them. [11]

In the midst of all this organizational publicity, Littlefield announced that he was going to California at the invitation of a Los Angeles dentist, Kate Buck, to begin another colony, but he assured his new partners that he would return. Chamberlain, who had doubts about Littlefield's ability to attract settlers to what had begun to look like a suburban housing development, stated that no one "reads *Ariel* in the Elks Club" and thought that the terms of the plan put it well beyond the means of the workingmen. Twenty-eight of the forty tracts were sold by 1912, with Chamberlain emphasizing the nonpolitical aspect of the colony. Despite the use of Emerson's motto on *Ariel* ("He serves all who dares to be true,") there was discord among the principals because Littlefield had misled them in his promises to make Kansas City his home and the base for *Ariel*. In fact, he was planning to remain in Los Angeles permanently. Hoffman, himself, was throwing his support behind a new cooperative community—this one in Florida—led by his old friend Thomas E. Will. Located near Lake Okeechobee in Palm Beach County, it was a speculative land venture that borrowed from the language of socialism to promote one-acre home lots and five-acre farm lots. Fruitcrest, Florida, was more the work of some aging socialists trying to make money than a colony promoting cooperation as a way of life.

By 1914, Littlefield was in California, and Chamberlain was in difficult financial circumstances and bitter at Hoffman and Littlefield. The California Fellowship Farm was on seventy-five acres of land near Puente, and it never had a membership of more than fifty. There were nudists and religious enthusiasts among the group, and, according to Robert Hine, "its members found the plots too small for profitable farming and, consequently, either left or bought larger pieces of adjacent property."[12] There were similar "Little Landers" colonies established in California between 1909 and 1916, inspired by the writings of William E. Smythe.[13] It is unclear just why Littlefield moved to California, but, by 1913, he had switched his emphasis from subsistence homesteads to his "Ministry-by-Mail," a mixture of "metaphysics and economics" that took his message through the post. In flowery Whitmanesque prose, "Ariel" as now he called himself, encouraged his readers to reach out and possess the spirit of the future: "Dear One—Awake at Dawn with thanks for another day of loving. I break fast, then sing myself a sky ship to sail to what's beyond. And now at the lectern of my typewriter, I say a joy-prayer, 'Bless and be blessed.' "[14]

In 1930, he started a magazine, *Joy*, and shortly thereafter became a supporter of Howard Scott's Technocracy, Incorporated. In 1939, the Red Rose Press was still sending out messages to the Joy Band Fellowship. Writing in July 1900, J. William Lloyd expressed his preference for a "universal type" of man who despised the boundaries of sex or race, who sympathized with the wronged masses, who was iconoclastic, and who was in politics a "reformer, revolutionist, socialist, abolitionist, and seeks radical remedies."[15] Littlefield fitted that type with his flamboyant socialism, his printer's interest in design, his universal religious interests, and his utopian zeal to "get an acre and live on it." Sinclair, Littlefield, Willard, Tingley, all began in the East, all had strong interests in socialistic and materialistic answers to social problems, but, in the end, all found utopia by turning inward and by moving with the sun.

In the introduction to this book, I noted that communities established in the late nineteenth century were "townships" that emphasized participation, shared symbols, common rituals, and common goals. These groups—if they were to be successful—had to lay stress on those characteristics that Rosabeth Kanter noted in *Commitment and Community:* sacrifice, investment, renunciation, mortification, and transcendence. In addition, these township colonies were part of a long-lived utopian tradition, and the individuals who led and joined such colonies were part of an ancient tribe. George Littlefield embodied in his life and career that history and the desire of these communards to find freedom in community. The biological axiom that ontogeny follows phylogeny can be seen in his life.

Littlefield believed (like the other utopians of the period) that there was an inevitable development of society toward a cooperative state based on man's progressive nature. Furthermore, he believed that the frontier still offered a place where experimentation could occur and (in his final days) that California offered both a physical and a spiritual landscape ripe for cultivation. Littlefield paradoxically remained in opposition to the dominant trends of his own culture while embracing (with his Fellowship Farms scheme) certain aspects of its commercial and entrepreneurial character. He maintained a Jeffersonian faith that land could liberate if properly cultivated, that artisanal values had a place in an industrialized world, and that spiritual values, whether in a labor church or in Whitmanesque optimism, offered succor and salvation.

George Littlefield was (like the country) in transition, and his impulse toward community can be seen as a sign of utopian faith and questing. His efforts at community and reform were not merely escapist and reactive but practical attempts (by his lights) to solve some personal and social problems. Communal and cooperative settlements are—in the minds of their founders and participants—practical alternatives to the world's impractical ways. Charles Lane, the cofounder of Fruitlands, once editor of the *London Mercantile Price-Current*, had rejected that version of practicality for his own more fanciful one. Every one, except Lane and Alcott, thought Fruitlands eminently *unpractical*, yet could it be said to have been derived from the same impulses that drove Cyrus Teed to see his Bureau of Equitable Commerce as a solution to the labor problem. They all saw that there was a "labor problem," though the dimensions of it were different in both periods and Lane and Teed came up with different answers.

Those communities founded between the outbreak of hostilities of the Civil War and the hostilities of the First World War were, like Littlefield, in transition. Longfellow had written in 1840 words that bear re-repeating when one considers the myriad ventures that surfaced during the years 1860–1914: "What will be the final outcome of all these movements it is impossible to forsee; some good end, I trust, for they are sincere men, and have good intention."[16] The same could be said for these latter-day reformers. As early as 1882, Littlefield's intentions were obvious when he introduced a profit-sharing plan for his printing establishment. By joining the Nationalist movement, he embraced a secular reform that attracted both generals and Theosophists. As a Unitarian minister, he was not unlike Edward Biron Payne, who, in 1895, was a member of the group that drafted the constitution for the Altrurian Community. After its failure, Payne became more "spiritual" and ended his days as a spiritualist. His wife, Ninetta Eames, was a spiritualist medium.

One could say that Littlefield's journey from 1882 to 1914 (when he went to California) was an archetypal utopian one. There was his steady movement away from the center, his shift from orthodoxy to marginal religious affiliation, and his rejection of capitalism for entrepreneurial cooperation. During this period, he sought a higher and more comprehensive (to use an Emersonian phrase) spiritual and social agenda with cooperation at its heart. His first reform crusade (as represented by his activities at Haverhill) was based on a desire to engage with the world and its problems, to denounce the mean-spirited and capitalist order, and to place the church at the center of the new order. His United Church of America hoped to create a counterculture based on a new age coalition then in revolt against the religious and social orthodoxies of the day. His Unitarian congregation turned its back on his plan, and he resigned. Littlefield had attempted to start an "enclave of difference" within the ongoing institutional structure, and it had been rejected. Now he was forced to start his own community to create an anti-institutional institution.

Communal reformers have always had at least two strategies available to them. They have, to use Rosabeth Kanter's typologies, had either a "mission" ideal or a "retreat" ideal. The first was based on the premise that utopians had to be active, had to engage the world with programs, ideas, and agendas; the second presumed a "passive" and meditative pose that not only drew away from society but forced the community in on itself. "Farming by the Square Foot" on a Fellowship Farm plot reiterates the physiocratic ideal and the Progressive faith in efficient cultivation, in the utilization of land for public and private good. It harkens back not only to Jefferson but to the faith (mistaken sometimes) of the Jewish agricultural settlers in Kansas and the Topolobampo plan. Land and the cottages placed on them meant both freedom and security. Freedom and security could be won if men and women worked together, if they pooled their resources and shared responsibilities. To own a home and plan a small garden was the emerging suburban ideal for workers, but, in the capitalist and competitive world, it was not enough—a community of common believers was essential.

A surer way, and one that did not depend solely on the institutions of society, was to establish a utopia, a place that would be both safe haven and an example for others to follow. It could become what Hoffman called a "fort from which to rally for the emancipation of the race."[17] Littlefield eventually abandoned the fort when he could not make a go of it and set out for another promised land, California. Possibly, he hoped to revitalize himself (he was then fifty) or escape the consequences of his plans before they collapsed around him. As an apostle of simple living in community, he was following through on William Demarest Lloyd's advice that the ills of modern America had to be faced by transforming hearts and minds: "A thorough, stalwart resimplification of life governed by simple needs and loves is the imperative want of the world."[18]

There could be no better place for revitalization, for the simple life, than in California. As Kevin Starr has so amply illustrated, it offered both an abundant landscape and a utopian set of possibilities.[19] William E. Smythe had published *The Conquest of Arid America* in 1900, advocating intensive farming based on scientific irrigation, and had, in 1909, started the Little Lander Colony at San Ysidro, near San Diego. Job Harriman's Llano was launched in 1914 in the aftermath of his unsuccessful race for mayor of Los Angeles. There were other semicooperative ventures started in the state at this time, particularly in the southern part, as California was being exploited for its natural resources. But California was more than a place; it was an idea that refreshed and one that encouraged new starts. Charles Fletcher Loomis called it the "new Eden of the Anglo-Saxon home seeker."[20] Littlefield was a New Englander who, like many others, before and after, turned to the Golden State for solace and inspiration. It was a place where new religions did flourish.

Littlefield, like some other utopians of his age, was an antimodernist in the way that Jackson Lears has outlined in *No Place of Grace*.[21] Littlefield rejected the emerging social order and tried to supplant it with what he believed was a new faith, a new common creed. In so doing, he was forced to find, like others before him, some balance between retreat and mission, between progress and old values.

Members who joined communal groups after 1860 risked something in order to achieve a settled life, and (in nearly all cases) they moved in order to gain it. They moved from hearth and home in search of deeper and more secure social arrangements than they could find in Chicago, Dayton, or Odessa. They moved into groups that were a curious compound of both radical and conservative tendencies. Their radicalism was rooted in their ability to break with the old order and establish (or reestablish) a new one. By their very nature, they were tradition breakers, schismatics intent on challenging the given order. As organizations, they promised security, safe harbor from the world, and they appealed to that conservative desire to be rooted in a community, to find fellowship and engagement with others and with a leader. Whereas the American world after the Civil War was fluid, the community appeared solid; whereas the world was quixotic and changing, the colony seemed true to its promises (or at least promised to be so); whereas the world was unsettled, the program offered was reassuring and provided a place from which either self or society could be altered.

Appendix

All the groups listed have been verified to have started operation. Those that only issued statements or prospectuses have not been included.

1. Harmonial Vegetarian Society (1860–64), near Maysville, Benton County, Arkansas.
2. Point Hope Community, or Berlin Heights Community (1860–61), Berlin Heights, Erie County, Ohio.
3. Icaria-Corning (1860–78), Village of Icaria (four miles west of Corning), Adams County, Iowa.
4. Adonai Shomo Corporation, or Community of Fullerites (1861–97), Petersham (the land now owned by Harvard University), Worcester County, Massachusetts.
5. Ora Labora Community, or Christian German Agricultural and Benevolent Society of Ora Labora (1862–68), between Caseville and Wildfowl (now Bay Port), Huron County, Michigan.
6. Celesta (1863–64), Celesta (two miles west of Laporte), Sullivan County, Pennsylvania.
7. Amenia Community, or the Brotherhood of the New Life (1863–67), Amenia, Dutchess County, New York.
8. Berlin Community, or Christian Republic (1865–66), Berlin Heights, Erie County, Ohio.
9. Brocton Community, or Salem-on-Erie (1867–81), Brocton, Town of Portland, Chautauqua County, New York.
10. Daviesite Kingdom of Heaven (official name is unknown) (1867–81), near Walla Walla (between Mill Creek and Russel Creek), Walla Walla County, Washington.
11. Reunion Colony, or the True Family (1868–70), near Minersville (now Oronogo), Jasper County, Missouri.
12. Mutual Land Emigration and Cooperative Colonization Company (1869–74), Nemaha County, Kansas.
13. Union Colony (1869–72), Greeley, Weld County, Colorado.
14. German Colonization Company, or German Colony of Colfax (1870–71), Colfax (seven or eight miles south of Silver Cliff), Fremont (now Custer) County, Colorado.
15. Kansas Co-operative Farm (later renamed Prairie Home Colony, also

called Silkville–Fourierist (1870–84), Silkville, Williamsburg Township, Franklin County, Kansas.

16. Progressive Community (1871–78), near Cedar Vale, Howard (now Chautauqua) County, Kansas.
17. Warm Springs Colony (1871), on the French Broad River, Madison County, North Carolina.
18. Chicago-Colorado Colony (1871–73), Longmont, Boulder County, Colorado.
19. Western Colony (later renamed St. Louis–Western Colony) (1871–72), Evans, Weld County, Colorado.
20. Friendship Community (1872–77), near Buffalo, Dallas County, Missouri.
21. Ancora Productive Union of the Industrial Public (1872), Ancora, New Jersey.
22. Bennett Co-operative Colony (1873–ca. 1877), two miles north of Long Lane, Dallas County, Missouri.
23. German Socialist Colony (1873–76), near Lynchburg, Virginia.
24. Social Freedom Community (1874–80), Chesterfield County (exact location unknown), Virginia.
25. Bon Homme Colony–Hutterites (1874–present), Bon Homme, Bon Homme County, South Dakota.
26. Women's Commonwealth, or the Sanctificationists (1874–1906), Belton, Bell County, Texas (later moved to Washington, D.C.).
27. Dawn Valcour (1874–75), at Colchester, Vermont, and Valcour Island, New York.
28. Orderville United Order (1875–84), Orderville, Kane County, Utah.
29. Wolf Creek Colony–Hutterites (1875–1930), near Freemen, Hutchinson County, South Dakota (later moved to Stirling, Alberta, Canada).
30. Investigating Community (1875), near Cedar Vale, Chautauqua County, Kansas.
31. Cedarvale Community, or Cedar Vale Benevolent and Educational Society (1875–77), Cedar Vale, Chautauqua County, Kansas.
32. Fountain Grove (1876–1900), two miles north of Santa Rosa, Sonoma County, California.
33. Modjeska Colony (1877–78), Anaheim, Orange County, California.
34. Esperanza (1877–ca. 1878), Urbana, Neosho County, Kansas.
35. Hays City Danish Colony (official name is unknown) (1877), on the Smokey Hill River (five to ten miles south of Hays), Ellis County, Kansas.
36. Home Colony (1877), South Frankfort, Michigan.
37. Rankin Colony (1878–79), Muskoda, Minnesota.
38. Elmspring Colony (later called Old Elmspring)–Hutterites (1878–1929), near Parkson, Hutchison County, South Dakota (later moved to Warner, Alberta, Canada).
39. Bible Community (official name is unknown) (?–1879–?), Plattsburg, Clinton County, Missouri.

40. Icaria–Jeune Icarie (1879–1887), on part of site of Icaria-Corning (no. 137), Adams County, Iowa.
41. Icaria–New Icarian Community (1879–95), near a site of Icaria–Jeune Icarie (no. 168), Adams County, Iowa.
42. Societas Fraternia (1879–?), four miles northeast of Anaheim, Los Angeles County, California.
43. Tripp Colony—Hutterites (1879–84), Tripp, Hutchinson County, South Dakota.
44. Rugby Colony (1880–87), Rugby, Morgan County, Tennessee.
45. Thompson Colony (1880–?), near Salina, Saline County, Kansas.
46. Washington Colony (1881–84), Town of Whatcom (now part of the city of Bellingham), Whatcom County, Washington.
47. Sicily Island Colony (1881–82), Sicily Island, Catahoula Parish, Louisiana.
48. Icaria–Speranza (1881–86), three miles south of Cloverdale, Sonoma County, California.
49. Beersheba Colony (1882–85), on Pawnee Creek (near present-day Kalvesta), Hodgeman County, Kansas.
50. Cremieux (1882–89), on the division line between Davison and Aurora counties, South Dakota.
51. Painted Woods (1882–87), Painted Woods (near Bismarck), Burleigh County, North Dakota.
52. Alliance, or Vineland Colony (1882–1908), Alliance, Salem County, New Jersey.
53. Rosenhayn (1882–89), Rosenhayn, Deerfield Township, Cumberland County, New Jersey.
54. Bethlehem Yehudah (also spelled Juhudah) (1882–85), South Dakota (exact location unknown).
55. York Society of Integral Cooperators (1882–?), Taney County, Missouri.
56. New Odessa Community (1883–87), Cow Creek (near Glendale), Douglas County, Oregon.
57. Mutual Aid Community (1883–87), near Glen Allen (now Glenallen), Bollinger County, Missouri.
58. Joyful, or Association of Brotherly Co-operators (1884), near Bakersfield, Kern County, California.
59. Tidioute Colony—Hutterites (1884–86), four miles south of Tidioute, Warren County, Pennsylvania.
60. Shalam (1884–1901), near Dona Ana, Dona Ana County, New Mexico.
61. Pioneer Association (1885–?), Mille Lac, Wisconsin.
62. Kaweah Co-operative Commonwealth (later reorganized as Industrial Coperative Union of Kaweah) (1885–92), near Visalia (now part of Sequoia National Park), Tulare County, California.
63. Columbia Co-operative Colony (later renamed Nehalem Valley Co-operative Colony) (1886–ca. 1892), Mist, Columbia County, Oregon.

64. Jamesville Colony—Hutterites (1886–1918), near Utica, Yankton County, South Dakota (later moved to Rockyford, Alberta, Canada).

65. Milltown Colony–Hutterites (1886–1907), Milltown, Hutchinson County, South Dakota.

66. Puget Sound Cooperative Colony (1887–90), Port Angeles, Clallam County, Washington.

67. Lord's Farm, or Woodcliff Community (1889–ca. 1907), Woodcliff Lake, Bergen County, New Jersey.

68. Koreshan Unity–San Francisco (1890–91), San Francisco, San Francisco County, California.

69. Kutter Colony–Hutterites (1890–1918), near Mitchell, Hanson County, South Dakota (later moved to Redlands, Alberta, Canada).

70. Rockport Colony–Hutterites (1891–1934), near Alexandria, Hanson County, South Dakota (later moved to Magrath, Alberta, Canada).

71. Union Mill Company (1891–97), Nehalem, Tillamook County, Oregon.

72. Co-operative Brotherhood of Winter Island (1893–ca. 1898), upper portion of Suisun Bay (two miles west of Antioch), Contra Costa County, California.

73. Hiawatha Village Association (1893–96), Hiawatha, Schoolcraft County, Michigan.

74. Shaker Community at Narcoossee (1894–1912), Narcoossee, Runnymede Township, Osceola County, Florida.

75. Altruria (1894–95), Mark West Creek (six miles north of Santa Rosa), Sonoma County, California.

76. Ruskin Cooperative Association (1894–99), Tennessee City and Ruskin, Dickinson County, Tennessee.

77. Colorado Cooperative Company (1894–1910), Nucla, Montrose County, Colorado.

78. Koreshan Unity–Estero (1894–present), Estero, Lee County, Florida.

79. Altruist Community (1894–95), Gibsonville, Genessee County, Michigan.

80. Home Employment Co-operative Company (1894–ca. 1906), Long Lane, Dallas County, Missouri.

81. Glennis Cooperative Industrial Company (1894–96), Eatonville, Pierce County, Washington.

82. Grander Age Colony (1894–98), Co-opolis, Mississippi.

83. Israelites, or New House of Israel (1895–ca. 1920), between the towns of Livingston and Leggett, Polk County, Texas.

84. Willard Co-operative Colony (1895–96), Andrews, Cherokee County, North Carolina.

85. Fairhope Industrial Association (later renamed the Fairhope Single Tax Corporation) (1895–present), Fairhope, Baldwin County, Alabama.

86. Christian Corporation (1896–97), Lincoln, Lancaster County, Nebraska.

87. Magnolia at Shepherd, Texas (1896).
88. Christian Altruist Colony (1896), Madison, Wisconsin.
89. Liberty Cooperative Association (1896–97?), Hustburg, Tennessee.
90. Christian Commonwealth Colony (1986–1900), Commonwealth (twelve miles east of Columbus), Muskogee County, Georgia.
91. Freedom Colony (1897–1905), six miles northwest of Fulton, Bourbon County, Kansas.
92. Equality, or Brotherhood of the Cooperative Commonwealth (later reorganized as Freeland) (1897–1907), Equality (two miles southwest of Edison), Skagit County, Washington.
93. American Settlers Association, or Duke Colony (1898–99), Duke (now Ruskin), Ware County, Georgia.
94. Cooperative Brotherhood, or Burley Colony (1898–1908), Burley, Kitsap County, Washington.
95. Point Loma, or the Universal Brotherhood and Theosophical Society (1898–1942), Point Loma (site now occupied by Point Loma College), San Diego County, California.
96. Shaker Community at White Oak (1898–1902), White Oak, Camden County, Georgia.
97. Salvation Army Colonies (1898–1910), Fort Amity, Colorado; Romie, California; Fort Herrick, Ohio.
98. Montecello Colony (1898), Montecello, Jefferson County, Florida.
99. Mutual Home Association, or the Home Colony (1898–1921), Carr Inlet (four miles southwest of Gig Harbor), Pierce County, Washington.
100. Ruskin Commonwealth (1899–1901), Ruskin, Ware County, Georgia.
101. Straight Edge Industrial Settlement (1899–1918), New York City, New York.
102. Friedheim (1899–1900), Virginia (exact location unknown).
103. Lystra (1899–1902), Virginia (exact location unknown).
104. Commonwealth of Israel (1899–ca. 1900), Adulum, Mason County, Texas.
105. Christian Social Association (1899–1904), Wisconsin (exact location unknown).
106. Spirit Fruit Society (1899–1908), Lisbon, Elkrun Township, Columbiana County, Ohio (later moved to Ingleside, Lake County, Illinois).
107. Niksur Co-operative Association (1899), Lawrence (now Wahkon), Mille Lacs County, Minnesota.
108. Kinder Lou (1900–1901), Kinderlou (four miles west of Valdosta), Lowndes County, Georgia.
109. Freeland Association (1900–ca. 1906), Freeland, Whidby Island, Island County, Washington.
110. Arden (1900–present), Arden, New Castle County, Delaware.
111. Southern Co-operative Association of Apalachicola, or Co-operative Association of America (1900–ca. 1904), Apalachicola, East Point, Franklin County, Florida.

112. The Roycrofters (1900–1915), East Aurora, Erie County, New York.

113. Maxwell Colony–Hutterites (1900–1918), Hutchinson County, South Dakota (later moved to Headingly, Manitoba, Canada).

114. New Elmspring Colony–Hutterites (1900–1918), near Ethan, Hutchinson-Hanson County line, South Dakota (later moved to Magrath, Alberta, Canada).

115. Zion City, or Christian Catholic Apostolic Church in Zion (1901–6), Zion, Benton Township, Lake County, Illinois.

116. Rosedale Colony–Hutterites (1901–18), Hanson County, South Dakota (later moved to Elie, Manitoba, Canada).

117. House of David (1903–28), Benton Harbor, Berrien County, Michigan.

118. Temple Home Association, or Halcyon Theosophists (1903–13), Halcyon, San Luis Obispo County, California.

119. Spink Colony–Hutterites (1905–18), Spink County, South Dakota (later moved to Fort MacLeod, Alberta, Canada).

120. Beadle Colony–Hutterites (1905–18), Beadle County, South Dakota (later moved to West Raley, Alberta, Canada).

121. Huron Colony–Hutterites (1906–18), Huron, Beadle County, South Dakota (later moved to Elie, Manitoba, Canada).

122. Richard Colony–Hutterites (1906–18), Sanborn County, South Dakota (later moved to Lethbridge, Alberta, Canada).

123. Helicon Hall Colony (1906–7), near Englewood, Bergen County, New Jersey.

124. Buffalo Colony–Hutterites (1907–13), Beadle County, South Dakota.

125. Fellowship Farm Association (1907–18), Westwood, Norfolk County, Massachusetts.

126. Tahanto (1909–34), Harvard, Worcester County, Massachusetts.

127. Milford Colony–Hutterites (1910–18), Beadle County, South Dakota (later moved to Raymond, Alberta, Canada).

128. Order of Theocracy (1910–31), Fort Myers, Lee County, Florida.

129. Free Acres Association (1910–50), New Providence (now Berkeley Heights) Township, Union County, New Jersey.

130. Halidon (1911–38), Westbrook, Cumberland County, Maine.

131. Lopez Community (official name is unknown) (1912–ca. 1920), Lopez, Lopez Island, San Juan County, Washington.

132. Spring Creek Colony–Hutterites (1912–20), near Lewiston, Fergus County, Montana (later moved to Rockford, Alberta, Canada).

133. Krotona Community of Adyar Theosophists (1912–24), Hollywood, Los Angeles County, California (later moved to Ojai, Ventura County, California).

134. Los Angeles Fellowship Farm (1912–27), northeast of Puente, Los Angeles County, California.

135. Warren Range Colony–Hutterites (1913–18), Fergus County, Montana (later moved to Cardston, Alberta, Canada).

136. James Valley Colony–Hutterites (1913–18), James Valley Junction, Beadle County, South Dakota (later moved to Elie, Manibota, Canada).

137. Metropolitan Institute of Texas, or the Burning Bush (1913–19), one mile southeast of Bullard, Smith County, Texas.
138. Bohemian Co-operative Farming Company (1913–16), one mile west of Maryland, Cumberland County, Tennessee.
139. Llano del Rio Company (1914–18), Llano, Los Angeles County, California.
140. Pisgah Grande (1914–21), near Santa Susana, Ventura–Los Angeles County line, California.
141. Army of Industry (1914–18), near Auburgn, Placer County, California.

Notes

CHAPTER 1

1. Arthur Bestor, Jr., "Patent Office Models of the Good Society: Some Relationships between Social Reform and Westward Expansion," *American Historical Review* 58 (April 1953): 526. For one refutation of Bestor's thesis, see Louis Filler, "Pilot Plans, Utopias and Social Reform" (paper presented at the Newberry Library Conference on American Studies, Chicago, March 1953).

2. John L. Thomas, "Romantic Reform in America, 1815–1865," *American Quarterly* 18 (Winter 1965): 679. Mark Holloway, *Heavens on Earth* (New York, 1962), 213.

3. Henry D. Lloyd, "Address" (presented at Ruskin, Tenn., 19 June 1897; now held at Ruskin Colony). Bernard K. Johnpoll and Lillian Johnpoll, *The Impossible Dream* (Westport, Conn., 1981).

4. Alan Trachtenberg, *The Incorporation of America* (New York, 1982), 180.

5. Robert Wiebe, *The Segmented Society* (New York, 1975), 19.

6. Ibid., 59.

7. Ibid., 169.

8. Robert Wiebe, *The Search for Order* (New York, 1967), 79.

9. R. Laurence Moore, *Religious Outsiders and the Making of Americans* (New York, 1977), 209–10.

10. Page Smith, *As a City upon a Hill* (Cambridge, Mass., 1966).

11. Edward Bellamy, *Looking Backward* (Boston, 1931), 10–11.

12. William James, *The Varieties of Religious Experience* (New York: Modern Library, n.d.), 27.

13. Keith Thomas, "An Anthropology of Religion and Magic," *Journal of Interdisciplinary History*, 6, no. 1 (Summer 1975): 102.

14. John Winthrop, "A Model of Christian Charity," in *The Founding of Massachusetts*, ed. Edmund Morgan (Indianapolis, 1964), 203. Kenneth Lockridge, *A New England Town* (New York, 1970), 1.

15. Alexis de Tocqueville, *On Democracy, Revolution and Society*, ed. John Stone and Stephen Mennell (Chicago, 1978), 55.

16. Rosabeth Kanter, *Commitment and Community* (Cambridge, Mass., 1972).

17. John L. Thomas, *Alternative America* (Cambridge, Mass., 1983), 365.

18. Ibid., 345.

19. Ibid., 128.

20. Walter Thomas Mills, *Product Sharing Village* (Chicago, 1894).

21. Laurence Vesey, *The Communal Experience* (New York, 1973).

22. Thomas, *Alternative America*, 366.

23. Kevin Starr, *America and the California Dream* (New York, 1986), and *Inventing the Dream* (New York, 1985); Carey McWilliams, *Factories in the Field* (Boston, 1939).

24. Bryan Wilson, *Religious Sects* (London, 1970).

25. Henry W. Longfellow to Stephen Longfellow, 10 October 1840, cited in *The Letters of Henry Wadsworth Longfellow*, ed. Andrew Hilen (Cambridge, Mass., 1966), 257–58.

26. "I will not prejudge them successful. They look well in July. We shall see them in September. I know they are better for themselves than as partners. Their saying that things are clear, and that they are sane, does not make them so. If they will serve the town of Harvard, and make their neighbors feel them as benefactors wherever they touch them, they are safe as the sun" (*Journals of Ralph Waldo Emerson*, ed. Edward Waldo Emerson and Waldo Emerson Forbes [New York, 1909], 6:421). For a comparative analysis of the views of Emerson, Thoreau, and Alcott on community, see Taylor Stoehr, "Transcendentalist Attitudes toward Communitism and Individualism," *Emerson Society Quarterly* 20, no. 2 (1974): 65–90. For Fruitlands, see Aurele Durocher, "The Story of Fruitlands," *Michigan Academician* 1, no. 3 (Spring 1969): 37–45.

27. Frederick Douglass, "What I Found at the Northhampton Association," reprinted in *From Utopia to Florence*, by Alice McBee (Philadelphia, 1975).

28. For a contemporary account of the Matthias sect, see William L. Stone, *Matthias and His Imposters* (New York, 1835). For Truth's career, see Arthur Fausett, *Sojourner Truth* (New York, 1938), 64–93.

29. John H. Noyes, *Confessions of John H. Noyes* (New York, 1849), 141. See also Elizur Wright's account of Noyes in New York in his letter to A. A. Philips, 29 October 1837, Thomas Collection, Library of Congress, Washington, D.C. The best study of the young Noyes is Robert L. Thomas, *The Man Who Would Be Perfect* (Philadelphia, 1977).

30. Horace Greeley, *Recollections of a Busy Life* (New York, 1868). 145. New York seems to have disgusted numerous utopians. Albert Brisbane's first contact with the city was when the "paddle wheel of his steamer churned up from the mud of the river the bloated corpse of a Negro woman" (Arthur Bestor, Jr., "Albert Brisbane: Propagandist for Socialism in the Forties," *New York History* 28 [April 1947], 131).

31. See my introduction, "The Familisterie: Radical Reform through Cooperative Enterprise," to *Papa's Own Girl*, by Marie Howland (reprint, Philadelphia, 1975); and Paul Gaston, *Women of Fairhope* (Athens, Ga., 1984), 19–65.

32. Maren Lockwood Carden, *Oneida: Utopian Community to Modern Corporation* (Baltimore, 1969), passim; and Robert S. Fogarty, "Oneida: A

Utopian Search for Religious Security," *Labor History* 14, no. 2 (Spring 1973): 202–27.

33. Arthur Morgan cites the novel—without specific evidence—as a possible source for *Looking Backward* (see his biography of Bellamy, *Edward Bellamy* [New York, 1944], 369).

34. "A cooperative market farm on the Hackensack Meadows, conducted with ordinary prudence and skill would be a great success. Are there no workingmen in our midst among the number now complaining that the city is overstocked with labor, who can take hold of and develop this idea" ("Cooperative Farming," *New York Weekly Tribune*, 1 September 1869).

35. Herbert W. Schneider and George Lawton, *A Prophet and a Pilgrim* (New York, 1942).

36. Russell Blankenship, *And There Were Men* (New York, 1942), 79–94.

37. The problem of defining a communal settlement has never been satisfactorily settled. Kenneth Lockridge's study of Dedham, Mass., *A New England Town: The First Hundred Years* (New York, 1970), states that it was "also a utopian experiment, hardly less so than the famous Amana, Oneida and Brook Farm experiments of the nineteenth century. The founders of this community set out to construct a unified social organism in which the whole would be more than the sum of the parts" (1). Ronald G. Garnett, *Cooperation and the Owenite Socialist Communities of Britain, 1824–1845* (Manchester, 1972), tries to rule out, however, Fourierist joint-stock companies from communal history. Kanter, *Commitment and Community*, 241–46, is the most intelligent discussion so far, and I have used a combined historical and sociological approach in deciding my own choices. However, Bryan Wilson's brilliant work in the sociology of religion should be a starting point for anyone interested in sect or cult formation (see *Religious Sects*).

38. There is no single study of this tendency among American thinkers, though several works throw light on the subject. See James Gilbert, *Designing the Industrial State* (Chicago, 1972); and Howard Segal, *Technological Utopianism in American Culture* (Chicago, 1985).

39. Horace Greeley, "Moral Aspects of Cooperation," *New York Weekly Tribune*, 31 July 1867, and "Cooperation," *New York Weekly Tribune*, 13 October 1869.

40. For an understanding of perfectionism, see John L. Peters, *Christian Perfectionism and American Methodism* (New York, 1943); and Merrill Gaddis, "Christian Perfectionism in America" (Ph.D. diss., University of Chicago, 1929). John L. Thomas provides a good working definition: "Perfectibility—the essentially religious notion of the individual as the reservoir of possibilities—fosters a revolutionary assurance that if you can re-arrange society by the destruction of oppressive order then these possibilities will have a chance and you will get progress" ("Romantic Reform," 656). For charismatic definitions, one should look at Max Weber's classic essay "The Sociology of Charismatic Authority," in *From Max Weber: Essays in Sociol-*

ogy, ed. Hans Gerth and C. Wright Mills (New York, 1946); and F. C. Anthony Wallace, "Revitalization Movements," *American Anthropologist* 58 (1956): 264–81.

41. *Buckeye State* (Lisbon, Ohio) (25 October 1890).

42. Deposition by Robert McWhirter, 10 December 1887, Bell County Courthouse, Belton, Tex.

43. Howard Quint's *The Forging of American Socialism* (Columbia, S.C., 1953) and Charles LeWarne's *Utopias on Puget Sound* (Seattle, 1978) are both sound studies.

44. Albert Kimsey Owen, *Integral Cooperation* (New York, 1885), 8.

45. For information about the indefatigable Longley, see H. Roger Grant, "Missouri's Utopian Communities," *Bulletin of the Missouri Historical Society* 66 (October 1972): 20–48; and Hal Sears, "Alcander Longley, Missouri Communist," *Bulletin of the Missouri Historical Society* 25 (January 1969): 123–37.

46. For an extended discussion of communal journeying, see Robert S. Fogarty, "Behold a White Horse: Communal Journeys," in *Prospects 10: Annual Studies in American Culture* (New York, 1986).

47. Wallace, "Revitalization," 265.

48. Ibid.

49. L. L. Bernard and Jessie Bernard, *Origins of Sociology* (New York, 1943), 313.

50. Ibid.

51. Neil Smelser, *Theory of Collective Behavior* (New York, 1962).

52. Bryan Wilson, *Religion in Sociological Perspective* (Oxford, 1983), 111.

53. Ibid., 111, 120. A recent study of the Unification Church bears out Wilson's conversion thesis. See Eileen Barker, *The Making of a Moonie: Brainwashing or Choice* (London, 1985).

54. Trachtenberg, *The Incorporation of America*, 180. Bestor, "Patent Office," 120.

CHAPTER 2

1. Henry David Thoreau, *Journal, 1837–1844*, ed. John C. Broderick (Princeton, N.J., 1981).

2. Philip Gleason, "From Free Love to Catholicism: Dr. and Mrs Thomas L. Nichols and Yellow Springs," *Ohio Historical Review* 70, no. 4 (October 1961): 283–307, 290.

3. For this phase of the Nicholses' career, see ibid.

4. George M. Pierson, *The Moving American* (New York, 1973), 229–57.

5. George W. Noyes, ed., *Religious Experiences of John Humphrey Noyes* (New York, 1923), 14.

6. *Dictionary of American Biography*, 9:338–39, s.v. "Nathaniel Taylor."

7. See Maren Lockwood Carden, *Oneida: Utopian Community to Modern Corporation* (Baltimore, 1969); Lawrence Foster, *Religion and Sexuality* (New York, 1981); and Fogarty, "Oneida."

8. For a compelling and thorough account of overland migration, see John Unruh, *The Plains Across* (Urbana, Ill., 1979).

9. See John O.Gooch, "William Keil," *Methodist History* 5, no. 4 (July 1967); and R. J. Hendricks, *Bethel and Aurora* (New York, 1933).

10. Henricks, *Bethel and Aurora*, 4.

11. Ibid., 52.

12. Ibid., 60–61.

13. "Who can doubt the saving grace of their music as they sang and played their way through the desert spaces, with savage tribes on all sides, able to utterly destroy them at any hour of the day or watch of the night" (ibid., 63).

14. Schneider and Lawton, *Prophet and Pilgrim*, 14 (this is the standard account of Harris's career). Michael Barkun's *Crucible of the Millennium* (Syracuse, N.Y., 1986) focuses on the millennial aspects of the 1840s.

15. Schneider and Lawton, *Prophet and Pilgrim*, 458.

16. Joseph Gambone, "Octagon City," *American History Illustrated* 10, no. 12 (August 1975): 11. Clubb's philosophy was a simple one: "We do not declare that man is already free, either in dietetics or morality. He is enslaved by appetite and habit" (Henry S. Clubb, "Vegetarianism," *Water Cure Journal* 18, no. 5 [November 1854]: 105).

17. Cited in Russell Hickman, "The Vegetarian and Octagon Settlement Companies," *Kansas State Historical Society* 2, no. 4 (November 1933): 379.

18. Ibid.

19. Miriam Davis Colt, *Went to Kansas* (Watertown, N.Y., 1862), 284–85.

20. Ibid., 21.

21. Ibid. Colt also reports that the bloomer dress was worn by many colonists.

22. Gambone, "Octagon City," 15. Colt reported that, at the colony's demise, "Mr. Clubb had no money to refund, but let us have some corn starch, farina, a few dates, and a little pealed barley" (*Went to Kansas*, 120).

23. Christopher Johnson, *Utopian Communism in France: Cabet and the Icarians, 1839–1851* (Ithaca, N.Y., 1974).

24. H. Roger Grant, *An Icarian Communist in Nauvoo* (Springfield, Ill., 1971), 15, 16.

25. Ibid., 19.

26. Robert Hine, *California's Utopian Communities* (Pasadena, Calif., 1953).

27. During this period, other German groups established themselves in cooperative fashion. The first settlers at Anaheim, Calif., were German farmers who had organized at San Francisco in 1857 and who purchased

1,165 acres. Once they settled on the land, however, they dropped the co-operative features. See Charles Nordhoff, *Communistic Societies of the United States* (reprint, New York, 1961), 361–63.

28. The major sources for the history of St. Nazianz are Frank S. Beck, "Christian Communists in America: A History of the Colony of St. Nazianz, Wisconsin" M.A. thesis, St. Paul Seminary, 1951); and William A. Titus, "St. Nazianz: A Unique Religious Colony," *Wisconsin Magazine of History* 5 (December 1921): 160–65.

29. Beck, "Christian Communists," 42.

30. Ibid., 47.

31. Ibid., 114.

32. While a member at Berlin Heights, James Towner, later a significant figure at Oneida, wrote, "We have been talking and writing a long time now, about the social equality of woman and freedom and justice, and considering what we must do to bring about those much desired objects. And many of us, perhaps the most of us, are waiting for the time to come when we can do something; we are waiting for Association, for community, for social reorganization of some sort. . . . Are we not beginning to see that, that instead of this waiting, we must go to work right HERE and NOW" ("Something Practical," *Social Revolutionist* 3 [1854]: 31).

33. The Germania Colony was led by Benjamin Hall and had originally come from Groton, Mass. They had a twelve-hundred-acre farm and several small industries. Material about them can be found at the Wisconsin Historical Society.

34. Frans H. Widstrand to Ignatius Donnelly, 7 August 1862, Donnelly Papers, Minnesota Historical Society.

35. Edwin Rozwenc, *Cooperatives Come to America* (Mt. Vernon, Iowa, 1941), 115.

36. Most leaders of the Knights preferred producer and consumer co-operatives; however, Gerald Grob has noted that, "during the first half of the 1880s therefore, a large part of the Knights' energies were channeled into cooperative activities" (*Workers and Utopia* [Evanston, Ill., 1961], 44).

37. T. Wharton Collins, "Bible Communism," *Cooperator* 8, no. 142 (18 April 1868): 142.

38. Horace Greeley, "English Cooperative Societies," *New York Weekly Tribune*, 5 February 1868.

39. In 1869, the Mutual Land Emigration and Cooperative Colonization Company was organized in London by James Redford and James Murray. About fifty families came during that year, but the cooperative features ended by 1874. They held in common 740 acres in Nemaha County, Kans. The Wakefield Colony, organized the same year, was to have been cooperative, but it gave up on the idea because of opposition from some colonists. See William Chapman, "The Wakefield Colony," *Kansas Historical Collections* 10 (1942): 496.

40. Schneider and Lawton, *Prophet and Pilgrim*, 37, 94.

41. Ibid., 94.

42. Ibid.

43. Ibid., 24.

44. Ibid., 29, 36.

45. Ibid., 47.

46. Ibid.

47. Ibid., 109.

48. Ibid., 117, 118.

49. Ibid., 125, 129.

50. Ibid., 133.

51. Ibid., 159.

52. Ibid., 177.

53. Ibid., 198.

54. *Celesta: Now and Then*, 26.

55. A primitive painting of the community site was done in 1864, suggesting the outlines of the settlement: "On the inside of the right angle and close to its apex is Armstrong's combination store, printing office and upstairs auditorium. It is a large appearing [sic], two and a half story building, with eight windows on the sides and four at the ends. . . . In the center one is Armstrong's home, and has a latticed front stoop with shrubbery at either side" (ibid., 23).

56. Ibid., 20.

57. Ibid., 18.

58. William A. Hinds, *American Communities and Cooperative Colonies* (New York, 1878), 397.

59. The Bishop Hill Colony was begun in 1846 by Swedish immigrants who objected to the lack of piety in the Lutheran state church. Jansson led them from Sweden to Henry County, Ill., where they built an impressive community. By 1848, they had colonists in residence; however, they lost their leader in 1850, when he was shot by an apostate with grievances against him. See Paul Elmen, *Wheat Flour Messiah* (Carbondale, Ill., 1976); and M. A. Mikklesen, *The Bishop Hill Colony* (Baltimore, 1892).

60. The major source for the history of the Walla Walla Jesus is Blankenship, *And There Were Men*.

61. Ibid., 88.

62. A group of German Methodists under Emil Baur founded a community at Huron County, Mich., after preparing for their move for almost ten years. They came from Ohio and Pennsylvania and homesteaded three thousand acres. By 1863, they had built ten homes and gained some financial support from the wealthy Harmony Community. Commonly known as "Ora and Labora," the community lost members in the Civil War and never collected adequate capital to sustain itself. See Carl Wittke, "Ora and Labora: A German Methodist Utopia," *Ohio Historical Quarterly* 67 (April 1958): 129–40. In the same year (1862), German Mennonites from Russia settled in South Dakota.

63. Horace Greeley, "Moral Aspects of Cooperation," *New York Weekly Tribune*, 31 July 1867.

64. Horace Greeley, "Cooperation," *New York Weekly Tribune*, 13 October 1869.

65. James F. Willard, ed., *The Union Colony at Greeley, Colorado, 1869–1871* (Greeley, Colo., 1926), xv.

66. Ibid., xiii.

67. Ibid., xvii.

68. James Willard, *Experiments in Colorado Colonization, 1869–1872* (Boulder, Colo., 1926), 62–65.

69. Ibid., 82.

70. Ibid.

71. Willard, *Union Colony*, 3.

72. Ibid., 11.

73. Ibid., 165–76, 239.

74. Ibid., 283, 305.

75. Dolores Hayden, *Seven American Utopias* (Cambridge, Mass., 1976).

76. The best general study of Silkville is Garrett Carpenter, *Silkville: A Kansas Attempt in the History of Fourierist Utopias, 1869–1892*, Emporia State Research Studies, vol. 2, no. 2 (Emporia, Kans., December 1954).

77. See Carl Guarneri, "Who Were the Utopian Socialists: Patterns of Membership in American Fourierist Communities," *Communal Societies* 5 (Fall 1985): 65–81.

78. Another French colony was reportedly organized along cooperative lines in 1869, with fifty families settled near Salina, Kans. All were to work and share the land together for a five-year period, but little was heard about the colony after its initial settlement. See Nell Waldron, "Colonization in Kansas from 1861 to 1890" (Ph.D. diss., Northwestern University, 1932).

79. Ibid., 43.

80. E. P. Grant, *Cooperation: or a Sketch of the Conditions of Labor, with a Notice of the Kansas Cooperative Farm of M. Ernest V. de Boissiere* (Williamsburg, Kans., n.d.).

81. Waldron, "Colonization in Kansas," 51.

82. E. V. Boissiere and E. P. Grant, *The Prairie Home Association and Corporation Based on Attractive Industry* (Williamsbury, Kans., n.d.).

83. Carpenter, *Silkville*, 62.

84. Marcus Thane, "Travel Letter," *Chicago Monthly Dagslyset* (1872), Brown Collection, University of Illinois Library, Urbana, Ill.

85. George P. Garrison, "A Women's Community in Texas," *Charities Review* 3 (November 1893): 30.

86. Deposition by Robert McWhirter, 22 November 1889, Bell County Courthouse, Belton, Tex.

87. B. W. Hayward vs. Ada V. Hayward, divorce suit, Belton, Tex., 22 November 1889.

88. Garrison, "Women's Community," 32.

89. Ibid., 38.

90. "The Women's Commonwealth," *Ainslee's Magazine* (September 1906), 34.

91. Ibid. See also Jayme A. Sokolow and Mary Ann Lamanna, "Women and Utopia: The Woman's Commonwealth of Belton, Texas," *Southwestern Historical Quarterly* 36 (April 1984), 371–92.

92. Margarita Spalding Gerry, "The Women's Commonwealth of Washington," *Ainslee's Magazine* (September 1902), 136.

93. Ibid., 139.

94. Ibid., 137.

95. Dolores Hayden, *The Grand Domestic Revolution*. (Cambridge, Mass., 1981). The guiding light behind the cooperative housekeeping movement, Melusina Fay Peirce, noted that "there is just as much money to be made out of household cooking, washing and sewing of today as there was out of household spinning, weaving and knitting of past centuries and American men, with their restless acquisitive energy, have already found it out" (*Cooperative Housekeeping* [Boston, 1884], 133).

96. This section is taken, in part, from my introduction to Cyrus Teed's *Cellular Cosmogony* (reprint, Philadelphia, 1975).

97. See Howard Fine, "The Koreshan Unity: The Chicago Years of a Utopian Community," *Illinois Historical Journal* 68, no. 3 (June 1975): 213–27.

98. *The Bennett-Teed Discussion* (New York, 1878).

99. Ibid., 8.

100. A. H. Andrews, "Reminiscences of a Charter Member," *Flaming Sword* (October, November, and December 1945), 2.

101. *Guiding Star*, vol. 2, no. 1 (January 1888).

102. Ibid.

103. Ibid.

104. See Teed's *Principles of Koreshan Messianism* (Estero, Fla., n.d.).

105. Koresh [Cyrus Teed], *The Messianic Appearing and Personality* (Estero, Fla., n.d.).

106. Ibid., 1.

107. Frank D. Jackson and Mary Everts Daniel, *Koreshan Unity, Communistic and Co-operative Gathering of the People: Bureau of Equitable Commerce* (Chicago, 1895), 11.

108. Ibid., 15.

109. Teed's brother belonged to this order and was reportedly an agnostic ("Their Theology," n.d., manuscript, Anita Newcomb McGee Collection, Library of Congress).

110. "Articles of Agreement," McGee Collection.

111. A. H. Andrews, "Reminiscence," *Flaming Sword* (October, November, and December 1946), 8.

112. A. H. Andrews, "Reminiscence" (April, May, and June 1946), 8.

113. A. H. Andrews, "Reminiscence" (January, February, and March 1946), 5.

114. Teed, *Cellular Cosmogony*.

115. Koresh [Cyrus Teed], *Emmanuel Swedenborg His Mission* (Estero, Fla., 1919), 57.

116. Koresh [Cyrus Teed], *Mnemonic of the Science of Memory* (Estero, Fla., n.d.), 2.

117. See Koresh [Cyrus Teed], *The Immortal Mankind* (Estero, Fla., 1909).

118. See "Mobilizing for the Final Conflict," *Flaming Sword* (October 1946), 8.

119. Ignatius Donnelly, *Caesar's Column* (Chicago, 1890).

120. Donald Myers, *The Positive Thinkers* (New York, 1980).

121. Mark Twain, *The Innocents Abroad* (New York, 1903).

122. "Jerusalem in Prose," anonymous manuscript, Jerusalem National and University Library, Jerusalem.

123. 'Still Long for Holy Land," *Chicago Daily News*, 18 December 1879, 2.

124. Anna Spafford to Hannah Whitehall Smith, 25 January 1883, Smith Collection, Oxford. The Gadites were Yemenite Jews who encountered opposition from Jews in Jerusalem, who insisted that they were Arabs, not Jews. See Bertha Spafford Vester, *Our Jerusalem* (Lebanon: Middle East Export Press, 1950), 142–49.

125. *Westminster Gazette*, 16 September 1907.

126. *Independent* 7 March 1889.

127. Ibid.

128. Mary F. Murphy and Anna Spafford vs. Dr. Samuel Hedges, Chancery Court, Chicago, 1896.

129. "Jerusalem in Prose."

130. Vester, *Our Jerusalem*, 187.

131. Newspaper clipping, n.d., Hannah W. Smith Collection (private), Oxford.

132. *Tongues of Fire* (February 1900).

133. Arnold White, *The Almighty and Us* (Ft. Lauderdale, Fla., 1979).

134. Ibid., 79.

135. Ibid., 223.

136. Ibid.

137. Ibid., 62.

138. Victor P. Abram, introduction to *The Golden Light upon the Americas*, by Frank W. Sanford (Gloucester, Mass., 1974).

139. Ibid., 19.

140. Ibid., 23.

141. Ibid., 206.

142. J. H. Neary to Esme Howard, 25 August 1908, FO 115-1509 x/k 1689, Public Record Office, London.

143. J. B. Keating, "Shiloh, or Fortified Kingdom of God," 21 August 1908, Public Record Office, London.

144. Ibid.

145. White, *The Almighty*, 274.

146. Ibid.

147. Quoted in Melvin Lasky, *Utopia and Revolution* (Chicago, 1976), 232, 281.

CHAPTER 3

1. Henry Villard, "Foreign Reports," *Cooperative Congress Reports* (1872): 95.

2. Ibid.

3. Ibid.

4. *New York Weekly Tribune*, 20 July 1870, 1 September 1869, and 21 April 1869.

5. Herman Haupt, *Cooperative Colonization* (Philadelphia, 1872), 3. Haupt cited an article in the April 1872 issue of *Harpers* by Edward Howland but favored the joint-stock arrangement over community of property: "The radical defect of nearly all schemes of association has been the attempt to accomplish too much. Societies founded on the principle of community of goods can only succeed amongst the religious enthusiasts, who regard the things of the world of little value, and practically carry out the injunction to love thy neighbor as thyself" (Haupt, *Cooperative Colonization*, 2).

6. Haupt, *Cooperative Colonization*, 2.

7. "Colonizing the South," *New York Weekly Tribune*, 9 August 1871.

8. *Credit Foncier of Sinaloa*, 1 December 1889.

9. T. Wharton Collins, "The Two Economies," *Labor Balance* 2, no. 2 (July 1878).

10. "Editorial Notes," *Labor Balance* 2, no. 14 (January 1878).

11. Hinds, *Cooperative Colonies*, 154.

12. The town of Petersburgh, Kans., received $1,500 from Thompson. It had been founded by a Chicago workingmen's group in Edwards County with aid from the Atchison, Topeka, and Santa Fe railroad. See William Zornow, *Kansas: A History of the Jayhawk State* (Norman, Okla., 1957), 188–89.

13. "A New Colonization Plan," *New York Times*, 6 June 1879.

14. Ibid. Throughout the 1880s, Newton would promote colonization. Writing in 1881 (R. Heber Newton, "Communism," *Unitarian Review and Religious Magazine* 16, no. 6 [December 1881]: 515), he stated that the cyclical nature of civilization had brought it back to an appreciation of communism and that recent religious cycles had confirmed this tendency: "After Nettleton, in 1817, came Robert Owen in 1824, after Finney came the Fourierite enthusiasms, in 1842–43; after the great awakening in 1857 the social movement which might have followed was withheld by the Civil War; after the practical Moody has come the practical cooperative efforts now being widely made. First, the regeneration of the soul, then the regeneration

of society." In this essay, Newton was simply reiterating the theory of communal development that John Humphreys Noyes outlined in *American Socialisms* (Philadelphia, 1870).

15. George Jacob Holyoake, "The Need of Two Nations," *Worker: Advocating Cooperative Colonization* 1, no. 1 (October 1879).

16. *New York Times*, 17 November 1879.

17. See *Topeka Commonwealth*, 14 March 1880; and Waldron, "Colonization in Kansas." A variant on this continuing antiurban theme would be tried by John Bookwalter, an Ohio philanthropist, who tried to settle farmers on his vast landholding in Nebraska so that they could live in European agricultural villages. Musetta Gilman, "Bookwalter: Agricultural Commune in Nebraska," *Nebraska History* 55 (Spring 1975), 91–105.

18. "Cooperative Colonization," newspaper clipping, 29 October 1879, Holyoake Collection, Bishopgate Library, London.

19. *Chanute Times*, June 1877.

20. *Star of Hope*, January 1878.

21. "Invitation to Communism," *Star of Hope*, January 1878.

22. R. E. La Fetra, "Communism: The Way Out of Panics, Wages, Slavery and Hard Times," *Star of Hope*, January 1878.

23. *Thayer Head Light*, 12 April 1878.

24. Sources for Longley's life can be found in Sears, "Alcander Longley"; and Grant, "Missouri's Utopian Communities."

25. Avrahm Yarmolinsky, *A Russian American's Dream* (Lawrence, Kans., 1965), 16, 45.

26. When he left his New Jersey boarding house for the Longley community, two other residents (also Russian) reportedly left for a community in Minneapolis run by E. P. Boyd patterned on Oneida; ibid., 15. Also ibid. 20, 30–31, 71, 73.

27. Ibid.

28. The major source for Pio and the Kansas experiment is Kenneth Miller, "Danish Socialism and the Kansas Prairie," *Kansas Historical Quarterly* 38 (Summer 1972): 156–68.

29. Ibid., 166.

30. Leo Shpall, "Jewish Agricultural Colonies in the United States," *Agricultural History* 24 (July 1950): 123.

31. Elbert Sapinsley, "Jewish Agricultural Colonies in the West," *Western States Jewish Historical Quarterly* 3, no. 3 (April 1971): 157–69.

32. Gabriel Davidson and Edward Goodwin, "A Unique Agricultural Colony," *Reflex Magazine* (May 1928), 30.

33. Shpall, "Jewish Agricultural Colonies," 126.

34. See Gabriel Davidson, *Our Jewish Farmers and the Story of the Jewish Agricultural Society* (New York, 1943); Joseph Brandes, *Jewish Colonies in New Jersey* (reprint, Philadelphia, 1971).

35. There are individual monographs on most of the colonies that supplement Shpall's ground-breaking work. See Dorothy Roberts, "The Jewish Colony at Cotopaxi," *Colorado Magazine* 18 (July 1949): 123–31; Gunther

Plaut, "Jewish Colonies at Painted Woods and Devils Lake," *North Dakota History* 32 (January 1965): 114–39; A. James Rudin, "Bad Axe, Michigan: An Experiment in Jewish Agricultural Settlement," *Michigan History* 56 (Summer 1972): 119–30.

36. Shpall, "Jewish Agricultural Colonies," 129, 131.

37. Ibid., 132, 133.

38. Davidson, *Our Jewish Farmers.*

39. Yarmolinsky, *A Russian American's Dream,* 100, 101.

40. Ibid., 105.

41. Edward Spencer Beeseley, "The Life and Death of William Frey, An Address Delivered at Newtown Hall," 1 November 1888.

42. "He had his own theories for all practical affairs. He had his rules about the number of hours he had to work, to rest, to eat, to dress, to make a fire in the stove, and how to light a lamp. At the same time Simonson was exceedingly shy with people and modest. But once he made up his mind nothing could shake him" (Leo Tolstoy, *The Resurrection* [New York, 1966], 475).

43. Yarmolinsky, *A Russian American's Dream,* 114, 101.

44. Ibid., 112.

45. Brian Stagg, "Tennessee's Rugby Colony," *Tennessee Historical Quarterly* 29, no. 2 (1967): 209–26.

46. Material on Rugby can be found at the Tennessee State Library and Archives. See W. H. G. Armytage, "New Light on the English Background of Thomas Hughes's Rugby Colony in East Tennessee," *East Tennessee Historical Society Publications* 21 (1949).

47. Foreign correspondent, *New York Weekly Tribune,* 18 August 1869.

48. Originally published in the *Boston Daily Advertiser,* Smith's remedy for unemployment was a "redistribution of labor: its diversion where in surplus from trade and manufacturing to tillage of the earth, the basis of all industries" (Franklin W. Smith, *The Hard Times* [Boston, 1877], 68. Smith believed that "associate migration" was particularly apt for Americans and was encouraged by the development of two towns, Vineland, N.J., and Greeley, Colo. His scheme, however, was predicated on private ownership of the land and a return on the capital invested.

49. Board of Land Ownership Constitution, n.d., Tennessee Historical Society.

50. Thomas Hughes, *Rugby, Tennessee* (New York, 1881), 21, 25.

51. Bishop of Tennessee to Thomas Hughes, 24 September 1880, Tennessee Historical Society.

52. Quoted in Brian Stagg, *A Distant Eden* (Rugby, Tenn., 1973), 5.

53. *New York Tribune,* 3 April 1877.

54. Ray Reynolds, *Cats Paw Utopia* (El Cayon, Calif., 1971), 7, 12.

55. Ibid., 23.

56. Albert Kimsey Owen, *Integral Cooperation at Work* (New York, 1885), 132.

57. John W. Lovell, "A Co-operative City and the Credit Foncier Company," *Credit Foncier of Sinaloa*, 12 October 1886, passim.

58. Owen, *Integral Cooperation*, 9, 13, 30.

59. Ibid., 14.

60. Edward Howland dedicated his massive 1868 biography of Grant to Marie: "Whose daily life and conversation demonstrate the truth of the philosophy of freedom" (*Grant as Soldier and Statesman* [Hartford, Conn., 1868]).

61. See Morgan, *Edward Bellamy*, 221.

62. Pierre Godin, *Social Solutions* (New York, 1873). *Social Solutions* was later reprinted by John Lovell in an inexpensive edition and gained a wide readership.

63. Edward Owen Greening, *The Cooperative Traveller Abroad* (London, 1888), 49.

64. *Credit Foncier of Sinaloa*, 19 January 1886.

65. *Credit Foncier of Sinaloa*, 8 June 1886.

66. *Credit Foncier of Sinaloa*, 7 September 1886.

67. Julius Wayland to A. K. Owen, 24 November 1893, Fresno State University Library.

68. Alvin Wilber quoted in Reynolds, *Cats Paw Utopia*, 62.

69. Ibid., 64, 63.

70. See Patricia Michaelis, "C. B. Hoffman, Kansas Socialist," *Kansas Historical Quarterly* 44 (Summer 1975): 166–82.

71. Christian B. Hoffman to A. K. Owen, 16 February 1891, Hoffman Collection, University of Kansas, Lawrence.

72. Owen, *Integral Cooperation*, 12, 25.

73. Reynolds, *Cats Paw Utopia*, 97.

74. "Open Letter to Albert Kimsey Owen," Albert Kimsey Owen Papers.

75. *New City*, suppl. (8 December 1893), 1:25.

76. *Credit Foncier of Sinaloa*, 7 December 1886.

77. H. D. Lloyd, *Address, June 19, 1897* (Ruskin, Tenn., 1898).

78. As early as 1890, colonies were being planned as the result of the popularity of *Looking Backward*. One wealthy California woman, Olive Washburn, had plans to convert her seventeen-hundred-acre ranch into a colony and "raise, as nearly as possible, all the necessities of life within the confines of the colony, so that the colonists need not go outside for anything." Her ranch was in the mountains near San Diego, and in the fall of 1890 there were six families on her property (see *Dubuque Weekly Times*, 29 October 1890). Another colony was chartered in Topeka, Kans., in 1893 under the Bellamy Colony Company, with the intent of founding a cooperative farm in the Cherokee Strip. There were three hundred to four hundred people in the company (all Populists), who were going "to carry the banner of the People's Party into that new territory" (*Washington Star*, 1 September 1893).

79. "Autobiography of Cyrus Willard," typescript copy, Antioch College Library.

80. Ibid.

81. "Our mission is to waken the minds of the people to the fact that they are industrial slaves and that industrial slavery must be abolished. The details will be wrought out in the heat of debate and discussion and perhaps storm and battle as the blacksmith shapes the shoe of the anvil" (Cyrus Willard to Edward Bellamy, 22 March 1889, Bellamy Papers, Houghton Library, Harvard University).

82. Writing to Bellamy ten years earlier, Willard had said, "He [Gronlund] knows as I do and every other Socialist that has studied the growth of these ideas as well as orthodox political economy that Nationalism is ¾ Socialism and ¼ Communism but he did not say so" (ibid.).

83. N. W. Lermond, "How to Build Here and Now a Cooperative Commonwealth," 22 December 1896, Brotherhood of the Cooperative Commonwealth.

84. Ibid. (quoting Muller).

85. William Muller, "One Way to the Co-Operative Commonwealth" (1893), Ault Collection, University of Washington Library.

86. See David C. Byers and Willis F. Dunbar, "Utopia in Upper Michigan," Michigan Alumnus 63, no. 14 (Winter 1957): 168–74.

87. During the late 1880s, Mills had run the American School of Politics, which had Josiah Strong on the faculty. It was devoted to the study of contemporary politics and focused on the issues of temperance, immigration, and civil service reform. In the course of their study, students were expected to look at cooperation because the "greatest fact in current economic life is not competition but combination" (Walter Thomas Mills, "The American School of Politics," Statesman 3, no. 2 [August 1888]: 341).

88. Byers and Dunbar, "Utopia in Upper Michigan." Some colonies started in this period were like the earlier Greeley, organized along cooperative lines for a single purpose. The Colorado Cooperative Company near Pinon was organized as a stock company, its sole purpose being the construction of an irrigation ditch. It was supported by reformers like Annie Diggs of Kansas and other socialists, who thought that the colony project should be more cooperative; others, however, like C. E. Smith, who had been at Topolobampo, tried to keep it a private venture.

89. In 1896, Mills moved on to begin work on his Peoples University at St. Anne's, Ill., some sixty miles south of Chicago. Students worked the land and lived off their own labor. It was described as a "colony" by the New York Herald, 1 November 1896. At the same time, a Christian Altruist colony was being started by John Holm in Madison, Wisc. Little is known about it.

90. For a discussion of the colony, see Coming Nation, 10 March 1895.

91. Hine, California's Utopian Colonies, 104.

92. Ninetta Eames Payne, *The Soul of Jack London* (Kingsport, Tenn., 1933), iv.

93. For a full account, see Duane Mercer, "The Colorado Cooperative Company," *Colorado Magazine* 45, no. 4 (1967): 293–306; and C. E. Julihu, *National Magazine* 11 (1899): 29. The Altrurian ideal remained in full force into the twentieth century, with one group, the Association of Altruists, organizing at Morrestown, N.J., in 1900 to "build ideal agricultural and urban areas . . . to transform society from competitive methods to altruistic cooperation" (Alexander Kent, "Cooperative Communities in the United States," *Bulletin of the Department of Labor* 35 [July 1901]: 635).

94. Hine, *California's Utopian Colonies*, 113.

95. J. Herbert Rowell, "Everybody's Opportunity, or Quick Socialism" (Chicago, 1901), 12.

96. Ibid.

97. Ibid., 23.

98. Kingsmill Commander, "Labor Unions and Cooperative Industries," *Cooperator* (Burley, Wash., n.d.), 1–4.

99. Charles LeWarne, "Labor and Communitarianism, 1880–1900" (paper presented at the meeting of the Organization of American Historians, Atlanta, April 1974).

100. Ibid.

101. The best study of the cooperative influence on American labor is Clifton Yearley's *Britains in American Labor* (Baltimore, 1957). Interest in cooperatives did not always translate into support for colonies. Some Chicago socialists, e.g., saw such efforts as a hindrance to social change: "A cooperative commonwealth cannot be made to order. . . . those who attempt this impossible task only obstruct the path of progress with their vain creations, thus impeding the work of the organized socialists who seek to show the masses that much of the structure of the cooperative commonwealth is around them, ready to be completed as rapidly as their intelligence is awakened to their share in the work" (cited in Ralph Scharnau, "Thomas J. Morgan and the Chicago Socialist Movement" [Ph.D. diss., Northern Illinois University, 1969], 290).

102. Yearley, *Britains*, 296.

103. George Jacob Holyoake, *Among the Americans* (Chicago, 1881), 12, 50.

104. See "Cooperation in the Cities," *Coming Nation*, 27 February 1897, 240.

105. J. J. Martin, "Objects of the Colony," 30, typescript, Martin Papers, Bancroft Library, University of California, Berkeley. For a critical look at Haskell's career, see Johnpoll and Johnpoll, *The Impossible Dream*, 180–204.

106. *Sunday Advertiser*, 12 July 1891.

107. Ibid.

108. Hine, *California's Utopian Colonies*, 99.

109. Ibid., 93.

110. *Washington Post,* 22 November 1891.

111. Despite its limited success, it served as the inspiration for the Winters Island Colony founded by Erastus Kelsey and Kate Lockwood Nevins. Kelsey was a leader in the Oakland Nationalist Club and Nevins an organizer for the Farmers Alliance. Kelsey, who owned the island, and Nevins, a former architect, signed up one hundred skilled laborers from the Bay Area to colonize but saw the Panic of 1893 destroy their plans. At its height, the colony probably had about thirty in residence because the great bulk of the members were unable to pay their monthly dues. It seems to have lasted until 1898.

112. Will Purdy, "Kaweah: A Saga of the Old Colony," Bankcroft Library, University of California, Berkeley.

113. Chester MacArthur Destler, *American Radicalism, 1865–1901* (Chicago, 1966), 183.

114. Ibid., 274.

115. Lloyd, *Address, June 19, 1897.*

116. See *Coming Nation,* 22 February, 28 March and 21 July 1896. The ten-member Home Employment Co., located at Long Lane, Dallas County, Mo., was a successor to the twenty-year-old Bennett Co-operative Co., founded in the wake of the 1873 depression. Home Employment was socialist in theory, cooperative in practice, and published a newspaper, *Industrial Freedom.* See Grant, "Missouri's Utopian Communities."

117. *Coming Nation,* 25 June, 30 April, 12 May, and 3 September 1898.

118. *Coming Nation,* 14 May 1898.

119. *Coming Nation,* 3 February and 8 March 1894.

120. See H. Roger Grant, "Portrait of a Worker's Utopia: The Labor Exchange and the Freedom, Kansas Colony," *Kansas Historical Quarterly* 43, no. 1 (Spring 1977): 56–66. There was an additional labor-exchange colony proposed for Berryville, Carroll County, Ark. See *Coming Nation,* 26 February 1896.

121. *Fairhope Courier,* January 1898.

122. *Coming Nation,* 16 December 1893.

123. *Coming Nation,* 16 and 23 December 1893.

124. Margaret Spence, "The Guild of St. George: Ruskin's Attempt to Translate His Ideas into Practice," *Bulletin of the John Rylands Library* 40, no. 1 (February 1957): 19.

125. Francelia Butler, "The Ruskin Commonwealth: A Unique Experiment in Marxian Socialism," *Tennessee Historical Quarterly* 1 (1964): 332–42.

126. *By Laws of the Ruskin Association* (Ruskin, Tenn., 1894), 1, 2, 10.

127. Theodore McDill, "The Happiest Days of My Life" (1932), typescript, Tennessee Historical Society, Nashville, Tenn.

128. J. W. Bramm, "The Ruskin Co-operative Colony," *American Journal of Sociology* 8, no. 4 (January 1903): 674.

129. Issac Broome, *Last Days of the Ruskin Cooperative* (Chicago, 1902), 51.

130. Ella Jennison, "Women of the Ruskin Community," *Coming Nation*, 10 August 1895.

131. Ibid.

132. *Coming Nation* also carried a "Children's Department" column with items of news from young socialists: "My pa has taken the *Coming Nation* ever since he heard of the paper. He likes it better every week. I call it his Bible" (10 August 1895).

133. *Coming Nation*, 26 February 1896.

134. Another colony, the Liberty Cooperative Association, was founded early in 1896 and was still in existence in May 1897. Located thirty-five miles west of Ruskin at Hustburg, Tenn., it had few members, but it did have a school, and, according to one report, those members said that they had "come to stay." See *Coming Nation*, 22 February 1896 and 29 May 1897.

135. McDill, "Happiest Days."

136. During June and July 1896, St. Louis hosted the Republican National Convention, the Direct Legislation Convention, the Populist National Convention, and the National Cooperative Congress. For the Populist party convention, see *Coming Nation*, 4 July 1896.

137. *Coming Nation*, 1 August 1896.

138. *Coming Nation*, 8 August 1896.

139. One such report focused on the east Texas cooperative association called the Magnolia Colony at Shepherd, Texas: "This colony is in fine timbered country and is improving steadily. Farming, gardening, dairying and poultry raising are the present industries. A steam saw and planing mill were put in early this fall and the manufacture of wagons implements, furniture will follow" (*Coming Nation*, 23 May 1896). Unfortunately, in 1897 the *Coming Nation* had to report the colony's failure because the membership fee, at $300, had been set too low.

140. *Coming Nation*, 17 July 1897.

141. Quint, *Forging of American Socialism*, 293, 303.

142. Charles Sotheran, *Reminiscences of Charles Sotheran* (New York, 1915), 36.

143. Cyrus Willard to Edward Bellamy, 3 August 1897, Houghton Library, Harvard University.

144. See N. W. Lermond, "Brotherhood Plan," *B.B.C. Tract Library* 1, no. 2 (December 1897); George Candee, "Workings and Trends of B.B.C. Cooperative Colonization Made Clear," *B.B.C. Tract Library* 1, no. 4 (February 1898); Frank Parsons, "Brotherhood," *B.B.C. Tract Library* (March 1898).

145. George Quimby to H. W. Halliday, 5 December 1897, Ault Collection, University of Washington Library.

146. Harry Ault, "You Can't Change Human Nature," n.d., manuscript, Ault Collection, University of Washington Library.

147. Ibid.

148. Ibid.

149. LeWarne's *Utopias on Puget Sound* covers the rise and fall of both socialist agitation and community settlements in the Pacific Northwest in considerable detail.

150. During 1895–96, there were a spate of colonies formed. During June and July 1895, e.g., four colonies, including the Willard Colony, announced that they were looking for members. The others were the Prosperana Association in San Francisco, an agricultural colony in Twiggs County, Ga., and one at Portersville, Calif., looking for "ideal men and women" for a labor-exchange project. See *Coming Nation*, 29 June 1895, and 6 July 1895.

151. Samuel Walker, "George Howard Gibson, Christian Socialist among the Populists," *Nebraska History* 55, no. 3 (Winter 1974): 553–72.

152. Ibid., 565.

153. John Fish, "Communism in Georgia" (paper presented at the meeting of the Organization of American Historians, April 1975).

154. See Paul D. Bolster, "Christian Socialism Comes to Georgia," *Georgia Review* 26, no. 1 (1972): 60–70.

155. The Willard Colony was located on twenty thousand acres and drew its membership from temperance advocates. A major fire destroyed a barn containing feed and tools in 1895, and that event hastened their decision to merge. Located in Cherokee County, N.C., it opposed trusts, natural monopolies, and liquor traffic. This staunch prohibitionist colony had its origins in the Protestant Union Church and, during its two-year existence, had about fifty members. Many subsequently joined the Christian Commonwealth Colony.

156. Fish, "Communism in Georgia," 5.

157. Paul Gaston, "Fairhope: A Work in Progress" (paper presented to the Southern Historical Society, Atlanta, 15 November 1980).

158. *Fairhope Courier*, 1 June 1898.

159. *Fairhope Courier*, August 1894.

160. Blanche Alyea and Paul Alyea, *Fairhope* (Birmingham, Ala., 1956), 10.

161. *Fairhope Courier*, 1 June 1898.

162. Gaston, "Fairhope," 7.

163. *Fairhope Courier*, September 1903.

164. Ross Paulson, *The Vrooman Brothers, Radicalism and Reform* (Lexington, Ky., 1968).

165. Bradford Peck, *The World a Department Store* (Boston, 1900; reprint, New York, 1971). For a discussion of the industrialist/entrepreneurs who penned utopian romances after Bellamy, see Kenneth Roemer, *The Obsolete Necessity* (Kent, Ohio, 1976).

166. For an earlier variant on this theme, see "Brotherhood of the Co-operative Commonwealth," *Coming Nation*, 22 August 1896.

167. See Kim McQuaid, "Industry and the Co-operative Commonwealth," *Labor History* 17, no. 4 (Fall 1976): 510–29.

168. Peck, *Department Store*.

169. See Florence Cohen, *A Fearful Innocence* (Kent, Ohio, 1981). Not far from Albertson's home at Overbrook, Frederick Reed and his wife were conducting what the *New York World* described as a free-love colony: "At one time 100 members lived in the shady groves of Overbrook and now there are 25—twelve men and thirteen women, mostly young and good looking. Reed, a former schoolmaster from Boston frequently lectured on Browning and Emerson, but he yearned to found a new sect with no restrictions upon the lives of the members" (newspaper clipping, 1907, McGee Collection).

CHAPTER 4

1. Lasky, *Utopia and Revolution*, 19.

2. John L. Thomas, "Utopia for an Urban Age," *Perspectives in American History* 6 (1972): 143.

3. *Dawn Valcour Community Circular*, 1 January 1875.

4. Ibid.

5. Earle Vance, "The Dawn Valcour Agricultural and Horticultural Association," *North Country Notes*, no. 87 (October 1872).

6. Newbrough also anonymously authored an antifeminist tract, "Women's Wish versus Man's Will," published in New York in 1859 by "A Buckeye." The Brown University Library has a copy. *The Lady of the West* (Cincinnati, 1855) is a true nationalist potboiler that exalts America and attacks Indians, Know-Nothings, foreigners, infidels, and suffragettes. It also suggests that America has a special mission to the world: "Ah! proud indeed should America be to think that his country is the grand asylum for the whole world" (269). Newbrough followed *The Lady of the West* with another historical romance, *The Fall of Fort Sumter* (New York, 1867).

7. John Ballou Newbrough, *A Catechism on Human Teeth* (New York, 1869). His answer to tooth decay is "cleanliness and temperance in eating."

8. The major sources for Newbrough's life are James Dennon, *The Oashpe Story* (Seaside, Oregon, privately printed, 1965); K. D. Stoes, "The Land of Shalam," *New Mexico Historical Review* 33, no. 1 (January 1958): 1–23 and 33, no. 2 (April 1958): 103–27; and Daniel Simundson, "Strangers in the Valley: The Rio Grande Republican and Shalam, 1884–1891," *New Mexico Historical Review* 95, no. 3 (July 1970): 197–207.

9. John Ballou Newbrough, *The Oashpe* (New York, 1882).

10. Dr. Rutherford, "A Cooperative Orphanage," *Cooperative Congress Reports* 1 (1879).

11. Elizabeth Rowell Thompson, *Kindergarten Homes* (Boston, 1873), 86.

12. Ibid., 91–98. See also Elizabeth Rowell Thompson, *The Figures of Hell, or the Temple Bacchus Dedicated to License and Manufacture of Beer and Whiskey* (New York, 1882).

13. Elizabeth R. Thompson and Loring Moody, *Heredity* (Boston, 1882), 54.

14. Thompson, *Kindergarten Homes*, 12, 124.

15. Emma Hardinage, *Modern American Spiritualism* (New York, 1870).

16. See Robert Delp, "Andrew Jackson Davis: Prophet of American Spiritualism," *Journal of American History* 54, no. 1 (June 1967): 43–53.

17. Ibid., 48.

18. Cited in Lee Priestley, "Shalam—the Land of Children," *New Mexico Magazine* 34 (December 1961): 2.This occurred in January 1883.

19. *New York Times*, 24 November 1882.

20. Newbrough, *The Oashpe*, 6.

21. Ibid., 41.

22. Cited in Dennon, *The Oashpe Story*, 18.

23. *Sante Fe New Mexican*, undated clipping, New Mexico Historical Society, Santa Fe.

24. John H. Newbrough, *The Book of Gratiyus* (Las Cruces, 1891), 9.

25. Ibid.

26. "New Movements," *Buddhist Ray* 3, no. 5 (May 1890). The ever-present Alcander Longley had an essay on "Practical Communism" published in the journal early in 1891, and there is a brief reference to Issac Rumford, founder of the Joyful Community at Bakersfield in 1884, who now appears as a "psychometrist."

27. Also in 1899, a group of Baptists under the leadership of James Tracy and J. W. Fairchild founded a colony at Adulam, Mason County, Tex. It had a membership of 150 and land holdings of nine hundred acres and "aimed at democracy in government and equality in rights and privileges." It lasted until 1901. See Ralph Albertson, *Mutualist Communities* (reprint, Philadelphia, 1973).

28. This discussion of Spirit Fruit is taken largely from Robert S. Fogarty and H. Roger Grant, "Free Love in Ohio: Jacob Beilhart and the Spirit Fruit Society," *Ohio History* 89, no. 2 (Summer 1980): 206–21.

29. See William Hinds, *American Communities and Co-operative Colonies* (reprint; Philadelphia, 1975), 556; Jacob Beilhart, *Life and Teachings* (Burbank, Calif., 1925), 20–21.

30. Beilhart, *Life and Teachings*, 21, 22–23.

31. Ibid., 24, 25.

32. For an extended discussion of the holiness movement, see Raymond J. Cunningham, "From Holiness to Healing: The Faith Cure in America, 1872–1892," *Church History* 43, no. 4 (December 1874): 499–513.

33. Beilhart, *Life and Teachings*, 27–28.

34. Ibid., 35.

35. *Buckeye State* (Lisbon, Ohio), 22 December 1904.

36. Beilhart, *Life and Teachings*, 47, 58.

37. Ibid., 75. See also Jacob Beilhart, *Anarchy, Its Cause, and a Suggestion for Its Cure* (Ingleside, Ill., privately printed, 1908).

38. Beilhart, *Life and Teachings*, 71.

39. *Spirit Fruit* (Lisbon, Ohio), June 1899.

40. See *Buckeye State*, 13 December 1900.

41. *Buckeye State*, 2 June 1904, 3 November 1904; *The Lakeside Annual Directory of the City of Chicago* (Chicago: Chicago Directory Co., 1900), 1610.

42. *Buckeye State*, 11 April 1901.

43. *Buckeye State*, 2 June 1904; see also 26 November 1908.

44. *Buckeye State*, 2 June 1904.

45. Ibid.

46. *Buckeye State*, 9 June 1904.

47. *Buckeye State*, 16 June 1904.

48. *Buckeye State*, 3 November 1904.

49. Quoted in *Buckeye State*, 22 November 1904.

50. *Daily Sun* (Waukegan, Ill.), 17 August 1905; *Buckeye State*, 5 October 1905; and Beilhart, *Life and Teachings*, 101–3.

51. *Cleveland Leader*, 20 June 1905; and Hinds, *American Communities*, 558–59.

52. *Waukegan Daily Sun*, 6 June 1906.

53. *Waukegan Daily Sun*, 1 June 1905.

54. *Cleveland Leader*, 20 June 1905.

55. *Waukegan Daily Sun*, 24 November 1908.

56. *Waukegn Daily Sun*, 25 November 1908.

57. Quoted in the introduction to Jacob Beilhart, *Spirit Fruit and Voice* (Roscoe, Calif.: Freedom Hill Pressery, 1926), 2:9.

58. Letter from Robert J. Knowdell, Santa Cruz, California, to Mr. and Mrs. Bowgren, Antioch, Illinois, November 11, 1973. Rockwell sold a portion of the Illinois land in 1912. By that time he had moved to Idaho.

59. *Buckeye State*, 9 March 1905.

60. Beilhart, *Life and Teachings*, n.p.

61. Ibid., 92–93.

62. Ibid., 9, 41, 44.

63. Edward Carpenter, *Homogenic Love* (London, 1894), *Sex, Love and Its Place in a Free Society* (Manchester: Labour Press Society, 1894), *Civilization: Its Cause and Cure* (London, 1897), and *Love's Coming-of-Age* (Chicago, 1902). For a discussion of Carpenter's connections with English utopian experiments at St. George's Farm in Totley, the Norton Colony at Sheffield, and the Fellowship of the New Life in London, see also W. H. G. Armytage, *Heavens Below: Utopian Experiments in England, 1560–1960* (Toronto, 1961).

64. Emile Delavenay, *D. H. Lawrence and Edward Carpenter: A Study in Edwardian Transition* (New York, 1971), 191–92.

65. Beilhart, *Life and Teachings*, 163, 170.

66. Ibid., 53.

67. *Philistine*, June 1905.

68. Beilhart, *Life and Teachings*, 76–77.

69. For a discussion of Lloyd and his utopian ideas, see Laurence R. Veysey, *The Communal Experience* (New York, 1973).

70. Leonard Abbott, "J. William Lloyd and His Message," *Mother Earth* (December 1908). The Stelton Community was an outgrowth of the Ferrer Association begun in 1910 by anarchists in New City. The group moved to New Jersey in 1915. Leonard Abbott was one of its leaders.

71. Beilhart, *Life and Teachings*, n.p.

72. For an outstanding discussion of the anarchist tradition, see Veysey, *The Communal Experience*. For the Moses Harmon circle in Kansas in the 1880s, see Hal Sears, *The Sex Radicals* (Lawrence, Kans., 1977).

73. *Waukegan Daily Sun*, 24 November 1908.

74. Hine, *California's Utopian Colonies*, 43.

75. Point Loma prefigured many of the contemporary communities in its emphasis on internationalizing its message. It drew its audience from various nations and perspectives. It was, in many ways, like Christian Science.

76. Frederick Booth-Tucker quoted in Marie Antalek, "The Amity Colony" M.A. thesis, Kansas State Teachers College, 1968), 44.

77. Ibid., 44.

78. See H. Rider Haggard, *The Poor and the Land* (London, 1905), and "The Salvation Army and Land Settlement," in *Sketches of the Salvation Army Social Work* (London, 1908).

79. The most thorough account of the Salvationists in America is Herbert Wisbey's *Soldiers Without Swords* (New York, 1955).

80. See Wilbur Copeland, *Handbook of Prohibition Facts* (New York, 1892).

81. William Hinds, *American Communities and Cooperative Colonies* (Chicago, 1908), 549.

82. *Straight Edge*, 4 January 1900.

83. *Straight Edge*, 17 February 1900.

84. *Straight Edge*, 21 March 1901.

85. *Straight Edge*, February 1906.

86. *Straight Edge*, January 1908.

87. *Straight Edge*, May 1905.

88. *Straight Edge*, January 1928.

89. *New York Independent*, 14 July 1906.

90. Helicon Hall Community, *Prospectus*, (Englewod, N.J.: Helicon Home Colony, 1906).

91. Ibid., 8.

92. Upton Sinclair, *Autobiography* (New York, 1962), 150.

93. Leon Harris, *Upton Sinclair: An American Rebel* (New York, 1980), 95.

CHAPTER 5

1. See Henry Bedford, *Socialism and the Workers of Massachusetts* (Amherst, Mass., 1966), 179.

2. *Ariel* 2 (1896): 6.

3. *Ariel* 6, no. 8 (March 1902): 6–7.

4. George E. Littlefield, *Fellowship Farm Facts* (Stelton, N.J., 1912), 10.

5. George E. Littlefield, *Today and Tomorrow* (Stelton, N.J., n.d.).

6. *Ariel* 7, no. 2 (October 1902): 5.

7. Ibid. See also David Shi, *The Simple Life* (New York, 1985), 175–247.

8. George Littlefield, "Farming by the Square Foot," in *On the Land* (Stelton, N.J., n.d.). Visitors to the colony in 1907 included Charles F. Nesbit of the Arden Colony in Delaware, Alexander Burns of the anarchist Home Colony in Washington. Other groups were Llewelyn Westwood, Massachusetts, begun in 1906, and Norwood, Massachusetts, in 1910. There may have been a small farm group at Sommerville, Mass., that started up in 1907. By 1912, the "movement" shifted to Stelton.

9. Littlefield, *Fellowship Farm Facts*, 7.

10. Christian Balzac Hoffman, "Let the Common People Unite," in *In the Open* (Stelton, N.J., n.d.), 18.

11. "Poor devils like myself, who are begging some public utility company for a chance to live, are forced to keep our ideas to ourselves. There is, beyond a doubt, a tacit understanding to avoid hiring, or keeping on the pay rolls any man with Socialist ideas. I see every day how the system works" (Norman H. Chamberlin to Christian B. Hoffman, 12 July 1912, Hoffman Papers, Kansas Collection, University of Kansas Library).

12. Hine, *California Utopias*, 47.

13. For more information about Smythe, see Robert S. Fogarty, *Dictionary of American Communal and Utopian History* (Westport, Conn., 1980), 106.

14. "Morn Matins," *Ariel Press* (Santa Barbara, Calif., n.d.).

15. *Free Comrade* 1, no. 4 (July 1900): 4.

16. Henry W. Longfellow to Stephen Longfellow, 10 October 1840, in *The Letters of Longfellow*, 257–58.

17. Christian Balzac Hoffman, "Let the Common People Unite," *In the Open* (Stelton, N.J., n.d.).

18. Ibid.

19. Starr, *Americans and the California Dream.*

20. Starr, *Inventing the Dream.*

21. Jackson Lears, *No Place of Grace: Antimodernism and the Transformation of American Culture* (New York, 1981), 66–73.

Manuscript Collections

Cooperative Society, Manchester, Holyoake, Craig collections
Ethical Culture Society, London
Jewish National and University Library, Jerusalem
University of London Library
Salvation Army Archives, London
Smith Collection (private), Oxford

Sources

Writing in *Death in the Afternoon*, Ernest Hemingway noted that the "dignity of an iceberg is due to only one-eighth of it being above water." The same can be said for scholarly works since they rest on a foundation that is rarely apparent to the naked eye. This book is based on two decades of research and on the work of other scholars. One of the basic premises of this book, namely, that there were many, not few, groups, was outlined in my "American Communes, 1865–1914" *Journal of American Studies* 9, no. 2 (August 1975); since then I have visited additional archival sites, expanded the focus of the study, and published material (here included) in the introductions to several volumes in the multivolume reprint series *The American Utopian Adventure* (1975), in essays in *Ohio History, Prospects 10: An Annual of American Culture* (1985), and *New Religious Movements* (1989).

Since 1970, an enormous amount of material (both primary and secondary) has been published concerning the history of communal settlements. Increasingly important scholarly work in this area has been based on primary sources, but there are still books and essays that rely on secondhand accounts. For example, any researcher trying to understand the relation between communal settlement and socialist aspirations must read Julius Wayland's *Coming Nation*. It is a tremendous source of information not only about Ruskin but about personalities and movements in the 1890s. Similarly, the pages of the *Credit Foncier of Sinaloa* and the *Fairhope Courier* tell us not only about Topolobampo and Fairhope but also about their relation with other reforms. Most colonies did not have such journals, but some, like Silkville, did leave a prospectus literature and occasional reports. Much of the material in this book has been hunted out of ephemera collections and clipping files. Recently, a new journal, *Communal Studies*, first under Mario DePillis and now under Michael Barkun, has begun to publish primary source material in addition to critical articles and reviews.

There is no single source, or compendium, of communal societies. Oto Okugawa's listing in my *Dictionary of American Communal and Utopian History* is, however, the most comprehensive one, and I have relied on it for my listing in the Appendix. I have added additional colonies that I have discovered since the publication of that first listing in 1980. I expect that there will be further additions to the list as other scholars work on the period and examine local newspapers. There is no reliable list for communities founded after the First World War, and there is clear evidence that cooperative and communal societies were started from 1920 to 1960. Community Services at Yellow Springs has acted as a clearing house for information for the intentional community movement. Its holdings are described in Jefferson Stelth's *American Lifestyles: A Guide to Research Collections on Intentional Communities, Nudism, and Sexual Freedom* (1985).

For the period between the Civil War and the First World War, one should begin with William Hind's 1908 compilation of communities found in his *American Communities*. Hinds listed not only communities but what he called "Promoters, Founders, Managers and Writers," a catchall category that drew in Ralph Albertson and Laurence Oliphant as well as Louisa May Alcott and Ray Stannard Baker. For a description of the source materials on which he based his book, see Mark Weimer's "The William Hinds *American Communities* Collection," *Communal Societies* 7 (1987): 95–103. Frederick Bushee's 1905 listing "Communities in the United States," *Political Science Quarterly* 20 (1905): 661–64, does highlight colonies founded after the Civil War, but there are errors in dating, and his comments about the "causes for closing" are misleading.

More reliable is Ralph Albertson's effort to draw up a comprehensive list based on the work of earlier compilers. Albertson was a long-time member of the communal and cooperative movement and had a keen sense about the problems confronting any chronicler faced with that fluid constituency called utopians: "No exact list exists or can be made, because of the great latitude in definition, and the unlimited variety in the nature and constitutions of communities. Many are born and die with no public record. . . . The data on many is fragmentary and often conflicting." His analysis of what he called "mutualistic colonies" closes, unfortunately, with a survey that does more to reveal his prejudices than it does to examine the groups. Brook Farm's membership, for example, is characterized as being a "congerie of misfits and cultured incompetents." That last description might well have fit Albertson and was Hawthorne's own assessment of himself, but it hardly represents a fair judgment. Albertson had participated in a failed experiment, and his comments have some value for that. See his "Survey of Mutualistic Communities in America," in the *Iowa Journal of History and Politics* 34 (October 1936). Therefore, the Okugawa list (now added to) constitutes the most reliable list, and further compilations should proceed from there rather than the often-cited and dubious Bushee and Albertson studies.

An indispensable guide to the general field (and one in need of updating) is the two-volume *Socialism and American Life* edited by Donald Egbert and Stow Persons in 1952. Their references to periodicals are an essential starting point for any study, and I have benefited greatly from their scholarship; yet the material they drew from for the post–Civil War period was quite limited. A valuable supplement to the periodical sources cited in *Socialism and American Life* can be found at the Labadie Collections in the University of Michigan. It is a typescript inventory (compiled in the 1940s) of materials on communities then in the collection. Frances Ingalls, the curator, made this listing. Subsequently, some materials disappeared from the library (most likely stolen), but the forty-page listing does contain a wealth of references to newspapers, magazines, and other sources for groups from the Shakers to the cooperators of the 1930s. For example, there is a particularly useful listing of groups extant in 1908 taken from *To-Morrow: A Rational Monthly Magazine* and the "Bureau of Group Organizations." The listing (though certainly not complete) does have addresses for both colonies and cooperators. For a more contemporary overview of the literature, there is my essay "Communal History in America," published in *American Studies: Topics and Sources* (1977) and then updated in a companion volume in 1980. For the literature of fictional utopias, see the authoritative and constantly updated volumes by Lyman Tower Sargent, *British and American Utopian Literature, 1516–1985* (1988).

Kenneth Roemer's comprehensive study *The Obsolete Necessity* (1976) contains not only an excellent analysis of the literary utopias of the period but also an annotated listing of works published between 1888 and 1900. Additional essays on utopian literature can be found in *America as Utopia* (1981), also edited by Roemer. The most recent updating of Lyman S. Tower's comprehensive *British and American Utopian Literature, 1516–1985* was in 1988. Rather than go back over the ground of my earlier essay, I will confine my remarks to works that are pertinent to the post–Civil War period and to works of a general nature that I have found particularly useful. Victor Turner's work in social anthropology has had great influence on some writers, but I find Bryan Wilson's books much more suggestive and complex. His *Sects and Society* (1961) and *Religion in Sociological Perspective* (1982) are major works that challenge both sociologists and historians alike. His sophisticated use of typologies represents a major break from the sect/church analyses used by Troeltsch and others. His current work on contemporary sect development in Japan represents a major scholarly effort. What his books have suggested is that communities may be more than one thing to more than one set of believers and that groups often have to be viewed not from a fixed historical or social perspective but from one that recognizes the process of change within the group over time.

There are two general works that cover the colonies started during this period. Mark Holloway's *Heavens on Earth* (1951) and Everett Weber's *Escape to Utopia* (1959) are both based on limited archival materials and fail to grasp larger issues and patterns. Three books were helpful in setting the cultural and political boundaries of this work. They are Robert Wiebe's *The Segmented Society* (1979), Allan Trachtenberg's *The Incorporation of America* (1982), and John L. Thomas's *Alternative America* (1983). All three—in quite different ways—focus on the notion of community and the ways that Americans sought to adjust to the pressures created by intense urbanization and industrialization. Robert Walker's *Reform in America* (1985) appeared too late to have an impact, but his discussion of utopian modes of thinking bears close reading by scholars. Both Howard Quint's *The Forging of American Socialism* (1953) and Bernard and Lillian Johnpoll's *The Impossible Dream* (1981) focus on the labor and socialist responses. Quint sees the response as heroic and praiseworthy, whereas the Johnpolls see the communitarian response as misguided and overstated. Whether misguided or heroic, there can be little doubt that laborers, socialists, and utopian engineers did, on occasion, turn toward communal solutions. Howard Segal's *Technological Utopianism in America* (1985) looks at the reformer's efforts to tame the beast. Cecilia Tichi's *Shifting Gears* (1987) examines the culture of waste and efficiency that Bellamy both damned and praised in *Looking Backward*.

The utopian search for a perfected place has been outlined in numerous works, with Frank and Fritzie Manuel's *Utopian Thought in the Western World* (1979) setting a high standard for scholarship and analyses. The works of Norman Cohn (*The Pursuit of the Millennium* [1970]), Ernest Tuveson (*Millennium and Utopia* [1949]), and Sylvia Thrupp (who edited *Millennial Dreams in Action* [1970]) provide a broad framework for understanding utopian ideas and ideals along with a discussion of millennialist notions. The American version of those ideals was first delineated by H. R. Niebuhr in *The Kingdom of God in America* (1937) and then elaborated on in more sophisticated fashion by Henry Nash Smith and Leo Marx in the early days of the American studies movement. The idea of the West as utopia produced a number of works like Charles Sandford's *The Quest for Paradise* (1951).

For studies about specific communal societies, every scholar begins with Arthur Bestor, Jr.'s, *Backwoods Utopias* (1950). His study of the sectarian movements of the early nineteenth century has been enlarged on by John F. C. Harrison in his study of Owenism, *Quest for the New Moral Order* (1969), and his comparative analyses of the millennialist origins of both Shakerism and Mormonism, *The Second Coming, Popular Millenarianism, 1780–1850* (1979). Dolores Hayden's innovative and imaginative *Seven American Utopias* (1976) looks at the built environment of American settlements and their efforts to construct—in a literal way—cities on a hill.

There is a large body of scholarly work on the Shakers, on Oneida, and on the Fourierists. A few works should be mentioned in connection with these groups. Lawrence Foster's *Religion and Sexuality* (1981) and Stephen Kern's *An Ordered Love: Religion and Sexuality* (1981) both examine Oneida, the Shakers, and the Mormons. Carl Guarneri has examined the Fourierists in detail, and his most recent work, "Who Were the Utopian Socialists? Patterns of Membership in American Fourierist Communities," *Communal Societies* 5 (Fall 1985), tells us—for the first time—just who they were.

The act of journeying has been sketched in great detail by both John Unruh in *The Plains Across* (1979) and Robert Hine's *Community on the American Frontier* (1980). Organized in 1844 in Missouri, the Bethel Community moved westward in 1856 to settle at Aurora, Oregon, until its dissolution in 1877. The best general study is still R. J. Hendrick's *Bethel and Aurora* (1933). A study by Iona Juanita Harkness Beale, "Certain Community Settlements of Oregon" (University of Southern California, Ph.D. diss., 1925), made good use of diary manuscripts by George Wolfer, Henry Kocher, and John A. Roebling and of personal interviews with colonists who had lived in the colony in the 1860s. Their musical history is sketched in Deborah M. Olsen and Clark M. Will, "Musical Heritage of the Aurora Colony," *Oregon Historical Quarterly* 74 (Fall 1978): 3. The Oregon Historical Society has a large collection of materials, including interviews.

Another German colony that moved westward was Amana, which made the trek from New York to Iowa in 1855 and stayed in its villages until dissolution in 1932. Bertha Shambaugh's *Amana, the Community of True Inspiration* (1908) has been superceded by Jonathan Andelson's massive and scholarly study "Communalism and Change in the Amana Society, 1855–1932" (University of Michigan, Ph.D. diss., 1974). Amana has been studied in considerable detail, with its economic history, its dialect, its birth rate, and its educational system all probed in a series of master's theses done at the University of Iowa. Archival sources on the group can be found at both the State Historical Society of Iowa and the University of Iowa. A third German colony (and one founded in the 1850s) was the Catholic colony of Saint Nazianz in Wisconsin. There is only one scholarly study available: Frank Beck's "Christian Communists in America: A History of Saint Nazianz, Wisconsin during the Pastorate of Its Founder, Father Ambrose Oschwald, 1854–1873" (St. Paul's Seminary, M.A. thesis, 1959). There are records of the group, including a diary from the postcommunity period, available at the Historical Society of Wisconsin (those records are in German). Much more work on this unique colony needs to be done.

While the Germans tended to organize communities around religious ideals and personalities, there was a counter thrust among the French that emphasized secular saints and ideologies. The Fourierists, the Icarians, and the Saint-Simonians all had an impact. Christopher Johnson's fine study *Utopian Communism in France: Cabet and the Icarians* (1974) sets the stage for this development. For the settlement phase, see Robert Hine's classic *California's Utopian Colonies* (1983) for chapters on the Icarians and the Saint-Simonians. Rondel Davidson's *Did We Think Victory Great?* (1988) is an examination of Victor Considerrant and the Reunion Colony at Dallas, Texas, in the 1840s and shows how the West and America served as a magnet for these idealistic Frenchmen. The labor question and the land question were central to the 1850s, as Eric Foner has shown in his *Free Soil, Free Labor, Free Men* (1970). Horace Greeley's role as prophet and publicist is examined in Glyndon Van Dusen's *Horace Greeley* (1953) Greeley's promotional efforts on behalf of cooperation are best traced in the *New York Weekly Tribune*, which had a large rural readership. The Colorado experiments have been well researched and chronicled. Manuscript material is available at the Western Historical Collection, the University of Colorado, in the James F. Willard Collection, and the C. B. Goodykoontz papers. Both Willard and Goodykoontz were professors at Colorado, and their *Experiments in Colorado Colonization, 1869–1972* (1926) and Willard's *The Union Colony at Greeley, 1869–1871* (1916) have excellent source materials. Meeker's letters to Greeley can be found at the Western History Department,

Denver Public Library. Other colony efforts (such as Cotopaxi, the Jewish colony of 1882) have material about them in the pamphlet files at the University of Colorado.

The most prominent French colony was Silkville. The Elijah Grant Papers at the University of Chicago and materials at the Kansas Historical Society form the basis for my discussion. Carlton Smith's Ph.D. dissertation "Elijah Grant and the Ohio Phalanx" (University of Chicago, 1950) is an important work. Garrett Carpenter's "Silkville: A Kansas Attempt in the History of Fourierist Utopias, 1869–1892" (Kansas State Teacher's College, M.A. thesis, 1951) is also rich in sources. Nell Waldron's study "Colonization in Kansas from 1861 to 1890" (Northwestern University, Ph.D. diss., 1932) has a chapter on Silkville. Grant's promotional writings for the colony should be examined in order to get a feel for his Fourierist message. See his 1870 pamphlet *Cooperation; or a Sketch of the Conditions of Labor, with a Notice of the Kansas Cooperative Farm of M. Ernest de Boissiere.* A Kansas scientist's account of his visit to the colony in 1871 is a valuable, though brief, report. See Charles V. Riley, *Fourth Annual Report of the Noxious, Beneficial and Other Insects, of the State of Missouri, 1871.* As a reformer and utopian, de Boissiere deserves a biography, but for the moment Carpenter's sketch of him is all that is available, plus George A. Huron, "Ernest Valeton Boissiere," *Kansas Historical Society* 7 (1939). Kansas was fertile ground for colonies in the post–Civil War period, and William Zornow's state history, *A History of the Jayhawk State* (1957), devotes space to these and other settlers who opened up the territory. A parallel (though noncommunal pattern) can be observed in Alberta Pantle, "History of the French-speaking Settlement in the Cottonwood Valley," *Kansas Historical Quarterly* 19 (February 1951).

While the French and German influence was being felt on the frontier, there was the continuing weight of English ideas and patterns. Owenism had left its mark as an idea, and the cooperative movement of the 1850s had in its ranks many British cooperators. See Norman Ware's *The Industrial Worker, 1840–1860* (1964). But a more powerful sentiment could be found in the English reform tradition that merged with the American one. Henry S. Clubb's essay on "Vegetarianism" appeared in the November 1854 issue of the *Water Cure Journal,* and he was later to write *The Vegetarian Almanac* (1855). Clubb came to America to promote his ideas and must surely have known the Nicholses, who migrated to Britain in the 1860s to finish their reform careers. See Stephen Nissenbaum, *Sex, Diet, and Debility in Jacksonian America* (1980).

The establishment of the temperance town of Vineland, New Jersey, in 1864 by Charles Landis gave reformers and individualists a boost, including Dr. Mary Tillotson and Marie and Edward Howland, who all lived nearby. A communal settlement, the Ancora Productive Union of the Industrial Public, was founded at Ancora, New Jersey, in 1872 by Samuel Fowler. An earlier community was founded in the same town by Thomas Taylor and Thomas Austin of Vineland. The first colony is referred to in the *Credit*

Foncier of Sinaloa (21 July 1885). Village radicalism took hold in Vineland and in several towns in Ohio. The tortured history of the Berlin Heights Association has been traced by William Vartorella, *Berlin Heights: Free Love and New Faith in Ohio* (1987). Francis Barry, the chief figure in the movement, was the spearhead behind an 1857 reform convention that brought spiritualism and free love together. He edited the short-lived *Age of Freedom* (1858), then *Good Time Coming* (1859), and then the *New Republic* (1862) from Cleveland, Ohio. Thomas Cook continued the tradition with a series of monthly publications from 1864 to 1868. They were titled the *Kingdom of Heaven*, the *Kingdom of Heaven or Little Philosopher*, the *True Union, or Scientific Socialist* and finally the *Optimist and Kingdom of Heaven*. All these journals were full of news and names about spiritualism and free love in the 1850s and 1860s. James Towner, for example, moved from Berlin Heights to the Oneida Community during the 1860s with his wife, Cinderella Sweet, the sister of the spiritualist Henrietta Sweet. For a comprehensive documentary history of free love, see Taylor Stoehr's *Free Love in America* (1979).

Visionary figures were plentiful in the years before the war. The Quaker Frederick T. Howland founded Adonai-Shomo in 1861 and later became an Adventist. Sources are scarce. The Adventist colony of Peter Armstrong left only an issue of the periodical *Now and Then*. Michael Barkun has looked at the Adventist and Millerite communities in his *Crucible of the Millennium* (1986). The saga of George Jones Adams and the Jaffa Colony is sketched in Harold Davis, "The Jaffa Colonists from Downeast," *American Quarterly* 70, no. 4 (October 1961). A brief account of one family's trip to the New Jerusalem in Palestine can be found in Thomas Edward Jacques's *A History of the Garden Peninsula* (1979). Mark Twain satirized them in *The Innocents Abroad* (1869). See Nadia Khouri, "From Eden to the Dark Ages: Images of History in the Work of Mark Twain," *Canadian Review of American Studies* 11, no. 2 (Fall 1980). A full history of the colony by a Latter-Day Saints historian, Reed M. Holmes, is titled *The Forerunners* (1982). There are letters from the U.S. consul about the colony in the Jewish National and University Library, Jerusalem. Another Mormon-related community—the Kingdom of Heaven—has had little research beyond Russell Blankenship's "The Walla-Walla Jesus" in *And Then There Were Men* (1942).

Thomas Lake Harris drew his inspiration from several sources and was known to Swedenborgians and spiritualists on both sides of the Atlantic. Herbert Schneider and George Lawton, *A Prophet and a Pilgrim* (1942), remains the standard source, though there are some insights into Laurence Oliphant that are revealed in the recent biography (1983) by Anne Taylor.

The Woman's Commonwealth has, in recent years, been the subject of much speculation. Court records at the Belton County Court House provide insights that go beyond George Garrison's excellent article "A Women's Community in Texas," *Charities Review* 3 (November 1893), which so much subsequent writing relied on. For a recent historical overview of the group see Jayme A. Sokolow and Mary Ann Lamanna, "Women and Utopia: The Women's Commonwealth of Belton, Texas," *Southwestern Historical Quarterly* 36 (April 1984). Their home and community in Washington, D.C., was the subject of an interesting article in *Ainslee's Magazine* (September 1902). There are no known extant manuscript sources, though a community scrapbook is reportedly in the hands of an Oklahoma couple and will serve as the basis for a book about the Sanctificationists.

Cyrus Teed's own writings are voluminous. His *Cellular Cosmogony* (reprint 1975) outlines the theory that sustained his vision. In a series of pamphlets and books like *Shepherd of Israel* (1896), *The Immortal Manhood* (1909), *The Law of Optics* (1912), and *Emmanuel Swedenborg His Mission* (1919)—just to cite a few—he elaborated on his religious and scientific theories. His periodicals, the *Guiding Light* and then the *Flaming Sword*, cover the Chicago and Florida phases of the group. For additional bibliographic citations and notes, see Howard Fine's detailed essay "The Koreshan Unity: The Chicago Years of a Utopian Community," *Illinois Historical Journal* 68 (June 1975). Elliot Mackle's study "Utopian Communities in Florida, 1894–1918" (Emory University, M.A. thesis, 1974) looks at the Edenic myths surrounding several Florida groups, including the Shakers, the colony town of Ruskin, and the Koreshan Unity. Sources for the community can be found at the Koreshan State Park at Estero, Florida, the Chicago Historical Society, the McGee Collection, Library of Congress, the San Francisco Public Library, and the Florida State Library.

Another group launched in Chicago in the 1880s was the American Colony on the Nablus Road in Jerusalem. It is the subject of Bertha Spafford's *Our Jerusalem* (1950). A typewritten manuscript "History of the Religious Society—Founder of the American Colony—Jerusalem" can be found at the Jewish National and University Library, Jerusalem. It was written by the daughter of a prominent member. Articles about the colony appeared in the Chicago papers. For a critical assessment, see the *Chicago Journal* (20 December 1887). A member of the British Parliament, William O'Brien, visited the colony in 1907 and gave his favorable comments to the *Westminister Gazette* in an article "An American Colony of Saints" (16 September 1907). A full history of the Holy Ghost and Us is scheduled for publication shortly by Shirley Nelson. Arnold White's autobiography *The Almight and Us* (1979) sheds light on the colony's decline. I have drawn on material at the Public Record Office, London (FO 115-1509-X/k 1689), for correspondence with British consular officers about the group. A 1974 reprint of Sandford's own vision, *The Golden Light upon the Two Americas*, is an important record of the final journey. A series of periodicals chronicles portions of their history. The Bowdoin College Library has broken runs of the *Everlasting Gospel*, *Glad Tidings*, the *Golden Trumpet*, *Tongues of Fire*, and *Truth*. Clippings from the Smith Collection (nearly all undated) cover the controversial faith-healing practices. The Holiness Movement that produced Sandford also generated other groups. A Texas colony is treated by Edwin Smyrl in "The Burning Bush," *Southwestern Historical Quarterly* 3

(1947). Religious enthusiasts formed colonies on Chincoteague Island, Virginia, and at Beals Island, Maine, in the 1890s. For a discussion of "Christ's Sanctified Church" led by Joseph B. Lynch, see the *Washington Evening Star*.

The colonization of the West took place in the context of both post–Civil War expansion and changing economic conditions. British participation in the American labor movement can be found by looking at Clifton Yearley's *Britains in American Labor* (1957) and a statement of cooperators' hope and strategy, *A Manual for Cooperators* (1879), by Thomas Hughes and Edward Vansittart Neale. Recent works such as David Montgomery's *The Fall of the House of Labor* (1987) make little of the cooperative ethic, whereas David Thelen's study of one state, Missouri, in *Paths of Resistance* (1986) emphasizes it. Organizations like the York Society of Integral Cooperation are discussed in Gerald Grob's *Workers and Utopia* (1969). Thomas Hughes's full career is examined in W. H. G. Armytage and Edward C. Mack's *Thomas Hughes* (1952). Hughes's own account of the Rugby experiment is in his *Rugby, Tennessee* (1881). Brian Stagg's "Tennessee's Rugby Colony," *Tennessee Historical Quarterly* 27 (1969), draws on the Rugby archives at the historic site and restoration. Other manuscript material can be found at the Tennessee Historical Society. A full modern history of the venture and the colony has yet to be written. Timothy Toswell of Rugby School, England, has reportedly completed the definitive work.

Hughes had only one colony project to his credit; Alcander Longley was an endless flow of projects. Roger Grant's "Missouri's Utopian Communities," *Missouri Historical Review* 64 (October 1971), and Hal Sears's "Alcander Longley, Missouri Communist," *Missouri Historical Society Bulletin* 25 (January 1969), cover most of the story. Longley's own *What Is Communism* (1870) is both a prospectus statement and an ideological one. William Frey has had an excellent biographer in the distinguished critic and translator Avrahm Yarmolinsky. Using the Frey papers at the New York Public Library, Yarmolinsky skillfully constructed *A Russian American's Dream* (1965). See also David Hecht, *Russian Radicals Look to America* (1947). Much of the research on the Jewish agricultural colonies has been brought together in Uri Herscher, *Jewish Agricultural Utopias in America, 1880–1910* (1981). There is an impressive body of monographic studies on individual colonies. Leo Shpall's "Jewish Agricultural Colonies in the United States," *Agricultural History* 24 (July 1950), remains the basic bibliographic guide, but since its publication articles such as Sanford Ragens's "The Image of America in Two Eastern European Periodicals," *American Jewish Archives* 17, no. 2 (November 1965), and James Rudin's "Beersheba, Kansas," *Kansas Historical Quarterly* 34 (Autumn 1968)—to cite just two—have added considerably more information. The American Jewish Archives in Cincinnati has the most complete set of sources.

Central to the literature of communal development in the 1890s is Julius Wayland's *Coming Nation*. The Special Collections Division of the State Historical Society in Nashville has a large body of materials relevant to the history of the colony, under the title "Ruskin Cooperative Association Records, 1896–1963." Francelia Butler's research notes and materials on Ruskin have been deposited at the University of Connecticut. In addition, there is a collection of letters about and by settlers in the Paul Schneider Papers at the Burton Historical Collection, Detroit Public Library. An occasional journal, the *Ruskin Bugle*, acted as a newsletter for former members, and it has valuable reminiscences. It is located at the Tennessee Historical Society and could well serve as the basis for looking at the colonists after they left Ruskin. Theodore McDill's reflective essay, "The Happiest Days of My Life" (written in 1932), is an important source for community life, as are the columns about life at Ruskin that appeared in the *Coming Nation*. Under the same name, a cooperative tomato-growing settlement was founded by George Miller, head of Ruskin College, in Glen Ellyn, Illinois. For basic information about the town, see Karl Grismer, *Tampa* (1950).

Another colony that has a substantial body of material available is Topolobampo. It had a rich history, and archival sources both in Mexico and the United States are now being used. The best place to examine the range of those sources is in Bennett Lowenthal's "The Topolobampo Colony in the Context of Porfirian Mexico," *Communal Studies* 7 (1987). Ray Reynold's *Cat's Paw Utopia* (1972) is the best modern study by a scholar who has collected and utilized a wide range of sources. Important collections are at the Huntington Library and the Fresno State University Library. The Owen Collection at Fresno contains some of Owen's correspondence with other colony leaders, including John Duss of the Harmonists, Issac Broome of Ruskin, J. W. Gaskine of Kaweah, and Charles Sears of Silkville. Owen's writings were numerous. His capacity for self-promotional activity was great, and he wrote in defense of his varied projects. See his *The Eagle Pass–Topolobampo Pacific* (1876), *Boyton's Patent Bicycle Railway* (1886), or *The Guernsey Market House Plan of Payments* (1887). During the 1890s, his penny pamphlet, *A Dream of an Ideal City* (1897), reached readers in Leeds and London, and his periodical *Credit Foncier of Sinaloa* (1885) is a running commentary of his promotional activities. His association with Marie Howland and Edward Howland was a fruitful one. Both their careers were varied. My introduction to a reprint edition of *Papa's Own Girl* (1975) provides the basic outline of Marie's life. Dolores Hayden's *The Grand Domestic Revolution* (1981) emphasizes her role in the cooperative housekeeping movement. Cyrus Willard's career as a labor reporter, commune member, and Theosophist is traced in his "Autobiography." A typescript copy is available in the Morgan Papers, Olive Kettering Library, Antioch College. Additional Willard material can be found in the Bellamy Papers, Houghton Library, Harvard University.

The Single Tax Colony of Fairhope is being studied by Paul Gaston, University of Virginia. The *Fairhope Courier* is available at the archives of the Fairhope Single Tax Corporation in Alabama. Like the *Coming Nation*, the *Courier* extended its coverage beyond town and colony to other reform issues. A preliminary and sensitive account of three Fairhope residents has been brought together by Paul Gaston in *The Women of Fairhope* (1984). A biographical sketch of Edward Howland (written by Marie Howland in 1891) gives valuable insights into their career together. The single tax movement spawned another colony (not cooperative) at Arden, Delaware, in 1900 and a community at Berkeley Heights, New Jersey, in 1910.

The political turmoil of the 1890s provided the cooperators with conditions that created wide-spread interest in their ventures. Charles LeWarne's study of communal groups in the Pacific Northwest, *Utopias on Puget Sound* (1978), covers the ground well. Older and more general works that have been helpful are Howard Quint's *The Forging of American Socialism* (1953) and James Dombrowski's *The Early Days of Christian Socialism in America* (1936). Both the secular and the religious motivations overlapped in creating some colonies, and one has only to read Nick Salvatore's *Eugene V. Debs* (1982) to see that Christian/socialist rhetoric in action. The Ault Collection at the University of Washington is an important source for the Cooperative Brotherhood Colony, and it has a substantial body of material on Jay Fox and the Home Colony. For Home, see Charles LeWarne, "The Anarchist Colony at Home, Washington, 1901–1902," *Arizona and the West* 14, no. 2 (Summer 1972). Paul Avrich's *The Modern School Movement* (1980) focuses on early educational radicalism.

There were a whole host of colonies started in the 1890s that deserve full histories. The Christian Commonwealth in Georgia and Ralph Albertson's role in it have been examined in several places, but never in detail. See his own comments in "The Christian Commonwealth in Georgia," *Georgia Historical Quarterly* 24 (June 1945), and Frances Cohen's look at his later and more spiritual interests in *A Fearful Innocence* (1981). Christian B. Hoffman's life has been reviewed by Patricia Michaelis in "C. B. Hoffman, Kansas Socialist," *Kansas Historical Quarterly* 44 (Summer 1975). There are colonies such as the Prosperanza Association, which had 480 acres of land in California and was (in the pages of the *Coming Nation*) looking for members in June 1895. Colonies like it and the East Texas Cooperative Association of Shepherd, Texas (1896), need local research.

Laurence Veysey's *The Communal Experience* (1973) is a superb study of two philosophies—mysticism and anarchism—and how they produced a movement, Vedanta, and a colony, Stelton. Veysey carries these twin impulses of mysticism and anarchism into his analyses of the 1960s and looks at their ability to create the counterculture. For the spread of spiritualism and the appearance of Theosophy are important features of the 1890s. For various reform efforts, see Hal Bridges, *American Mysticism* (1970), William Leach, *True Love and Perfect Union* (1980), and Hal Sears, *The Sex Radicals* (1977). William J. Lloyd and Leonard Abbott edited a newsletter, the *Free Comrade*, that exemplified this new spirit at the turn of the century. See Abbott's appreciation of Lloyd, *Comrade* (July 1902), under the title "J. William Lloyd: Brother of Carpenter and Thoreau." For the Angel Dancers of Woodcliffe, New Jersey, see David Steven Cohen, "The Angel Dancers," *New Jersey History* 95 (Spring 1977). Cohen concludes that the free-love stories were based on rumor and that the leader was a religious mystic rather than a lecher. Roger Grant's history of another free-love group, *Spirit Fruit* (1988), went beyond our joint essay "Free Love in Ohio: Jacob Beilhart and the Spirit Fruit Colony," *Ohio History* 89 (Spring 1980). The Woodstock Colony's Ralph Radcliffe Whitehead exemplifies the new artistic sense that emerged in the 1890s under the influence of Morris and Ruskin. Jackson Lear's *No Place for Grace* (1981) is an intelligent ordering of that history. Little is known about the Overbrook Colony at Wellesley, Massachusetts, except that press reports pinned the labels "aesthete" and "free lovers" on the group.

The Children's Colony at Shalam does not have a full history, though it has been treated in dissertations and articles. James Dennon's *The Oashpe Story* (1965) has been of great help in tracing the Newbrough and Howland stories. Newbrough's mystical writings in *The Oashpe* (1882) and Elizabeth Rowell Thompson's reform tracts are essential to any understanding of this group. Robert Delp's article "Andrew Jackson Davis: Prophet of American Spiritualism," *Journal of American History* 54, no. 1 (June 1967), helps place the spiritualist and reform traditions in relation to one another. There is a good sketch of Thompson in volume 3 of the *Dictionary of Notable American Women* that traces her benevolent activities, including her support for the American Association for the Advancement of Science.

The Straight Edge Colony is best viewed through the pages of its journal, the *Straight Edge*. The New York Public Library has a substantial run from 1899 to 1942, with, however, only occasional numbers after 1914. Wilbur Copeland's own writings can be found in periodicals like the *Independent* (3 November 1900) and the *Chautauquan* (14 June 1913) and in pamphlets like *A Personal Statement Concerning the Straight Edge* (1902). Though no manuscript material has been discovered, there is a wealth of information in the periodicals. Helicon Hall is just a lay-by in the larger life of Upton Sinclair. His own assessment of the venture is in his *Autobiography* (1962). Leon Harris's *Upton Sinclair* (1975) treats the full life and David Katz's *Seven Days a Week* (1978) the servant problem.

The Salvationists were eager to solve the labor problem since it bore heavily on families. Herbert Wisbey's *Soldiers without Swords* (1955) deals with the history of the Army in America, and Clark Spences' *The Salvation Army Farm Colonies* (1985) sums up all the relevant literature on the colonies. H. Rider Haggard's *The Poor and the Land* (1905) is a plea for the colony approach and a statement about the urban poor. Haggard visited the Fort Amity colony in 1905. California has always attracted colonies, and the Bancroft Library has assembled a vast array of sources. A substantial bibliographic and finding guide to the Bancroft and Doe Memorial Library was compiled by Patricia Bauer under the title "Cooperative Colonies in California" (n.d.). Material about Kaweah, the Mormons, the Theosophists, Fountain Grove, and numerous other groups (such as the 1875 colony at Calaveras County) are cited. The Martin and Haskell papers (cited above) are a separate body of sources. Point Loma is the subject of one substantial scholarly study, Emmet Greenwalt's *The Point Loma Community in California* (1955), and a history of the group is included in Robert Hine's *California's Utopian Colonies* (1953). The Llano Colony has had several histories, with Paul Conkin's *Two Paths to Utopia* (1964) the most satisfactory. An offshoot of Llano is the subject of Wilbur Shepperson's *Retreat to Nevado* (1966). A modern history of Llano del Rio that examined it from a colony rather than a Job Harriman angle is in order. Finally, the life and times of George Littlefield can be examined by looking at Henry Bedford's *Socialism and the Workers of Massachusetts* (1966) and the pages of his little journal, *Ariel*, available at the New York Public Library.

Index